ETERNAL LIFE: A NEW VISION

Books by John Shelby Spong

Honest Prayer

Dialogue in Search of Jewish-Christian Understanding
(with Rabbi Jack Daniel Spiro)

Christpower (compiled and edited by Lucy Newton Boswell)

Life Approaches Death: A Dialogue in Medical Ethics (with Dr. Daniel Gregory)

The Living Commandments

The Easter Moment

Into the Whirlwind: The Future of the Church

Beyond Moralism (with the Venerable Denise Haines)

*Survival and Consciousness: An Interdisciplinary Inquiry into
the Possibility of Life Beyond Biological Death* (editor)

Living in Sin? A Bishop Rethinks Human Sexuality

*Rescuing the Bible from Fundamentalism:
A Bishop Rethinks the Meaning of Scripture*

*Born of a Woman: A Bishop Rethinks the Virgin Birth and
the Role of Women in a Male-Dominated Church*

This Hebrew Lord: A Bishop's Search for the Authentic Jesus

Resurrection: Myth or Reality? A Bishop Rethinks the Meaning of Easter

Liberating the Gospels: Reading the Bible with Jewish Eyes

Why Christianity Must Change or Die: A Bishop Speaks to Believers in Exile

The Bishop's Voice: Selected Essays (1979–1999)
(compiled and edited by Christine Mary Spong) (Crossroad)

Here I Stand: My Struggle for a Christianity of Integrity, Love and Equality

*A New Christianity for a New World: Why Traditional Faith Is Dying
and How a New Faith Is Being Born*

The Sins of Scripture: Exposing the Bible's Texts of Hate to Reveal the God of Love

Jesus for the Non-Religious: Recovering the Divine at the Heart of the Human

ETERNAL LIFE: A NEW VISION

Beyond Religion, Beyond Theism, Beyond Heaven and Hell

JOHN SHELBY SPONG

HarperOne

An Imprint of HarperCollinsPublishers

HarperOne

ETERNAL LIFE: A NEW VISION. *Beyond Religion, Beyond Theism, Beyond Heaven and Hell.* Copyright © 2009 by John Shelby Spong. All rights reserved. Printed in the United States of America. No part of this book may be used or reproduced in any manner whatsoever without written permission except in the case of brief quotations embodied in critical articles and reviews. For information address HarperCollins Publishers, 10 East 53rd Street, New York, NY 10022.

HarperCollins books may be purchased for educational, business, or sales promotional use. For information please write: Special Markets Department, HarperCollins Publishers, 10 East 53rd Street, New York, NY 10022.

HarperCollins Web site: http://www.harpercollins.com

FIRST EDITION

Library of Congress Cataloging-in-Publication Data
Spong, John Shelby.
    Eternal life: a new vision / by John Shelby Spong. — 1st ed.
        p.   cm.
    Includes bibliographical references.
    ISBN 978–0–06–076206–3
1. Death—Religious aspects—Christianity. 2. Future life—Christianity.
3. Eternity. I. Title.
BT825.S74 2009
236'.2—dc22   2008051443

09 10 11 12 13 RRD (H) 10 9 8 7 6 5 4 3 2 1

*This book is dedicated to those special people who through
their deaths taught me not only how to die, but more
importantly, how to live and how to hope for life beyond
this life. Each is described in the preface along with a
brief statement about what their gifts were to me.*

John Hunter Griffith (1868–1935)
John Shelby Spong (1889–1943)
Malcolm Linwood (Buck) Baker (1944–1958)
Shari Ann Rountree (1961–1963)
Carol Faye Terry (1952–1966)
Cornelia Bertha Marie Brauer Newton (1926–1971)
James Grayson Campbell (1929–1976)
Joan Lydia Ketner Spong (1929–1988)
Doolie Boyce Griffith Spong (1907–1999)
Emily Jane Failla (1982–2006)
John Harvie Knight (1960–2006)
Rosalie Suzanne (Rozanne) Garrett Epps (1922–2008)

I am in debt to each of them.

JSS

CONTENTS

PREFACE

This may well be my final book! It is appropriate that it be about final things, and it is.

Yes, I know I have said "final book" before. This is indeed my fifth "final book." I have even written my autobiography. One is supposed to die after an autobiography is either written or published. I did not do that. Instead I went on to have what were probably the most exciting and creative years of my life both professionally and personally. During that time I wrote three other books. When this book comes out I will be in the seventy-ninth year of my life and, while I do not doubt that others can maintain far beyond that age the intellectual rigor and personal discipline that it takes to write books of great skill and competence, I couple my age with the fact that in this book the major themes of my writing career culminate. *Eternal Life: A New Vision* serves to close a circle around which I have been walking for some time and thus provides a proper conclusion to this phase of my life.

To write another book would inevitably force me to move into an entirely new field of study in a meaningful way. My experience has been that the subject of the next book is always opened to me by the study done in preparation for the present book, so that the new book seems to be but another chapter developing or perhaps expanding a similar theme. I must confess that although this also seemed to occur in the writing of this

book, the new subject was so vast and my previous engagement
with it so slight, that it would take years to master the necessary material to dare to write about it. Because that kind of
time is simply not available to me and my ability to undertake
the necessary study is limited, I can only file these new insights
and directions by title and invite someone else in succeeding
generations to make them the area of his or her expertise. So
let me simply note for history that this book on life after death
drove me deeply and in a new way into the Fourth Gospel.

I have previously been put off by the Christology of John's
Gospel, which has always seemed to me to suggest that Jesus
was the presence of an external deity pretending to be a human
being. I am aware of how influential John's Gospel has been
in Christian history in the formation of such doctrines as the
Incarnation and the Holy Trinity. That kind of Christology, I
have argued, has become all but inoperative in the light of the
insights of Copernicus, Galileo, Newton, Darwin, Freud and
Einstein, with which the Christian faith must contend if it wishes
to engage the real world of today. When, however, my study for
this book led me into the theme first of consciousness and then
of self-consciousness, heightened consciousness, and finally
into universal consciousness, Johannine statements attributed
to Jesus, like "The Father and I are one" and "If you have seen
me, you have seen the Father," began to make sense for me in a
new way. It was then that I wished that I might be a Johannine
scholar and write on John's Gospel from this new perspective.

A second facet of this was that as I was working on this
book, I also became further convinced that John's Gospel was
written on the basis of an early Jewish three-year lectionary
and that if we could place its content back into that context, it
would read very differently from the way most Christians read
it today. This means that despite the brilliance of people like
C. H. Dodd, Edwyn Hoskyns, William Temple and Raymond

Brown, just to name a few of the major Johannine scholars that I have read, the key to understanding this gospel has not yet been fully discovered, or even fully engaged. To see John first as a Jewish lectionary book and then to view it, not incarnationally, but through the eyes of heightened consciousness and the mystical perspective of seeing life united with the divine and sharing in eternity is, I believe, that key. To walk through this door would also mean that people would be led to see Jesus' essential identification with God not in incarnational terms, but as a new level of human consciousness. That constitutes not just an appropriate and new direction, but a flashing, even blindingly bright, new understanding. I will develop these ideas, but only briefly, in my final chapters of this book, but this was the experience that caused me to wish that I had the background and the time to look at the entire Fourth Gospel through this new lens. Christianity is for me no longer about an invasive deity; it is about a fully human one in whom God becomes profoundly present and inherently visible. The author of John's Gospel, I am now convinced, saw that and understood it. That is why this gospel is so very different from any other book in the New Testament. I simply file this titillating clue to the Fourth Gospel, to which attention must and will be paid in the future. Others surely will develop this possibility, and when they do, they will write this powerful Jesus story in a new and exciting way. If I could count on living five more years, I would surely want to do it myself. I indeed may try. Through this preface, however, I encourage others to engage this study and to walk this path. I will rejoice in their future success. With this caveat stated I can now say, without fear of contradiction, that unless something I have already written winds up being published, this is probably my final book.

It is in fact a kind of death experience itself to acknowledge that with the publication of this volume my career as the author of books may be now complete. I will continue writing my weekly Internet column as long as I am able and as long as my subscribers indicate that they want me to do so by continuing their subscriptions, but I doubt that more books will flow from my fountain pen onto legal pads, both of which mark me as a product of a previous generation. Twenty-two volumes, three of them coauthored, and translations now in most of the languages of Europe, plus Korean, Arabic and Indonesian, constitute a cohesive body of data sufficient to call it a career. Every author wonders how his or her contributions will be judged. I suspect that if future generations notice me at all, they will say, not what some of my critics say today, "He is too radical," but rather, "He was not nearly radical enough." I see future thinkers—yes, overtly Christian thinkers—already on the horizon and eager to go to places in their writing that it has not yet occurred to me to walk. I think especially of such people as Gretta Vosper in Ontario, Ian Lawton in Michigan, Eric Elnes in Nebraska, Carlton Pearson and Robin Meyers in Oklahoma, Jeff Proctor-Murphy and David Felten in Arizona, Hugh Dawes in England and Greg Jenks in Australia (Brisbane), whom I regard as the most creative church-related voices in the next generation. Each will make an enormous impact on the emerging Christian world. While that assessment of the gifts these people have to bring is clear to me now, time will surely make it clear to countless others. I have in my career pressed this Christian faith story, which I love so deeply, to the limits of my ability. I rejoice that I might have helped others to go even beyond my limits. Every person must live within the boundaries of his or her own time in history. I have built bridges from my Christian past into a new Christian future. I am pleased that in this book I believe I have come to the place where I can actually see into another realm, and just seeing it is quite enough for me.

My thanks go to a number of people beyond those I will mention in my somewhat autobiographical first chapter. First I express my gratitude to Andrew Scrimgeour, the dean of the libraries at Drew University in Madison, New Jersey. Andy has not only done research for me but over a period of years has placed one resource after another at my disposal. He has made the contents of the Theological Library at Drew University (a good Methodist school) available to me, as if I were a member of that university's faculty, complete with my own study carrel. I am much in debt to him and to Drew University.

Next there is Gerald F. White, an octogenarian, retired attorney in Elizabeth City, North Carolina. Gerald writes me three or four times a year and has been as encouraging in my current quest as he was eager to receive its final form. He urged me to send him a copy of the unedited manuscript for fear that he might not live long enough to see its publication. That request has been granted. He has lived long and well.

Then there is Billy Kingston, a professor at Trinity University in Dublin, Ireland, and his wife, Mary, who not only pushed me with questions at St. Deiniol's Conference Center in Hawarden, Wales, but also sent me two monumental books, one on the development of the ideas of life after death in the various religions of the world by Alan Segal, which became very important in my study, and the other an analysis of the idea of resurrection in both Christianity and Judaism by Kevin Madigan and Jon Levenson. Both books are listed in the bibliography.

None of the people to whom this book is dedicated are still numbered among the living. Yet each of them taught me vital lessons about how to live, how to die and how to hope. They are also the people whose deaths made it essential for me to wrestle with death openly and publicly. Outside their families and close friends none of them would be recognized as public figures, but they have been my teachers and through this book something of the gifts they have given to me will, I hope, be given to the world at large. Allow me the privilege of saying just a brief explanatory word about each of them. They are listed in the order of their time of dying.

John Hunter Griffith was my maternal grandfather. His death when I was not yet five was the first time I had experienced the loss of a human being. As this book will reveal, that was when I began this lifelong journey into the meaning and reality of my own mortality.

John Shelby Spong was my father. I am a "junior," but since he died when I was only twelve, that "junior" has never been used except by the Social Security office. My dad's death altered my journey in dramatic and life-changing ways. I regret that none of my children ever knew him. I also regret that for the most part I did not either.

Malcolm Linwood (Buck) Baker was a vibrant, athletic young teenager, a member of the high school swimming team, who was found floating facedown in a public swimming pool at a team practice. He was surrounded by countless people, yet no one noticed until it was too late. His parents, Ophelia and Noah, were special friends and very strong people.

Shari Ann Rountree was an infant barely two years of age. She died of poison accidentally ingested while in the care of her grandmother. She was the only child that her parents could ever have. No one was to blame for the poisoning. It was, rather, one of those events in life that will always be inexplicable. Her death seemed so cruel, so preventable in hindsight and so emotional that those close to her bore the scars for the rest of their days. So did I, for it raised the question of theodicy in an unanswerable way. Her grandmother and father are now deceased, but Ann, her mother, still lives with those scars. She has two adopted sons who later helped to transform her life.

Carol Faye Terry, the oldest child of Martha and Hubert Terry, was eleven years old when she received the diagnosis of Hodgkin's disease. She died the day before her fourteenth birthday. In Faye's death, so slow and yet so inevitable in its coming, I experienced the searing dimensions of death, but I also learned how beautiful and serene a young life can be.

Cornelia Bertha Marie Brauer Newton was the first adult person who allowed me, indeed invited me, to walk with her inside the experience of her own dying. Her husband was a doctor and she was the mother of three young children. It was because of Cornelia that I began to rethink the meaning of prayer. Though she is not mentioned in its pages, she was the inspiration for my first book and its title, *Honest Prayer.*

James Grayson Campbell was a radiologist at the Medical College of Virginia. He lived but one year from the date of his leukemia diagnosis until his death. Jim with his medical training obviously knew that he was dying and almost daily he shared with me what that meant during that short year. I wrote my first book on the resurrection of Jesus, entitled *The Easter Moment,* because of him. His wife Ruth, also a physician, still lives in Richmond, Virginia.

Joan Lydia Ketner Spong was my wife. I will say more about her in just a moment, but suffice it now to say that Joan ultimately found death to be a blessed release from a long and debilitating sickness. More than anyone else has done, however, she forced me to face my own limitations in ways that would never allow me to be the same again.

Doolie Boyce Griffith Spong was my mother. She was a gifted woman, who made the best of her less than ninth grade education to survive as a thirty-six-year-old widow with three young children, no money and no marketable skills. I watched her age with great admiration. She sold her house and most of her belongings to enter a retirement home with no obvious pain. Her values were never in things. Her world shrank through the years as she lost her sight, her hearing and her ability to walk until at age ninety-two she died. She taught me to recognize what really matters in life. I was privileged to be her son and hope that I have honored her with my life.

Emily Jane Failla was a vital, alive young woman whom I first met when she was about four years old. I watched her grow up into being a spectacular teenager, a brilliant university student and finally an outstanding public school teacher. She died at age twenty-four in a mountain climbing accident. Emily taught me that life is more about quality than it is about quantity, for she lived briefly but well. Her parents Kay and Frank and her younger sister Lauren remain special people to me to this day.

John Harvie Knight was the grown son of two of my closest friends, Millicent and Eliot Knight. John was married and the father of three young children. He was found dead in his home in the early hours of the morning on the day after Christmas. He had no previous health problems or warning signs. His death was both sudden and unexpected. The circumstances of his death made it impossible for me to hide from reality ever again inside pious clichés and emotionally dishonest assurances. Embracing that realization openly formed the content of my homily at his funeral and it made me realize that our unwillingness to look at death squarely reveals how meaningless most religious God-talk is, even among the faithful.

Rosalie Suzanne (Rozanne) Garrett Epps was the final funeral service in which I participated professionally. Her death occurred after this book had actually gone to the publisher. Rozanne epitomized the thoughts developed in this volume more than anyone I know. She lived fully and well. She was of that generation in which women balanced marriage, family and career. Rozanne wrote a regular column for a weekly newspaper into her eighties. She cultivated young friends when her generation passed away. She had a zest for life that few achieve. She took a staff position with the Legal Aid Society in the year she died. In my homily at her funeral in Richmond, Virginia, for the first time I used some of the insights developed in this book. They fitted Rozanne perfectly. She was a soul mate to me, a friend and even a mother to my daughter Ellen.

I am grateful to all of these people for being my teachers.

I also want to express my gratitude to my online publishers and editors at Waterfront Media in Brooklyn, New York—Mike Keriakis, Ben Wolin, Mark Roberts and Roseann Henry. Together they have made my weekly column a reality for seven years now. It was the writing of that piece every seven days that served to stimulate the ideas that eventually showed up in my most recent books, including this one. I remember in particular two columns, one entitled "A Conversation About Death in New Zealand" and the other "Emily Jane Failla: A Special Life." Far more than I realized, I have discovered that I process all of my emotions and clarify my thoughts by writing about them. In retrospect I now understand that I did the same thing earlier in my career through sermons.

For a number of years in my professional life I was privileged to have as my executive secretary a wonderful person named Marilyn (Lyn) Conrad. She and her husband, David, became personal friends as well. How pleased I was to learn that she was willing to put aside grandmother duty and the pleasures of her retirement to reenter the workforce long enough to type the first draft of this manuscript. Working with her on this book reminded me anew of what a joy it had been to work professionally with her for ten years and, not coincidentally, on five previous books.

I was immeasurably helped by my publisher, Mark Tauber, at HarperOne; my editor, Michael Maudlin; my project manager, Lisa Zuniga; and my copy editor, Kathy Reigstad.

Finally, I acknowledge publicly one more time the meaning, love and support that I receive from my family. Christine is my adored wife, as well as my professional partner and editor, my confidante, my closest friend and my deepest love. As this book will reveal, the depth of my relationship with her has been one of my windows into eternity.

I was also privileged for thirty-seven years to be the husband of Joan Lydia Ketner Spong, one of the people to whom this book is dedicated. Since this is probably my last book, I want to say just a word more about her. Joan's premature death to cancer in 1988 closed out an all too brief, but beautiful life, and the pain associated with her long and difficult final sickness has made it all but impossible for me to talk about her publicly in any depth until relatively recently. She is the mother of our three daughters and she, together with them, gave to me love in such abundance that I have been able to enter this ever-expanding circle called life in ways that I never imagined to be possible. I never want her memory to leave my consciousness. My love for Joan does not compete with my ability to love others; indeed it expands that ability. Because I will always love Joan, my love for Christine is even deeper and transformative.

Next there are those three daughters, whom I have loved from the moment they were born, Ellen Elizabeth, Mary Katharine and Jaquelin Ketner. That love later expanded to include their husbands or partners, Gus Epps (Augustus E. III), Jack Catlett (John B. II) and Virgil Speriouso, and then it found new dimensions in their children, my grandchildren, Shelby, Jay (John B. III), John and Lydia, and even in their pets, a cat Nolan (named for Nolan Ryan) and dogs Elsie Lou (a rather southern name), Browndog (a rather descriptive name), Jersey Rose (so named because she was a German shepherd puppy bred and raised in New Jersey) and Sammy (another German shepherd, named for Sammy Sosa). The members of this my primary family mean more to me than words can convey. What they are in the present generation is wonderful. What they will be in the second generation is exciting to ponder.

Then there are my stepchildren, who came so wonderfully into my life in my marriage to Christine and made it sweeter still: Brian Yancy Barney, his wife Julieann and their exciting and lively twins, Katherine Elaine and Colin David, who make my second tour as a grandfather rich and memorable; and Rachel Elizabeth Barney, that unsettled and unsettling rolling stone of a soul who knows no boundary in the adventures of life and who always calls me into an ever-deepening experience of living and risking. I am grateful for the joy each of them has brought to my life and to the life of their mother, my beloved Christine.

Finally, I thank you my readers, whose number is well over one million if just one person read each book that was purchased. I am grateful that you have allowed me to come into your lives through my books, which have been the primary means through which I have sought to call the members of this generation into an awareness that worship means expanding the meaning of their humanity. That is why the worship of God is important to me, and it is this God that I find present in Jesus, the fully human one, whose humanity became the point of contact with what we call the divine. As this book will seek to demonstrate, I have come to see this Jesus as the one who pushed the boundaries of self-consciousness so dramatically that he redefined both God and the meaning of human life. That is why the Christian claim has always been that in Jesus God is met, engaged and known. The issue here lies in breaking out of the traditional theistic definition of God, which blocks for so many the meaning of Jesus. It is the fully human one who makes the holy visible, the fully conscious one who enables us to see that the human and the divine are one, and the fully alive one who enables us to see that death is ultimately a dimension of life through which we journey into timelessness. It was the Fourth Gospel that captured this meaning of both Jesus and God best for me when that author described the purpose for which Jesus lived to be that of giving us life and giving it abundantly. I hope this book is in the service of that purpose.

John Shelby Spong
Morris Plains, New Jersey

ONE

SETTING THE STAGE— A NECESSARY PERSONAL WORD

Certain persons, no doubt, get dragged into glory.
Make me willing, sometimes even eager for the stretching journey . . .
There to be known.

Owen Dowling[1]

Before this book's content can be engaged intellectually by readers, its character must be understood existentially. It is such a personal story that I need first to set its subject, "Life after Death," into its own context. That context will also serve to explain to my readers why this was a book I had to write.

There is a sense in which this book has been in preparation my entire life. I began wondering about the meaning of mortality when I first encountered its reality in the death of a family pet sometime before I was three. I have since lived through a variety of death experiences, as every person does, in the course of my own biblically allotted three score and ten years, a time-span that I exceeded almost a decade ago. I am, however, still counting. I have been drawn, it seems relentlessly as a moth is drawn to a candle, into a study of death and thus into a consideration of that question to which religion seems to devote so much of its energy—namely, whether death might be a doorway into something more. In that study I now discover that I have moved far from those assurances that came to me via some external religious authority, for which I once claimed ultimate truth. First, in my evangelical, fundamentalist Christian upbringing I was taught to believe that the scriptures were in fact the inerrant words of God. At that point in my life, I could sing with no hesitancy a hymn like "Blessed Assurance, Jesus Is Mine," which identified my commitment to Jesus with a "foretaste of glory divine." The world of expanding knowledge and new learning, however, kept intruding into my evangelical security system, chipping away at my certainty. That understanding of scripture as inerrant ultimately proved to be little more than an untrustworthy leaking ship that had to be abandoned. Religious concepts become fragile indeed when education renders them no longer believable. Try as I might, sometimes with great fervor, remaining on board that biblical premise proved to be impossible. No human words, ancient or modern, I finally concluded, can ever capture ultimate truth, so I looked for a way out of that disintegrating biblical security system.

My exit from biblical fundamentalism actually came only when I discovered an alternative with equal power to which I could appeal. Its code name was "the authority of the church." In retrospect I recognize that this was nothing more than a ministep from one kind of fundamentalism into another, but it felt like a huge step for me at the time. I learned well the jargon of my new idolatry. "Not only did the church write the scriptures," I asserted, "but the church also decided which books would constitute its sacred text." Those assertions were in fact historically accurate, at least as far as the New Testament was concerned, but the conclusion I drew from those assertions did not really follow. "The church alone," I then stated, "has the authority to interpret the scriptures properly." My flanks, I thought, were now well protected. Even as I parroted these clichés, however, I must have been aware of the weakness of this argument. Surely I recognized that I needed far more certainty than this if I were going to make these claims believable among those who were not, as I then was, in love with the church. All I had really done was to replace one inadequate authority, the Bible, with another equally inadequate authority, the church. For the church to serve as my final authority it had to be invested with some version of divine infallibility, just as the scriptures had previously been invested with divine inerrancy.

The hysteria that always seems to attend such assertions caused me to ask some very different questions. Do people who require certainty in religious matters, and their names appear to be legion, really believe what they are saying? Do they not know that they are just pretending? If they do know they are pretending then why do they act the way they act? When their religious authority-claims are challenged, their typical response is not to enter a rational discussion, but to engage in revealing anger. Anger never rises out of genuine commitment; it is always a product of threatened security. The human *need* to believe in God and in such ultimate matters as life beyond death, I concluded, must be greater than the human *ability* to believe these things. When people get to the point where they do not really believe what they are saying, they still seem to believe in believing in what they are saying! They do not even recognize the difference. Nonetheless, I, like so many others, participated in this activity, and it worked for me for a number of years, serving during that time to still my restless search for answers that might keep my doubts in check and to convince me that there was an enduring and eternal truth that I would someday find. In retrospect I recognize that this inner need to believe was a factor inspiring my choice of a life path leading me into my career, first as a priest and ultimately as a bishop. In that profession, as in few others, I could wrestle openly and publicly with the questions of God and death and what, if anything, lies beyond death; and I could do it within the security of time-tested answers. I do not regret that choice for a minute, but that is because this career has in my particular experience had the power to lead me beyond all human answers and all human boundaries, including the boundary of religion itself, and into an unfettered search for truth and meaning that has no end. That is not everyone's experience with religion; indeed religion does not typically encourage such exploration. It did, however, for me.

While no life ultimately escapes the reality of death, it is particularly difficult to avoid dealing with it in a religious profession. The ordained ones in our society are cast in the role of death's interpreter in teaching, in pastoral care, in dealing with the diagnosis that announces someone's impending demise, in grief management, in exploring death's inconsistencies, in planning funeral services and in preaching on those occasions. Perhaps the secret hope of those in the church's ministry is that we can deal with death, while still hiding inside the sanctuary of pious words and carefully nuanced traditional answers.

Death, however, has a peculiar ability to call us out of hiding in ways we did not originally anticipate. Even funeral services draw us into a dialogue with the non-believing world far more than we once imagined. Because of the interconnectedness of human life, the people constituting the congregations at funeral services are not necessarily believers. They have come primarily because they were close to the deceased or to one of the bereaved. It is not the faithful who fill the pews at a funeral, but rather a cross section of human life. People of various faith traditions and of no faith tradition come to funerals, most in various stages of their own spiritual development. The clergy quickly learn that the traditional pious assertions of the past do not engage many of those in attendance at funeral services.

This insight was publicly revealed recently in Washington, D.C., at the funeral of one of America's best-known and most popular television journalists.[2] Because this journalist had been an active Roman Catholic, his funeral, a requiem mass, was conducted by the recently retired cardinal archbishop of Washington. When the time came for the worshippers to go to the altar to receive the sacrament, it was made clear that not all were welcome to participate. Only Roman Catholics were invited to this altar. This jarring note of our tribal religious past was widely disobeyed by the mourners, among whom were many other easily identifiable television and media personalities known not to be Roman Catholics and, in some instances, not even to be religious people. Drawn by their friendship with the deceased and perhaps by some inner need that the presence of death seems to elicit, they violated the rule and received the bread and wine. The Catholic League condemned them by name and this condemnation was subsequently picked up by newspapers, including *America*, the national Catholic weekly. These receivers of the sacrament at this Catholic altar were accused of "religious insensitivity to Catholic values" and of being "disrespectful of Catholic practices."[3] Funerals frequently prove to be far too public and too emotional to suit the comfort needs of those committed to sectarian religion. A liturgy designed for the mentality of a religious ghetto does not communicate well with those who live outside the ghetto. There are few hiding places for those who want to flee from reality into religion, though many still try to do so.

I have in the course of my professional career conducted more than a thousand funerals. They have been indelible experiences; I remember more of them than one might imagine. The first time I officiated at a funeral was in 1955 at Christ Church in Raleigh, North Carolina. I was only twenty-four and still a deacon. The deceased was an eighty-two-year-old woman named Nella Grimes Ward. She was a relative of members of the church in which I was just starting my ministry. I had called upon her two or three times before her death and had enjoyed talking with her. She was of the generation that felt honored by the visit of an ordained person and thus seemed flattered by my attentiveness. That, plus the fact that I was a symbol of her extended family's religious life, caused the family to invite me to "assist" the senior minister, a man named Stephen Walke, in the service. I remember being terribly self-conscious and wondering how the words I was using were being heard by those gathered in grief and remembrance. My realization now is that many of the people who came to that service had probably heard that liturgy so often that the words simply rolled off of them and would not have been recalled five minutes later. It might have been interesting to interview them afterwards to check the accuracy of this assessment.

The last two funerals in which I participated officially are the final two people to whom this book is dedicated. One, Rozanne Epps, was the death of a brilliant and vital woman in her middle eighties who had been rendered comatose by a stroke. Her life could be celebrated. The other was John Knight, whose unexpected death in his early forties was devastating to his wife, his children and his parents. In this situation it became painfully obvious that pious clichés do not penetrate genuine grief. Indeed they sound exactly like what they are, religious narcotics designed to dull pain. Between that first and these final funeral experiences of my professional life, separated as they were by fifty-two years, I discovered that I entered every death moment analytically as one observing, contemplating, wondering, questioning and being forced to listen both to the words people spoke and to the words being proclaimed through the church's liturgy, and to think about how each fit into and interpreted the realities of the moment. The words used in funeral services, both my own words and those of the liturgy, did not, I discovered and observed, always illuminate the trauma through which the bereaved were reeling.

I also learned in those final activities of people's reticence to talk about death in any context. It is not something about which most people feel comfortable, which in itself is revealing. Most people seem quite eager to delegate "death-talk" to the "professionals," in which category they tend to include undertakers, doctors and clergy. That always surprised me, for I, representing one of those three categories, felt so inadequate. I discovered, however, that just the fact that I was around death so frequently in their minds gave me an expertise they felt they did not have. I learned in that process that what they perceived that I represented was far more important than anything I said, or did, and even more important than who I was or what I thought. It was humbling to learn that my ministry was deeply symbolic and not really about either my being or my doing.

My task in grief situations so often was simply to help the bereaved make decisions they would have been quite capable of making on their own, had they not been immobilized by grief. Through my familiarity with the typical cycles of death, I could give them the assurance that they would get through the trauma and in time be whole again. Grief experiences, therefore, almost inevitably turned out to be bonding moments that formed deep memories and lasting friendships. One draws very close to those with whom one is privileged to walk "through the valley of the shadow of death." These were among the richest emotional moments of my life, and proved to be the primary place in which my professional life and my personal life overlapped.

In this regular engagement with death I became aware of two constant themes. First, death is a powerful and painful reality that hovers over life almost constantly, either in memory or in anticipation; second, the words that religious traditions, including my own, use are quite specifically designed to tame death, to domesticate it, to transform it and finally to transcend it. Death must, therefore, raise the deepest and most unsettling questions with which human beings deal. I chose a profession in which these things were inescapable because I had a compelling inner need to work in the arena where human beings must raise the questions of meaning, purpose, transcendence and God. In some sense I wanted to see if I could be both a person of honesty and a voice for organized religion—at least I wanted to live self-consciously in that tension. So I have danced with death for some time now, but I have rejoiced in life even more deeply. My first conclusion is that neither death nor life seems to make much sense without the other.

The fact that I have an overdeveloped left brain and an underdeveloped right brain also meant that death was to me always a subject that I felt could be mastered intellectually and I was determined to do just that. This was the agenda that drove me as long as twenty-five years ago to make what was surely a rash decision. I determined then that I would write a book—in my youthful arrogance, I even thought "the definitive book"— on death and life after death. I entered into this task with high levels of intellectual fervor. I spent between two and three years working on this project, reading extensively.

I first searched out the concept of life after death as it appeared in the Hebrew scriptures. I was amazed to find how scanty that material was. My Jewish ancestors in faith were so concerned about *this* life that they had little time to invest much of their energy in the fantasyland of life after death. One finds early in Hebrew history a sense of a place called Sheol, which simply meant the abode of all the dead. It was generally located, in the minds of the people, somewhere beneath the earth. This Sheol, however, was never a motivating realm or an anticipated destiny. One biblical account tells of a time when a medium, sometimes referred to as "the witch of Endor," was said to have called up from Sheol the shadowy presence of the prophet Samuel at the behest of a troubled King Saul (I Sam. 28). Samuel was in Sheol because he was dead and that was the abode of *all* the dead, but to Sheol and to the sense of life beyond death that it represented there was in the Jewish scriptures no commitment, no hopefulness, no comfort and no joy. It was not until the second century before the Common Era that individual life after death connected with honor and reward rose to become a factor in Jewish life. When it did, it was primarily driven by the concept of divine justice. The narratives in such writings as the books of the Maccabees (see II Macc. 7, for example) about young Jewish persons who, during this period of severe religious persecution, chose death as martyrs, rather than the public denial of their faith, became intolerable for Jewish people to embrace unless there was some redemptive feature connected to their deaths, such as receiving the reward of faithfulness in some afterlife. These insights were worthwhile to understand, but they did not illumine my writing task greatly. So I plowed on unbothered by the reality that I was going nowhere. Expanded knowledge does not necessarily lead to conclusions.

I next searched out the New Testament's teachings on life after death, only to discover that there is no consistency among its various authors. Paul certainly appears to say that "life in Christ" is eternal, but life outside of Christ simply terminates in death. Heaven is not defined in Paul and there is no hell in his writings at all. The fiery punishment that marks the traditional understanding of hell is mostly the gift of Matthew, with some heavy assistance from the book of Revelation. Matthew transformed the valley of Hinnom, which first enters the Jewish story in the book of Joshua (15:8, 18:16)—and which came to be used as a garbage dump, and thus was always burning—into Gehenna. Then Matthew and other religious leaders stoked the fires of Gehenna until they became the symbol of God's punishing wrath. Thus the fiery pits of hell were born. The Fourth Gospel, on the other hand, equated eternal life with "knowing Christ" or "believing in Christ" (John 6:47, 17:3). In John heaven was more about the quality of life than the quantity of days. The variety of ideas in the New Testament on so central a subject fascinated me, but once again these insights did not help my writing task.

Certainly it is true that resurrection lies at the center of the gospel portraits of Jesus, but even that subject, I discovered, is interpreted in a wide variety of ways by both Paul and the gospel writers. The earlier New Testament writers speak of the resurrection as an act of God, making it an event that does not happen in time and space. Its *effects* only, not its *substance,* could be experienced in time and space. The later New Testament writers speak of the resurrection as something that Jesus did, at a particular moment and in a particular place. Witnesses could, therefore, see and describe the event. In the earliest gospel there is no account of the raised Christ appearing to anyone at any time. Mark gives his readers only the portrait of an empty tomb, a resurrection announcement and a future promise.[4]

Matthew, writing a decade after Mark, is quite ambivalent about the meaning of resurrection. He doctored Mark's story of the women coming to the garden at dawn on the first day of the week to allow them to see a physically raised Christ, a feature that Mark had specifically denied (compare Mark 16:1–8 with Matt. 28:1–10). When Matthew relates a narrative about the raised Christ appearing to his disciples in Galilee, however, he speaks not of a resuscitated body at all, but of a transformed and heavenly being who appears out of the sky (Matt. 28:16–20). It is Luke first and John later whose work turned the resurrection of Jesus into a literal physical resuscitation (see Luke 24 and John 20). When we put these data together side by side we begin to recognize that there is no consistent meaning in the New Testament about even so central a part of the Christian tradition as the resurrection of Jesus. It was interesting to learn these things, how again this knowledge led nowhere.

This study next carried me into an exploration of the meaning of death and life after death in the other great religions of the world. It would not be fair to suggest that this was an exhaustive or comprehensive study, but it did consume the greater part of a year in my life. I read the Tibetan Buddhist Book of the Dead and the Hindu Bhagavad Gita. I explored the issues around reincarnation. It seemed to me that the primary purpose of reincarnation was to answer the fairness question, the same issue that heaven and hell served to answer in the West. Both are about reward and punishment—that is, they are designed to control behavior in this life, not to instruct us about the nature of eternity. All ideas of the afterlife as a place of reward for virtue, or punishment for sin, would have to die for me before I could go deeply into this subject. They did and I have, but that was to come years later.

Finally, I delved into the more modern work of those known as "parapsychologists." I even served as part of the faculty of a conference with several of these specialists at Georgetown University in the early 1980s. This conference had been created by the energy and interest of the late Democratic senator from Rhode Island, Claiborne Pell, better known for the Pell Grants that bear his name. Not only did I have the opportunity to listen to their lectures, but I also had the chance to engage them in long personal conversations. During this phase of my exploration, I roamed into that arena known as "out-of-body experiences" or "near-death experiences." I read significantly in the genre of literature that claims to document experiences of death and a return from death to reoccupy the same body after sending communications or having other adventures beyond death. I recognize the deep yearning that we human beings feel to have contact with those we love who have departed this life, so I listened to these stories with sensitivity and compassion. I found myself, however, more skeptical than convinced. I nonetheless ventured on since I felt I should examine every claim regardless of my personal response to it or how strange, sometimes bizarre, those claims might seem to be.

There were great benefits to me personally in each of these studies, but none ever led me to documentable data that might form the basis for a book. I could never narrow the topic to something about which I could write. Every new insight seemed to open different doors through which I needed to walk and to introduce me to new ideas that I needed to explore. So it was that an outline for a book never developed. I finally abandoned this project in frustration and went on to subjects about which I could write. I assumed that I would never return to this topic again.

In that period of my life I wrote what were surely my most creative books, which convinced me that abandoning this project had been the right decision. All of these books were in the service of translating biblical experience and theological concepts into the language of our time and place in history. When I wrote my autobiography, *Here I Stand: My Struggle for a Christianity of Integrity, Love and Equality,* the publication of which was designed to coincide with my retirement, I assumed that my book-writing days were over. Then, in the years following my retirement as a bishop, I became a full-time lecturer and even a published weekly columnist. This career shift led me in 2003 to sign a new, but intended to be final, contract with my publisher. It called for three books to be written between 2004 and 2009, at which time I would presumably complete my writing career. The first of the three books was the brainchild of my publisher and came out in 2005 under the title *The Sins of Scripture: Exposing the Bible's Texts of Hate to Reveal the God of Love*. The second expressed my passion to summarize the theological path I had walked for so long. This came out in 2007 under the title *Jesus for the Non-Religious: Recovering the Divine at the Heart of the Human*. Then the time came to make a decision about the subject of what was supposed to be the final book of my career.

It was the sense of incompleteness that still plagued me about my unfinished work on death and life after death that caused me to want to return to this subject as the content of my final book. I was much older, more balanced in the knowledge of who I was and approaching the inevitable winding down of my own biological clock, an experience we all face as life draws to a close. Those factors compelled me to want to revisit this subject and so I set upon the topic with the goal of a 2009 publication.

Back to my studies I went. I read the work about life after death of every major Western theologian of the eighteenth, nineteenth and twentieth centuries. I found most of it almost totally unhelpful. Only John A. T. Robinson in his book *In the End, God* and Helmut Thielicke in his book *Death and Life* offered me new insights. Most of these writers wrote against the background of a worldview that I no longer shared, and therefore they communicated little or nothing to me. It was not that these people were not brilliant in their day; it was that they still operated out of assumptions that were no longer available to me. It made me realize how far and how fast the theological world was moving. I even went back to read anew such classics as the *Summa Theologica* by Thomas Aquinas and *The Institutes* by John Calvin. Even in those masterpieces of Christian history it was as if they did not inhabit the same planet on which I lived. I then began to read in the area of brain development and human consciousness, and finally a glimmer of light began to dawn.

When I got to this point, I also began to have discussions that appeared to offer a very different pathway forward. I reconnected with old friends Daniel and Jacque Gregory. Dan was a research doctor and Jacque a health professional, and both of them had a keen interest in this subject, but not from a traditional religious perspective. Dan and I had, in fact, almost forty years earlier coauthored a little book on end-of-life decisions entitled *Life Approaches Death,* published privately in Richmond, Virginia. Later in his life, quite independent of me, since we contacted each other in those years only through Christmas cards, Dan had moved significantly into studies about life's origins and the meaning of both life and consciousness that had opened for him some new frontiers. He made me aware of this in a Christmas card after he had read my book *A New Christianity for a New World.* Then he shared with me his own writings and research. We met for a day in Pennsylvania and talked for four hours around a lunch table. He sent me other resources that had been helpful to him.[5] This was a significant step in this book's gestation.

The next building block for this book also developed over the years in what has probably been my most significant long-term friendship, that with Carter and Charles McDowell. Interestingly, Charles was also a medical doctor, now retired from private practice, an orthopedist who specialized in hand surgery. Carter is one of the best-read persons I have ever known, with a special interest in subjects as diverse as theology and urban planning. These two subjects are related in her mind, since both are about finding meaning in life. The McDowells and I have talked together over the years about death and about what if anything lies beyond it, especially as both of them watched their own mothers die. Carter and Charles have always been both skeptical and even dismissive of any suggestion that there might be life beyond this life. They have challenged every thought I have ever had on this subject, but none of the three of us will let the subject go. So the conversation goes on. Neither Charles nor Carter is closed to discovering new insights, and both are willing to admit that these insights might well point to something that is real; but they insist that life after death, if it is to have any meaning, must make sense to their well-honed twenty-first-century minds. Charles and Carter engage me deeply, and much of what I write reflects conversations I have had with them.

The final building block that was needed to get me to write this book was supplied by two very dear friends, each of whom, as this book was being written, was living under a critical diagnosis. I enlisted their help. The first was Milton Reece LeRoy, an Episcopal priest, an archdeacon and a former colleague of mine who, toward the end of his life, found his primary meaning not in the Episcopal Church, but in the Quaker tradition. The second was Owen Dowling, a retired Anglican bishop in Australia. These two people were staring death quite consciously in the face. Neither was flinching, and both agreed to write me regularly as they walked into their own dying and to chronicle in their own words their thoughts, fears and observations, noting for me the things that helped them engage the dying process and the things that did not. I have treasured their letters and their insights, and I have been helped enormously by them.

Despite all this work and all this assistance, I still kept hitting what seemed to me dead ends. I tried to understand why. One thought kept recurring: The only language I have to use in this book is the language of time and space. The subject I am seeking to address, however, is not bound by time and space. I was therefore attempting to describe a state that I have not entered and about which I have no firsthand data. I cannot evaluate these data because the world in which I live cannot process an experience that lies beyond its limits. Another recurring thought was that the realm that I was seeking to postulate beyond this life might not be real at all, but a fantasy of my own creation that is joined in by vast cultural forces. Perhaps that is why I could come to no final conclusions. My problem was that I either could not or would not face these limitations. After my second attempt to address this subject seemed to go nowhere, I began to suspect that only a person out of touch with reality would try to write about something for which there was no language and no empirical data. I will never forget the response of a 102-year-old friend of mine named Malcolm Warnock, when I last had dinner with him. He had always been a kindred spirit in an endless quest for truth. When I told him about this book and my desire to write about life beyond death, he laughed out loud. "That is the silliest thing I have ever heard," he said. "No one knows anything about it and no one can find out." I flinched at the impact his words had on me, but I began to think that Malcolm just might be right.

I was about to abandon this project for a second and final time, despite all my study and the extensive notes I had taken on all my reading, and despite my nagging sense that there was something here that compelled me, but that I just did not know how to access. Then, as seems so often to happen in the world of intuition, a simple word got me back on track. At a luncheon in San Francisco in 2007 with my publisher Mark Tauber, my editor Mickey Maudlin and my wife Christine, I shared my frustrations and my growing desire to abandon this project. In that conversation, in an almost offhand way, I said: "The only way I know that I could write this book is to do it in an intensely personal manner, and since I've already written an autobiography, I do not believe my readers would welcome a second one!" It was Mickey Maudlin who responded in a low voice, but matter-of-factly: "Then you must write it as a personal story." The conversation that followed fleshed out that idea. The autobiography was an external narrative of my life. This book would be an internal narrative, a "spiritual autobiography," if you will. That conversation broke the writer's block, the mental logjam, and made this book finally possible. I am grateful to both Mark and Mickey. It was because of that conversation that this book will have a highly personal quality about it. My hope is that as I tell my internal story, my readers will connect their own personal stories to mine so that this book might become their story too. I also hope that by going inside for clues and directions, I can illustrate the fact that reality can be approached in a number of ways and that we cannot bind reality with the limits of our own perceptions.

So let me give to you, my readers, my conclusion first in this opening chapter. If I were asked to respond to the question raised by the mythical biblical character named Job so many centuries ago (Job 14:14), I would now be prepared to give my answer. Job asked, "If a man [or a woman] dies, will he [or she] live again?" My answer is, "Yes!" Now let me take you on the journey that I have walked, which carried me both beyond religion and even beyond Christianity, as it is traditionally understood, but a journey that has brought me to a new vision of eternity, to the place where I can give that "yes" answer with both conviction and integrity.

Rest in Peace:
Owen Dowling

Live in Confidence:
Milton Reece LeRoy[6]

TWO

LIFE IS ACCIDENTAL

You cannot abandon what you do not know.
To go beyond yourself, you must know yourself.
Sri Nisargadatta Maharaj[1]

Where do we begin this journey? How does one even talk about that which is beyond the limits of human experience? Human beings have used religious claims for millennia to hide our lack of knowledge even from ourselves. Are those reassuring but spurious claims all that life after death is about? Self-delusion is always easy. Yet something draws us, even if it is only our fears, into this discussion, so we must identify a legitimate place to begin. I, for one, can only start with what I do know. I can with integrity journey into whatever might be *beyond* this life, only by going deeply *into* this life, into the here and now. I cannot look at death and its meaning except from the vantage point of one who is alive. I cannot talk about the divine except from the perspective of the human. So my point of departure is the assertion that I am alive; I am a living thing. That assertion is, however, a far more complex and mysterious reality than most people ever stop to contemplate or even to imagine.

There are many things in the world of nature that are alive, yet they reveal no sense of being aware of it. If a living thing has no knowledge that it is alive, it is safe to bet that it also does not know that it will die. The fact that human beings know that we will die is rather remarkable. It means not only that we know we are alive, but also that we must wonder about what life means, what death means and whether any of it has any purpose or meaning. Thus, to know that I am alive is itself a fact filled with wonder and mystery. It is this fact that enables me to raise such questions as: Why am I alive? What does it mean to be alive? What does it take to know that I am alive?

Human knowledge has expanded in a myriad of directions in recent centuries, cracking open the mysteries of the past and explaining things about which our ancestors wondered for thousands of years. We know what causes thunder and lightning, why the ocean tides ebb and flow. We know about germs and viruses, about birth defects and Down syndrome. We can even embrace to some degree the infinite size of the universe and the relative emptiness of space. Despite these enormous breakthroughs, the question about how life emerged out of lifeless, inert matter still remains to be solved. There are many theories, one of which may someday prove to be correct, but for now the search goes on and the debate rages.

What is the definition of life or of a living thing? Among the various attempts to answer this question there is common agreement that for something to be defined as living it must have the ability to reproduce itself in some way. A rock cannot cause another rock to come into being, so a rock is not regarded as living, at least in the biological sense. If one breaks a single rock into two rocks, the doubling does not mean that the absolute quantity of rock is expanding, but only that inert matter is being broken up. Living things, however—whether they are single cells, weeds, giant oaks, insects, birds, or highly

developed and complex animals—all have the ability to reproduce themselves. That is the basic biological definition of what
it means to be alive.

There is also about living things an unvarying and radical
sense of interdependence. Without plant life there would be no
animal life and vice versa. This interdependence is seen on the
most primitive of levels. The first living cells produced something called oxygen, which in turn made all future life possible.
Oxygen is not native to the earth's atmosphere. It is the gift of
living things. For literally billions of years, those original single
cells of life pumped oxygen into the earth's atmosphere, starting a process that enables us today to state that oxygen constitutes about twenty percent of the atmosphere of the planet
earth, and that figure is rising. So while it is both circular and
contradictory to say that life is what makes life possible, it is
still true. Thus, the alpha point of this study lies in the assertion that I know that I am alive, and it is imperative for me to
embrace all that this means. I begin my quest for life's omega
point by beginning at its alpha point. No conversation about
life after death can begin anywhere else.

René Descartes, a French philosopher of the seventeenth
century who is sometimes called "the first modern man," believed that he could be certain that he existed when he forced
all knowledge into what he regarded as the irreducible maxim,
expressed in his famous phrase "Cogito ergo sum," which
translated means "I think, therefore I am." I, however, want
to start my investigation into life at a place far more basic than
that of Descartes, for life is obviously far older than "thinking," at least as Descartes understood "thinking." Indeed, life
is quite different from simply thinking. I certainly experienced
life long before I experienced thought, or being, or for sure the
language in which to think. Step one for me then is to seek to
answer the question: What does it mean to know that I am

alive? Corollary questions might be: What does it mean for me to use the word "I"? What is it that makes the one who can say "I" a unique entity?

While the *source* of life might still remain in the realm of the unknown, the insights of science have made it quite clear that each individual specimen of life is an unpredicted and unpredictable accident. I can quite accurately be described as an "accidental human being." That is certainly not the way that traditional religious thinking approaches life, but that is what biology teaches us. I am not the product of anyone's design, and no thing or being has created me by intention. I am the product of the infinite laws of probability, with no apparent or obvious purpose. That is not a statement that will likely gladden the hearts of those human beings who hear it, for we are prone to create a sense of worth and purpose for ourselves that is not well served by the truth of our accidental and chance nature. The facts, however, make the chance nature of our life abundantly clear. Chance embraces us on both a macro and a micro level.

The macro side of our accidental lives is seen in that before my conception, indeed some sixty-five million or so years ago, a giant comet thought to be as large as the planet Mars appears to have collided with the earth. The chance nature of that impact changed the conditions supporting life on this planet dramatically. The earth was thrown off its regular orbit, its climate was altered and its life forms were scrambled. Those changes made the dinosaurs extinct, breaking forever the dominance of reptiles across the face of the earth. Destruction for some forms of life, however, always creates opportunities for other forms of life. That is nature's law. In this case the mammals had a new opening for which they were uniquely prepared. No one planned that cataclysm. It just happened. We need to embrace the fact that human beings, as one form of mammalian life, became possible in that chance collision, though that possibility was not readily apparent and nothing seemed to be aware of it at the time. When one views our earliest mammalian ancestor, a furry mouselike creature that inhabited the grasslands of what is now East Africa, it would be hard to predict the rise of Homo sapiens, yet we are its direct descendents. These are the facts that force us to recognize that it was a chance collision, occurring millions of years ago, that made my life and yours possible. We are accidental creatures.

This accidental quality of life is also present on the micro level. Chance was working at the moment of my conception, when the particular being of my life began. I know now (but I did not know it at the time for I did not know anything then) that I am the result of a chance connection of one living thing called a spermatozoon, or sperm for short, that came from my father, with another living thing, a single, somewhat fragile egg or egg cell that came from my mother. Neither the sperm nor the egg had any realistic hope for life until they connected. I have every reason to believe that the union of my father and my mother, which made this collision of his sperm with her egg possible, was a loving union. I also know, however, that only three times in their entire marriage did their sexual union actually result in a new life being created, so even these three successes had a high probability factor attached to them. It is also obviously true that many new lives have been conceived apart from love, so while love is valuable, it is certainly not necessary for starting a life.

Let me be clear in stating that no divine force directed or planned for the union of that particular sperm with that particular egg. It was nothing more or less than a chance connection. My father released literally millions of sperm with each ejaculation. Every one of these sperm carried with it a different genetic code. My mother released approximately one egg per menstrual cycle, or perhaps some four hundred and twenty-five to four hundred and fifty in her lifetime. Only one of them resulted in me. There was clearly no higher purpose involved that might have guided that single and particular sperm to penetrate that specific egg and to form, thereby, a living thing called a zygote. It was, for sperm and egg alike, the work of chance and chance alone. That appears to have been forever the nature of life.

Yet in a strange but essential way, that fertilization, occurring in the darkness of my mother's womb, defined me and my particularity in hundreds of inescapable ways. It set very real limits on who I was and on who I could become. It determined many things about the self I was destined to be. I made no choices in this. I exercised no influence over it and, of course, I did not have the capacity to think about this moment of conception. I am an accidental being. That is also true for every other living thing, human and non-human, plant and animal alike. According to the laws of nature all living things are products of chance. That is how life begins.

In that coming together of a particular sperm and a particular egg, much of my identity was set. My gender as a male, for example, was thereby determined. The sperm that produced me had a Y chromosome, so I was to be a male child. Once again, I had no choice in this matter, and the odds of being male or female are about fifty-fifty. The general outline of my body shape was also determined: my potential height, the ultimate shape of my head and torso, the color of my skin, my eyes and my hair. In my conscious life I do have a small, but certainly not an ultimate, ability to vary some, but not all, of these factors. Even those slight variations are within fixed limits. I can, for example, make my body fatter or thinner, healthier or less healthy, based upon my eating habits, my rate of consumption, and my willingness to exercise regularly and to sleep properly.

We are all, nonetheless, genetically programmed far more than most can imagine. I cannot achieve a height beyond that which the genes I received from my mother and father and the way that they interacted made possible. I cannot expand the given potential of my intelligence quotient (IQ). I cannot alter any of the givens of life, including, as research has shown us, my sexual orientation.

At the moment of my conception a biological clock within me began to tick, starting my relentless march toward death. I was unaware of this, for I had no thinking capacity, but an absolute limit was set on the time I would live on this earth in that chance meeting between the sperm and the egg. Death thus needs to be seen and understood as a natural, not an unnatural, part of the cycle of life. It is a given, not an abnormality. It is not an enemy to be defeated or to be overcome.

There were still other, as yet unnamed, givens in the birth process that are not, technically speaking, genetically determined, but they would still shape my life over time and they were also beyond my power to control. I did not choose my birth family, for example. I had no say in determining its values, tastes, educational achievements or standards, its economic status or even the diseases to which I might be genetically predisposed. I had no choice in the health practices of my parents that might have affected my well-being during the period of pregnancy that produced me. I am thus eternally bound to them, not just by genetics, but also by their practices, their tastes, their style of life and their status. Even if in my life I managed to transcend some of my origins, as many people do, they will forever remain my origins.

Once again these things may offend our well-cultivated human sense of our own dignity and worth. Human beings tend to repress whatever reality we do not like, and we pretend that some other version of truth is real. The fact remains, however, that the chance nature of each of our lives is not only a given, but a truth that cannot be denied.

To drive this insight more deeply into our awareness, let me offer one additional insight. I, like every other human life, began my journey into existence as a dependent parasite. I was attached to my mother by what would be called, at a later stage in my development, an umbilical cord. Through this literal lifeline I would receive nourishment, oxygen and other things necessary for my survival. The waste products of my body were destined for the placenta from which they were carried off by her bloodstream. I was a part of her. I had at the beginning of my life no awareness of myself as a self or indeed any awareness of anything else.

I thus went through a number of biologically determined stages with no knowledge of or control over any of them. I "quickened" in my mother's womb, or at least that was the word used in Elizabethan English to describe a new thing that occurred about halfway through my mother's pregnancy. When the Christian creeds speak of "the quick and the dead," they are not describing the two kinds of pedestrians in New York City traffic, but are referring to "the living and the dead." My mother experienced this "quickening" as kicking and that was her first moment of conscious awareness that there was now a life different and indeed distinct from her own that was being carried within her, a life that was no longer fully controllable by her. My separation had begun. It would take me far longer than it took her to come to a similar awareness of this fact. So far as I knew or could experience anything, I was still a part of my mother; I was occupying the only space that I then knew existed.

When the time came for my mother's body to expel me into this huge world about which I had no advance knowledge, I was, like the majority of fetuses, properly positioned headfirst in the birth canal. Mine was to be a normal, not a breech birth, though once again that was determined by natural forces over which I had no control, and breech births, so far as we know, do not leave lasting imprints on those who are born that way. Muscle contractions in my mother's womb forced me involuntarily outward. It was at this moment of birthing that I experienced some aspects of a wider world for the first time. I became aware of temperature variations, hunger pains, the discomfort of being soiled by the functions of my own body, helplessness and perhaps most of all, the sense of being separated, alone and lonely.

None of this could I process, but all of this I endured. We are aware that birth is not easy on the mother. We signify that when we choose words like "labor" and "hard labor" to describe the birth process. We are not as aware that the birth process is not easy on the newly born either. Indeed, it may well be traumatic for each of us.

Quickly, as if to compensate for this trauma of separation, my mouth was attached to my mother's nipple and I felt "at one" again. I was cradled in her arms, feeling the warmth of her body, which caused the anxieties of separation to abate to some extent.

That was as close as I could get to reentering the womb, though I am sure that if I had been able to give voice to my yearning, I would have stated that such a return was my desire. I obviously had no concept of what it meant to be "an individual" and no great desire to find out. Certainly I had no sense that this was to be a permanent status and thus my destiny. I also had no idea of just how large the world was into which I had so recently arrived or that there were people in it beyond my immediate family. I could be accurately defined as conscious, but my sense of *self*-consciousness lay a little later in my future.

That is how I arrived on the planet earth. Is anyone's story really much different? Have not those cycles been repeated billions of times in the earth's history?

A late-nineteenth-century German scientist named Ernst Haeckel coined the phrase "ontogeny recapitulates phylogeny," by which he argued that in the fetal life of the human being all of the stages of the entire evolutionary journey of a living thing, from that single cell into its present life form, were replicated. Though that idea is now dismissed in scientific circles, I would like to suggest that every human being does replicate the human journey of living things from consciousness into self-consciousness, and we do tend to relive the stages of human development and share in the traditional human struggles in search of meaning. So in order to understand what human life is we do need to look at that moment when conscious life on this planet emerged into self-conscious life, and to look closely at the way our earliest human ancestors processed their developing awareness.

That dramatic transition from consciousness into self-consciousness occurred not too long ago, relatively speaking. So I now turn away for a moment from my own accidental pathway into life and look at the origin of human life as a species. It too was marked with accidental qualities. The components of that long, three-billion-eight-hundred-million-year journey (give or take a year or so) of life from inanimate to animate forms and then into conscious awareness, until we finally took that critical step from consciousness into self-consciousness, are quite similar to the process that marked the birth of each of us first into life and then into self-awareness. In this sense ontogeny does recapitulate phylogeny. This analysis will accomplish two things. First, it will drive us to the startling and uncomfortable conclusion that we are not quite as unique as we think we are; second, it will force into our conscious minds this question: Can a creature who so clearly comes into being as a product of the accidental forces of nature ever seriously entertain the possibility that there is something inherently eternal about him or her? Our journey into the mystery of life and our quest to answer Job's question have a new urgency. Perhaps it is not a comfortable way to begin, but it is a necessary way, and so we take the first step and the search goes on.

THREE

ALL LIFE IS DEEPLY LINKED

I feel myself so much a part of everything living that I am not the least concerned with the beginning or ending of the concrete existence of any one person in this eternal flow.

Albert Einstein[1]

Scientists today estimate that the universe in which we live is between thirteen and fourteen billion years old. The planet earth, a tiny part of that universe, is between four and five billion years old. No living thing, however, appeared on this planet until about eight hundred million years after earth came into being. Human life (depending on what definition is used for that life) did not arrive on this planet until somewhere between two million and one hundred thousand years ago. This suggests that neither human life nor even life itself was the purpose for which the world was created. For most of us who view all things from our own centers of consciousness, this knowledge comes as a shock to our inflated sense of self-worth. It challenges both our self-serving anthropomorphism and our human delusions. It is, however, a truth that must be engaged.

The original life form was a single cell, which had within itself the capacity to subdivide its nucleus and thus to produce in its place two living cells. This process of cell division occurred literally trillions of times over hundreds of millions of years in the early history of this planet. Changes did happen in this life process, but they came at a less than snail-like pace. When those occasional changes did occur, however, they brought into being unprecedented things that were startlingly new, absolute originals. We still do not understand what initiated these dramatic changes or why suddenly, or even not quite so suddenly, these changes appeared. Life is still a profound mystery, even to those of us who are in the process of living it.

The first of these discernible changes came when the aforementioned single cells, which had been the same for hundreds of millions of years, began to form themselves into clusters of cells. This had the effect of allowing cell differentiation to enter the world of living things. This incredible first step into complexity meant that each cell no longer had to carry out all of the functions of cell life in solitary splendor. The various cell functions could now be shared or even delegated. Once this step had been taken, multicellular living things became a factor in the developing mystery of life. Hundreds of millions of years then passed again before another step occurred that changed the nature of living things forever. This change divided life into two distinct forms that we would someday refer to as animate and inanimate life. At the moment of this division the distinction seemed minuscule, almost too slight to be noticed. Even today when botanists and zoologists study those life forms that are on either side of that primitive division, it is difficult to apply terms such as *animate* to one and *inanimate* to the other. In time, however, that dividing line would become easily recognizable for the vast majority of creatures. All of this development of life took place in and was confined to the sea, since the surface of the earth was not yet hospitable to any form of life. So prolific were these life forms that the sea actually began to teem with living things.

The next major transition in the development of life occurred when living things exited the sea for dry land. That had become possible because the earth's surface had finally become capable of sustaining life. Inevitably living things began to feel the lure of the earth's inviting new environment. First, both plant and animal life began their very tentative journeys out of the oceans and into the riverbeds and estuaries. Only then, slowly and over many generations, did these life forms finally make their way onto the surface of the earth itself, always adapting to the changing environment with which they were constantly interacting. This exodus from the sea meant, for example, that egg-laying sea creatures slowly evolved into egg-laying amphibian creatures and then finally into egg-laying, land-based reptiles. A story describing the recent Arctic discovery of the fossil remains of the intermediate creature that bridged the gap between fish and reptile appeared in the press in late 2008. This creature, called *Tiktaalik roseae*, was deemed to have lived three hundred and seventy-five million years ago.[2] When this transition was complete and reptiles were established on the land, they were destined to thrive to the extent that, in the form of the great dinosaurs, they dominated the earth from about one hundred and eighty-five million years ago to about sixty-five million years ago. That was when, scientists believe, the previously mentioned life-altering collision with a huge comet occurred. In that enormously destructive moment, the giant reptiles became extinct, opening the door for the gradual rise into prominence of warm-blooded, internal egg–laying mammals. These mammals brought with them the potential for higher levels of both intelligence and consciousness than reptiles had ever been able to achieve.

A vigorous biological dialogue between these living things and the physical elements of the environment, including climate changes, caused mammalian life to proliferate into a wide variety of forms that are now recognizable and chartable species. These mammalian subgroups today are so distinct that despite having common ancestors they can no longer interbreed. In this way enormous varieties of life forms became part of this planet. The ability of living things to adapt to the ever-changing physical world was the key to both their survival and their evolutionary pathway.

At some point in this evolving process, that aspect of life which we today call consciousness appeared. Again no one knows quite when, how or why. Embryonic forms of consciousness seem to have been little more at the beginning than a physical response to the environment—something that caused a living thing to react. In other words, consciousness began as an adaptive, survival-related mechanism. Newly conscious forms of life lived in the medium of time, but they had no sense of time's passing. There were no references to and little memory of the past. There was no anticipation of or planning for the future. Some instinctual behavior may have looked as if it were time-related, but there was no freedom not to do such instinctual things as building nests in which to lay eggs or gathering nuts for the winter's hibernation. Time for these newly conscious creatures was no more than a one-dimensional, endless present. They responded only to the threat of the moment. They spent no time remembering yesterday's threat or anticipating tomorrow's traumas. The emergence of consciousness was an enormous enhancement of life in this world. Only in retrospect and from the human perspective does it seem limited. Once this breakthrough had been achieved, again vast amounts of time passed—literally hundreds of millions of years—during which this thing called consciousness continued to develop.

Somewhere between two million and four million years ago, out of the line of primates, a species emerged with an even larger brain capacity—creatures that were human-like, but not yet fully human. In these creatures would occur one more of those gigantic leaps in the fabric of existence that is called life. That was the critical moment when consciousness expanded into *self*-consciousness. It is hard to date the exact moment of this transition. Perhaps that is because it was probably not a moment, but occurred rather over a long sweep of time in which the seemingly ultimate barrier dividing consciousness from self-consciousness was more like a movable line. It was, however, the kind of line that could be crossed in only one direction; no single creature moved from self-consciousness back into mere consciousness. Some scientists date this transition into self-consciousness as recently as fifty thousand years ago, while others date it as long ago as two hundred thousand years. At some point, however, the line between consciousness and self-consciousness was crossed irrevocably. At that moment human life, newly defined by this presence of self-consciousness, appeared on the face of the earth. This was a dramatically new thing. The world would never be the same.

We try with the power of our imagination to recreate what it meant to be the creature in which—or should we now say in *whom*?—self-consciousness first appeared. What was it like? It obviously had many elements, but all of them were likely to have been frightening. First, the self-conscious ones experienced themselves as separate from the world of nature, of which until that moment they had been a constituent part. They now perceived themselves as standing over against a world that seemed to possess such enormous size that it dwarfed them, encouraging feelings of weakness and even helplessness. That world also seemed to possess enormous power, which made them aware of their own relative powerlessness. Perhaps our closest parallel is found in the human infant, who after being born into this world discovers simultaneously the feelings of separation, weakness, dependency and powerlessness. At the moment in history that I am now trying to imagine and to describe, however, these were the feelings of fully grown, but traumatized human beings. It was as if they had stepped out of their own skins and stood viewing those skins from some place beyond them. The immediate yearning was to find a way back into the womb of nature to restore their comfort zone. They wanted to rest securely inside something bigger than they felt themselves to be. The natural world from which self-consciousness had in fact separated them was filled with forces they did not understand and about which they had never before had to think. There was a sun, which they could observe as it rose in the east, traveled across the sky and set in the west. That sun brought the warmth and light on which they depended. Its disappearance at night brought fear, darkness and coolness. Our medieval ancestors would reflect this in their prayers to be delivered from things "that go bump in the night."[3] There was a smaller body in the sky that was eventually named the moon. It gave some light to the darkness of night, but that moon kept changing its size from a full disc to nothing but a sliver of light. Sometimes it looked as if some giant creature had taken a bite out of it. Then the light of this moon would disappear into absolute darkness, only to emerge on the third day into a new sliver of light that slowly grew, increasing its intensity on each of the following days, until its full light reappeared, only to begin once more to fade into darkness. Those turns of the moon became the first way that time was calculated. Something in the past was described as "many moons ago." Our calendars still reflect twelve turnings of the moon, plus five and a quarter days that human beings add to the year in a variety of creative ways to keep the calendar and the seasons relatively stable.

Out of that same mysterious sky came blowing wind, falling rain, flashing lightning and crashing thunder. Cutting through the dry land were creeks and rivers fed by the rain, which provided the sustaining gift of water. All of them flowed eventually into the great bodies of water at the edges of the land masses of the world. These oceans, as they came to be called, had seemingly eternal waves that broke in on that land with relentless, and occasionally furious, regularity. All of these things had been there in the world of nature forever, humans assumed; what was new and different was that now there were separate, self-conscious centers of awareness who wondered, questioned and sought to understand these physical things. This was what served notice that self-conscious creatures now had to understand, manipulate and control things in their world in a way they had never thought about before. They were asking questions of purpose, meaning and destiny. They were trying to discover who they were and how the rest of the world related to them.

I have two twin grandchildren who when they arrived at age four or five asked the question "Why?" a thousand times a day, a question unique to self-conscious creatures. That childhood inquisitiveness is reminiscent of the early stage in human development when everything was a mystery for which the question "Why?" was the appropriate human response. In some sense every human life, as I noted earlier, seems to replicate the stages of human development. I suspect the anxiety level experienced in the trauma of this birth into self-consciousness was beyond the ability of these first human beings to absorb. Life on the planet earth would never be the same once self-consciousness was established.

This was when the meaning of time began to permeate the newly self-conscious humans, adding mightily to the rising tide of anxiety. Self-conscious people recognized that life was transitory, a fact that animals do not recognize. To embrace the transitoriness of life was also to become aware that time flows in only one direction, carrying humans through life to life's end. The end of life is death, which is the inevitable destiny of every living thing, but only the self-conscious living ones could know that. An awareness of time also meant that the self-conscious ones could escape the boundaries of time in both directions. They could recall and even relive the past in their minds. They could anticipate and plan for the future. They could contemplate the concept of eternity. Try to imagine the impact that these realizations had on the human emotions in that startling moment of transition from consciousness to self-consciousness. Humans could now remember the fears and the predators of yesterday and make those memories part of their present, and they could embrace mortality and know that it was their inescapable destiny. Thus it became both the nature and the destiny of human beings to be not just frightened and fearful in the moment of danger, but chronically anxious and constantly fearful. Survival, apparently part of an innate drive in all living things, had now been raised to self-consciousness. With the advent of self-consciousness it became the nature of human beings to live in the constancy of anxiety and fear. Self-conscious creatures could no longer inhabit a one-dimensional present, as simply conscious creatures appeared to do. As today's descendants of those early humans recognize, it takes enormous courage to be human. Self-consciousness places our emotional lives into the eternal status of perpetual overload.

There were no role models to teach the newly self-conscious ones the skills needed to cope with their new reality. Originators must always break new ground. Human beings were now separated from the animal kingdom by a huge gulf. The biblical myth of creation catches this truth in that the first man, Adam, was said to have been given power over the birds of the air, the fish of the sea and the beasts of the field. Adam named those animals, as if he were their master, the ancient story says, and he proceeded to define all non-human creatures as living only for the convenience and the benefit of the self-conscious ones (Gen. 2). The newly human ones began to make claims about themselves that were meant to establish their uniqueness, their crucial difference. They said of themselves that they bore the image of the one who created them and who lived beyond this world, and thus they had some eternal worth. No living thing in the billions of years in which life had been on this earth had known or felt the things the self-conscious ones now began to feel. Human life was different from anything this planet had ever known.

As happens with every breakthrough into a new level of awareness, the fear present in the new is always more apparent than the opportunity that the breakthrough enables. I suspect that after the initial attempt to return to the womb proved impossible they next began to address the compelling desire to deal with the sense of separation and the anxiety of their radical loneliness. Perhaps that early response is expressed in the biblical myth that pictured the first man and the first woman as trying to return to the Garden of Eden where, the story suggests, they had once lived in a state they identified as being "at one with God," or at least at one with nature. Adam and Eve discovered the truth that self-consciousness is a one-way ticket to a new reality. The gates to the garden of mythical oneness were now locked and were, the myth said, guarded by an angel with a drawn fiery sword (Gen. 3:24). The truth of the admonition in the title of one of Thomas Wolfe's novels that "you can't go home again" was experienced as profoundly real at the dawn of self-consciousness.[4]

Humanity as a corporate concept does not really exist. It is a construct that finds expression only in and through individual human lives. The only way we can look at the impact of self-consciousness on human life as a whole is to look at its impact on a particular human life. From that we can extrapolate "human patterns." This means that the pathway into understanding human life in general is to journey so deeply into a particular human life that we are able to break into an awareness of that which is universal to us all. This also means that the only way I will know what it means to live is to discover what it means to die and, in a contrary manner, the only way I will know what it means to die is to discover what it means to live. If I am ever going to be able to talk about life after death with credibility, I must learn how to engage and live life before death.

Life after death has no meaning unless there is life before death. That is why my approach forces me to go back and forth between human history and my individual history. Self-consciousness and a new understanding of time gave human life a new dimension, forcing human beings to deal with mortality and even with the idea of extinction. How does human life cope with that? I can answer that only by looking through a personal lens. So I now return to tell the story of how I learned to wrestle with death until I found in that struggle the universal clues that illumined the threat, the fear and the power that death seems to hold on our lives, including what it means and how it might be transformed.

FOUR

DANCING WITH DEATH: THE DISCOVERY OF MORTALITY

Make an island of yourself, make yourself a refuge; there is no other refuge.

Siddartha Gautama, the Buddha[1]

My first actual experience with death came before I was three. With it came a slowly developing alteration in my definition of what it means to be alive. It is revealing to see what a child remembers about his or her first confrontation with death. When something lodges in the memory bank of a child not yet three, it has to have made an indelible impression. Death has the power to do just that.

We had a small aquarium in our living room. I was fascinated by the darting, colorful fish seemingly so content just swimming in their pool. They were lively little creatures, coming to the surface with what looked like puckered lips to eat the food sprinkled on the top of the water. I might well have known the word "fish" by this time, but I do not think these fish had names. One day, however, when I went down for breakfast, I stopped to look into this aquarium and one of those little creatures was floating on top of the water. I had never seen that before and I had no idea what it meant. I guess "normal" is finally defined as repeated behavior, but this was unexpected behavior and I must have judged it to be abnormal. My immediate response was to get my mother's attention. Without much conversation and in a matter-of-fact way, she simply went about the business of serving as a rather unceremonial undertaker. She dipped a little net into the water, drew out the inert body, carried it to the toilet and with one flush of rushing water sent that once-alive little fish away forever. It was all very sudden.

Things die I learned that day, and when they die, they disappear. The reality of death had entered my world and I began the inevitable human effort of trying to make sense out of that reality. My dance with death had begun. Death has to be processed, and process it I did. At this young age, however, I did not have a sufficient vocabulary, to say nothing of the intellectual capacity, to make much sense out of this experience, so processing it meant little more than filing it away in the recesses of my memory, along with any conclusions I may have drawn and any questions I might have had. A creature alive yesterday was not alive today and it would never be part of my life again. I had touched, in an existential way, the meaning of finitude, and I began to apply it and to raise questions I had never raised before.

No great value seemed to be assigned to that little goldfish. It was easily replaced and life moved on. No one seemed eager to dwell on it. I am not sure that I had yet even thought of *myself* as a living thing, much less that fish. I do remember this moment, though, all these years later, and I now believe I understand why. I had observed what it seems only self-conscious creatures can experience. Life is lived between a beginning and an ending. I had witnessed an ending. Human beings seem always to be aware that they are living between those two points. Human beings know that if they look backward, they had a beginning, a birth, and if they look forward, they will have an ending, a death. The other goldfish did not seem to notice the departure of one of their own, but human beings notice. That is one of the many things that appears to make human life very different from that of other animals. The intellectual equation is simple to work out, but difficult to embrace. Two statements form the boundaries: All living things die. I am a living thing. The conclusion is obvious and the logic is quite easy to recognize—but no, I did not draw the inevitable conclusion, not yet. I was, however, beginning to embrace finitude and mortality for the first time. This experience became part of what I would someday call my data bank, but it did not fit in easily, forcing me to return to it again and again as new data became available to me.

It is the nature of human life that new data demanding to be engaged will expand the meaning of all past experiences. These data will force us to look at life from a variety of angles. The idea that something can change from being a living thing to being a dead thing was not easily forgettable for the child I then was, or perhaps not easily repressible, not even if that living thing was only a goldfish. The idea simply never went away and time after time new experiences impinged on my conscious mind and reignited this unsolved mystery.

I was not very close to my maternal grandfather as a child. His first wife had died before he married my grandmother, and he had a number of grandchildren prior to my birth. He treated me, or so it seemed, with no great specialness. He was, however, a figure in our extended family, and he was a human being, not a goldfish. When he died of a stroke before I was five, he formed my first memory of a human being who died. I had no great sense of loss, since I knew him as only a distant figure, but my mother's tears and her obvious grief meant that, at least for her, his death constituted a significant loss. So it was my mother's reaction to his death that had the major impact on me. Like most kids under five, I did not really understand family relationships. It did not occur to me that my grandfather was to my mother what my father was to me. My grandfather's death did, however, confirm my growing knowledge that death was real and that all living things will die. When I asked, with what I suspect was viewed as great anxiety, if I too would die, my mother told me that death was something that happened only to "old people," so I had no cause to be anxious. It was, however, also clear to me that she was not comfortable talking about this, so I did not pursue it. I simply internalized her anxiety.

I did not go to my grandfather's funeral, so I did not see his body lying in his casket, nor did I observe his casket being placed into the ground and covered over with dirt. All I experienced was that my grandfather, like the goldfish, disappeared. I never saw him again. When I inquired about where he had gone, my mother said, "To be with God." That sounded comforting to me, primarily because God was called "Father." It was okay, my mother assured me, since my grandfather was now very happy. Those words had no real content for me, so once again I let them pass without further questions. I did wonder, however, what it meant to grow old. When would I grow old? Were my parents old? Could *they* die? That became a new source of anxiety about which I did not even want to ask. My mother, I now know, was only twenty-eight years old when her father died, and he—my grandfather—was not yet seventy. Age is quite relative. So is growing old.

Perhaps these conversations with my mother about death would have been more satisfactory and even comforting to me had she not chosen that time to begin to teach my siblings and me "to say our prayers" each night. Perhaps it was my grandfather's death that motivated her to do that at this time. Perhaps it started earlier, but the two became linked in my mind and fed each other. I am fairly certain that my mother made no connection between our conversations and the words of the prayer we were encouraged to learn, but *I* did, and I found it very unsettling. The prayer she taught us to pray contained these words:

> *Now I lay me down to sleep*
> *I pray the Lord my soul to keep.*
> *If I should die before I wake*
> *I pray the Lord my soul to take.*

That prayer made it quite clear that death was an option for me. It also associated death with going to sleep, with darkness and with the night, while identifying waking with the dawn, the daylight and even the resurrection. Later Easter hymns would confirm this word association. "Welcome Happy Morning" we would sing, and death would be identified with the "long shadows" of the darkness and with the night.[2] What this prayer did for me, however, was to erode my comfort zone, which had been constructed on the basis of the "fact," as it had been shared with me, that only old people died. This prayer suggested to me that every night might be my last. When I shared, rather obliquely, the anxieties that were clearly called into being by this prayer, my mother was surprised. She quite clearly had never thought about these words. They were just the words of a familiar children's prayer that she had once learned. Her explanation was, "These are words that little children have been taught to say to God for hundreds of years." I waited for further clarification.

"It was so long ago," she continued, as if this were a whole new idea that had just come to her, "that perhaps some children did die in that ancient bygone time before we had good doctors and good medicine." I thought, even then, that it was a fairly lame explanation. I have since learned that most religious explanations are just that, lame. For example, I had been told on various occasions that the Devil was always thwarting God's will and that God was all-powerful. How could both be true? The two statements simply do not go together logically. The purpose of religious explanations began to seem to me not to *explain* at all, but to divert questions, to cauterize pain and, if that failed, to repress reality. Since the words of my bedtime prayer did not seem to bother my mother, however, I made the decision not to be bothered by them either—though it was a little harder, I was discovering, to do this again and again.

Prayer, I would later surmise, was something like an experience of ritual hypnosis. While everyone said the words, no one was expected to believe them. Religious rituals, I was beginning to learn, were defined as part of the human need to deny, to cope and to pretend that all of these techniques are useful when reality presents us with something that is beyond our ability to manage emotionally. At this point in my life I simply could not separate the human need to pretend from the human search for truth. Organized religion would also forever fuzz over that distinction.

When I was seven and in the second grade at Dilworth Elementary School in Charlotte, North Carolina, the reality of death once more invaded my fortress mentality, as it does periodically for everyone. My dance with death reached a new crescendo and the security blanket that appeared to couple death with age was pulled off once and for all, leaving me fearful, shivering and vulnerable. A classmate of mine had a new "Flexi Flyer," probably one of his most cherished Christmas presents.

For those not familiar with this toy, it was like a sled, but on roller skates rather than blades or runners. It snowed very little in my North Carolina hometown, so traditional sleds were neither very useful nor common. A Flexi Flyer worked just like a sled, but without the need for snow. It could be guided by one's feet while sitting up or by one's hands when lying down headfirst. All that was needed for a great ride was a paved hill. Sidewalks offered that, but so did streets. That classmate and a friend, both seven-year-olds, found a secluded hill on Euclid Avenue. I can still envision the spot. The thrill of the ride was enticing. Euclid Avenue, however, fed into a heavily trafficked street named Tremont Avenue. On one ride down that hill, these boys went zooming into that busy thoroughfare and were killed instantly by an oncoming car. I am sure the driver did not know what had happened as that low-to-the-ground Flexi Flyer entered the well-traveled street at a rapid clip. At school the next day my teacher told us why our classmates were not there and why they would not be back ever again. The message I received that day was that seven-year-old boys can and do die. Those classmates had not been old. "It was an accident," I was told. "No one was to blame." Yes, they were foolish to play in the streets, but they did not understand the danger. There was a lot of exhortation in school that day about safety, about accidents and about the danger of playing in the streets. I tried to put all of these pieces together. I did not attend either of the two funerals. I did not know the families of these boys, so I saw no wrenching grief. I did, however, have more data to process—threatening data—but suppression of reality works, and repression of uncomfortable experiences also works, and life moves on.

It is hard to recreate just how close a boy can be to his dog, but the death of my dog Pupa, when I was approaching eleven, was the next episode that made my own concern with mortality an inescapable part of my growing awareness. A dog is certainly more significant than a goldfish and this dog was a far larger part of my daily life than even a distant grandfather. I played regularly with Pupa. He greeted me with wagging tail and obvious affection each day when I came home from school. This dog was part collie and part German shepherd, big enough to romp with me in the yard, to wrestle with me on the ground and even to lick my face. This dog had been part of my family longer than I had been. Indeed, his name came from the fact that my older sister, Betty, was not able to say "puppy" when this dog arrived in our family, so Pupa it became. I had never known a time when Pupa was not there, nor did I anticipate that such a time would ever come. Pupa was like my bed or another piece of furniture: he was simply a part of the household. This dog was now over twelve years old, but I did not know anything about the life span of dogs. When he was found dead one morning, however, the issue of death was once more inescapably brought into my awareness. There was no foul play, just death by natural causes. This was my first experience of the active grief we call bereavement. I wept over this loss. It was also the first time I saw a burial. Dad dug the grave. Dead things go into the ground, I observed. We marked Pupa's grave with stones, flowers and even a little cross made of sticks. I did not quite understand what the cross meant; it was just something you put on a grave, I assumed. A gaping hole was in my life, however, where once Pupa had been.

By the time of Pupa's death I was a regular attendee at Sunday school and was beginning to hear stories about a place called heaven and, to a lesser degree, a place called hell. My evangelical Sunday school teachers were adults and I was still under the illusion that adults knew everything about life. So I asked one of them shortly after Pupa's death if I would ever see Pupa again. Both of them assured me that I would, but their answers seemed to possess no real conviction. They were more concerned with my grief than with the reality of a future life. If assurance was helpful, they were ready and willing to offer it. Children, however, know the difference, so I was left unconvinced. All I knew was that my dog was no more. People told me I could always get another dog. Dogs, it seemed, were regarded as interchangeable. That was a new thought, but not a comfortable one. Pupa was a member of my family. Were family members replaceable? I did not ask that, but I did wonder. The shadow of death now seemed longer, darker, perhaps even more inescapable. It was enveloping me and in the process I was embracing what it means to be human. That is never easy. Human beings must dance with death before they will ever be able to rejoice in life or laugh with it.

I was twelve when death struck my family once more. This time it was my father who died. He had had heart trouble and had been a bed patient for months. I did not know, however, what that meant. I certainly did not expect him to die. There were some ominous signs near the end of his life, but I did not know how to read them. My Uncle Ernest, my father's youngest brother and my favorite uncle, came to visit very frequently. My Aunt Jean, my father's sister, happened to be there on the night he died. My father had been the central focus in our family of five. He was the breadwinner, though I did not know what that meant. He traveled in his job, mostly by car, occasionally by train. We were used to his absences, but he always came back. He would leave on Monday morning and return either on Thursday or Friday evening. We looked forward to that return each week, not only because we missed him, but also because he would bring surprises. We did not feel whole when he was away.

In retrospect, I recognize that he traveled very little in the last year of his life. I did not really know why or what it signified.

I also now realize that he was not a healthy man. He was quite overweight, two hundred and twenty-five pounds on a five-foot nine-inch frame. Double chins were always a part of my image of him. He got no exercise of which I was aware. I did not understand, or even have the ability to embrace, what his sickness did to the economics of our family. I was aware, though, that our house was rearranged to put him in a bed in the living room, removing from him the necessity of climbing stairs. His death was announced to me in the early hours of the night by the scream of my mother to my Aunt Jean to come quickly. I shuddered at what that cry meant, but paralyzed, I did not rise from my bed to find out. At dawn my Aunt Jean came to my room to tell me that my father was dead. Once more death had invaded my consciousness, but this time in such a central place that I would never again be able to relegate it to the edges of my life.

Comforters came in great numbers over the next few days. When they turned away from the adults, which tended to include my older sister, Betty, and spoke to me—the oldest son— or to my brother, Will, who was nine, many of them seemed compelled to describe how happy my father was now that he was no longer sick. The word "heaven" also entered the conversation frequently, being referred to as a place of ultimate bliss. It was, people said, the highest destiny for which one's life could hope, for there the presence of God could be constantly enjoyed. Something about this was amiss, however, even in my young mind, for if we really believed that, why were we so sad? If Dad was so happy, why were those who loved him, like my mother and my older sister, so distraught? Religious thinking seemed to me to be detached from reality. I tried to process the heaven-talk, which seemed to abound, but the harder I tried, the less sense it made. One person even suggested to me that God must have needed my father to be with God. I wondered why God's need should take priority over my need. That seemed like a strange deity to me. Later in my life I would hear an elderly woman tell a nine-year-old boy the same thing in almost identical words about his father, who had died of a heart attack at a relatively young age. This lad, whose name was John Nelson, responded by saying: "Well, damn God!" The lady reacted as if she expected lightning to strike him on the spot—or perhaps her, for listening to such words. I, however, thought that this was the best answer I had ever heard to this kind of pious nonsense. A God who needed Johnny's father more than Johnny did was a demonic figure for whom condemnation was an appropriate response.

There was certainly nothing about any of these heaven-is-a-good-thing responses to the death of my father that made much sense to me then, nor do they now. If death was such a great benefit, I wondered why the doctors had tried so hard to keep my father alive. I was told that his death was God's will. That made me wonder even more. Does God will everything that happens? Why would God will the death of a man who was a father of three young children, the husband of a thirty-six-year-old woman and the financial support of his family? This sort of God made no sense to me, especially when I tried to correlate this image with the very strict, moralistic God that I seemed to encounter regularly in my particular church. The God I met in church was portrayed to me as a rewarding and punishing, supernatural, parental deity. I had had implanted into my tender young soul a far greater sense of the fear of this God than I had of this God's love. My church was quite clear about what constituted virtuous behavior, and my father had violated all its rules, some routinely. That too was a source of fear, and made the heaven-talk not only not helpful, but filled with dread.

The highest human virtue that my church seemed to proclaim, and the thing that God appeared to approve most, was regular church attendance. My father had little use for churchgoing, managing to get there only on Christmas and Easter, and then under duress. The Christian life, my church proclaimed, was marked by personal habits that shunned the major vices, which were defined as alcohol, tobacco, gambling, cards and the use of profanity. My father was, in fact, an episodic alcoholic, a two-pack-a-day cigarette smoker, one who loved to play slot machines at the local Elks' club, as well as one who gambled regularly with his friends around a poker table or a bridge table. He was also known to be quite profane, even taking the name of the Lord in vain! My church had taught me about God's record-keeping ability. Nothing escaped the divine eye, I was told. Every deed was written down, my Sunday school teachers said, and it was documented by angelic witnesses. I supposed this was to make it impossible to argue with God. That record book would be read out on the day of our deaths as part of the ritual of judgment. When callers coming to our home to express their regrets now told me what a fine Christian man my father was and that I should be comforted by the conviction that he was to receive his reward, the words simply did not add up. If the church's stated standard of judgment was applied to my father, then my father was guilty of being, time after time, on the other side of what they called the law of God. My church was quite clear about the fate of sinners like that. By these standards my father was bound for judgment and hell. It was a confusing time for me. Pious talk of heavenly bliss collided with the church's definition of sin and its message of judgment and punishment. If religion was designed to comfort me, it failed. It brought me, rather, into intense emotional conflict. Church efforts to control behavior with a theology of reward and punishment seemed to me to eviscerate its message about the God whose name is love. The fact remains that my church did not comfort me in my grief. It rather enhanced my anxiety.

I was deemed, as had been the case when my grandfather died, to be too young to attend my father's funeral, so I still had no idea of what happened at a funeral or what its purpose was. I assumed it was "an adult thing." Death, I came to understand, was something to be hidden from children and even denied. These tactics only enhanced my imagination and filled me with new questions.

I was also told at this time by family visitors that "Spong men don't live long." These people pointed to the fact that my father's father, the grandfather I never knew, had died at fifty-nine. They did not mention that he died in the influenza epidemic following World War I. My father's brother, my Uncle Belser, died at forty-nine, but he had been in an accident. It is interesting how data are bent to prove the thesis being developed. Even aside from that data-bending, it was a strange message, devoid of comfort, but I accepted it at face value, and thus my dance with death became quite pronounced and quite personal. I was never again apart from the shadow of this statement, or was it a prediction? Spong men don't live long! Death was from this moment on not repressible for me.

I began to feel that I was programmed for an early death. This perception manifested itself in both an unconscious and a conscious rush through life. I finished my university education in just three years by taking an excessive academic load and by enrolling in one summer session. I got married shortly after graduation at age twenty-one. All of my children were born by the time I was twenty-eight. I did not want to leave my children fatherless as I had been left. I was ordained less than two weeks after my twenty-fourth birthday, was elected a bishop at age forty-four and fully expected to die, as my father had, by age fifty-four. My friends, observing this "young man in a hurry," saw me as a rising star. My critics dismissed me as one who was inordinately ambitious. Neither group understood that I felt programmed for an early death by conversations burned into my mind at the time of my father's death. I suspect I was also motivated by this sense of death's impending reality to enter the profession that claimed to possess the answers to all of the questions that death raised. I know I wanted to find those answers. Though I was beginning to be at odds with the religious answers I had been receiving from my particular church, I was not yet at odds with religion itself.

One of the reasons for this was that just before my father's death I, a lad not yet twelve, had the chance to taste and to experience a very different kind of religion from that in which I was raised. It came through an odd and eclectic set of circumstances that led me into a new church, one to which I migrated alone, without any family member going with me. It made an indelible impact on me, however, because it was so different and I became aware that religion was not as monolithic as I had previously imagined. I was becoming a religious roamer. What I did not then recognize was that this is what human beings have always been. I was really just replicating in my individual life the history of my species. It is the nature of self-conscious life to cope with the issues of meaning and mortality by engaging in a religious search. I had reached the point where my search would begin in earnest. To that unfolding story that has so many dimensions, I now turn.

FIVE

THE LURE OF RELIGION

You need chaos in your soul to give birth to a dancing star.

Friedrich Nietzsche[1]

It is not just life itself that is accidental, but so are many of its experiences. The process through which my own religious options were broadened was clearly one of those accidental things. It began at an opportune moment through no decision that I made. It is, therefore, a story worth relating.

In May before my father died in September we were visited by his older sister from Pennsylvania, my Aunt Laurie. Her visit was a sign that his sickness was critical, but I was not aware of that. Under pressure from this fairly aggressive lady I found myself on a Friday morning being taken to St. Peter's Church in downtown Charlotte, a church I had never been inside in my life and one that was well outside my normal orbit. It was not outside my Aunt Laurie's, however. My father's family had moved in 1899 from Montgomery, Alabama, to Atlanta, Georgia. Remaining there less than a year, they moved in 1900 to Charlotte when he was about my age and his older sister Laurie was perhaps thirteen, and this had been the church that they attended. Laurie, unlike my father, had strong and positive memories of it, especially of the fact that they had a well-known music program that featured a boys' choir. She determined that I should be a member of this choir, so on that May Friday she and I boarded the bus for the trip to the city center. St. Peter's was only two blocks from "the square" around which Charlotte was organized. In that historic church I was introduced to the director of the boys' choir, was auditioned by him and by noon had been enrolled in the choir. I attended my first rehearsal on Saturday morning, the very next day. By Sunday I was vested, processing down the aisle and singing at that church's major Sunday service before a large congregation. It was a swift transition.

My response to all of this was quite enthusiastic, so much so that in just three weeks I had made the decision to be confirmed in that church and that action had been carried out by the bishop, Edwin Anderson Penick. That departure from my former church did not seem to be upsetting to my family, even though it broke our tenuous religious solidarity. Because of the prior connection with my father's household it was looked upon as a kind of family homecoming.

The only person who actually did seem to be upset about my decision was my former minister, a dour Scotsman named Robert Bruce Owen. Even in his displeasure, however, there was consolation: I discovered that I mattered to him at least statistically.

The boys' choir did not sing in the summer, so I had only three Sundays in May and two in September to attend this church before I lost my father. That slight connection was, however, enough to give me some ballast, which enabled me to absorb the "comforters" who came to me in my grief over my father's death with their rather harsh judgments. My exposure to this new religious experience was too brief at that time to be substantive, but the initial impressions were already operative.

Because the boys' choir sang at the major worship service of this church every Sunday morning, in this new religious setting I came to experience "church" and "liturgy," whereas in my former church I had experienced "Sunday school" and "Bible teaching." The difference was overwhelming. My new church building was larger, grander, more ornate, darker and more mysterious than any place I had ever seen. Its upward sweep, its gothic-like dimensions, its stained-glass windows displaying both biblical and heavenly scenes, literally transported me to that realm about which religion seemed to allude, but to represent so inadequately in words. It would also provide me in just a few months with the first of my father substitutes. My choir master was a grandfatherly type figure with white hair and a great affection for both music and his boy choristers. His name was William Wall Whiddit. When my father died, although I had been in this choir for such a short time, I discovered that Mr. Whiddit listened to my musings and my questions with sensitivity, though he said little, and in the process he won my trust.

When All Saints' Day came in November[2] some six weeks after my father's death, the anthem the boys' choir performed had words that were quite different from the reward and punishment mentality that had all but overwhelmed me in my family church. The anthem was "Souls of the Righteous in the Hand of God," by T. Tertius Noble. It was a moving piece of music that referred to the hope, expressed in words taken from the Apocrypha (Wis. 3:1–7), that in God's hands no harm could touch those who had died, for it proclaimed them to be "at peace." Before we sang it on that particular Sunday, I got up the courage to ask Mr. Whiddit if the anthem could be dedicated to my father. "Of course," he said without a moment's hesitation. Even though no notice of that dedication appeared in writing anywhere, when we sang it I felt as if it had been written in the sky for the entire world to see. I began to say that at last I had not only attended my father's funeral but had also sung at it.

I am sure that this powerful new interest of mine in things religious did not escape my mother's notice. For Christmas that year she gave me two gifts. The first was my own personal Bible. It was a thick, leather-bound King James Version (I did not know there was any other!) of the Bible, complete with tissue-thin pages, a concordance, maps and even some artwork, which brought these stories to life in ways I had never before experienced. The words of Jesus, printed in red letters, seemed to leap off each page, demanding attention. I must have been a strange twelve-year-old, because I was thrilled with this gift. I cannot imagine any of my children or grandchildren respond-ing to such a gift with similar enthusiasm. Her second gift that year was a very romantic, today I would call it schmaltzy, pic-ture of Jesus, which I hung on the wall above the headboard of my bed so that Jesus could literally watch over me while I was sleeping. This portrait was of a northern European Jesus displaying fair skin, blond hair and blue eyes, and it came com-plete with both a heavenly light illumining his face and a halo, or at least a nimbus, around his head. I am confident that it was from this portrait that I got the impression that Jesus, far from being a Jew, must have been a Swede. With this picture domi-nating my room, the activity of singing in church every Sunday and my commitment to the daily reading of my new Bible until I had read it in its entirety, I became an unquenchable religious seeker at the age of twelve.

I still viewed the Bible quite literally, since I did not yet have any other intellectual perspective through which to look at its sacred pages. So Adam and Eve were literal figures of history, hu-manity's first parents. I never even wondered where Cain found his wife. Noah's ark, the Bible said, had come to rest on Mount Ararat, and so it did not surprise me that people still looked for it there. God had, quite literally, dictated the Ten Commandments to Moses on Mount Sinai, presumably in Hebrew since that was the only language that Moses spoke. Jesus was obviously born of a virgin, which presented me with no problems. He also, I assumed, did all the miracles attributed to him. I never wondered why Mark and Matthew offered two different stories describing the miraculous feeding of the multitude. In the first of these stories Jesus used five loaves to feed five thousand men, plus women and children, on the Jewish side of the lake, after which his disciples gathered up twelve baskets of fragments. In the second he used seven loaves to feed four thousand people on the Gentile side of the lake, after which his disciples gathered up seven baskets of fragments (see Mark 6:30–44 and 8:1–10 and Matt. 14:13–21 and 15:32–39). Luke and John collapsed these two stories into one (see Luke 9:10–17 and John 6:1–13). I was also convinced that Jesus had conquered death in the resurrection, which I was sure was a physical resuscitation of his three-days-dead body, and that he then ascended into the sky of a three-tiered universe. I did not then know that the story of the ascension was added to the developing tradition by the author of Luke/Acts, probably in the tenth decade of the Common Era, some sixty-plus years after the crucifixion. This was all in the book, and while these stories fascinated me, it did not occur to me to question their literal accuracy. I was not just a human being who was religious; I was a religious human being. Religion was not tangential to my being; it was at the heart of my being. If I had to relate myself at this stage of my journey to the various stages in the history of the human journey, I would say that I had arrived at a point that could be located in the premodern phase of human history. I did not know enough about either the Bible or the way the world operated to see any conflict between the two. I was committed to reading that Bible in its entirety, however, and it was not long before troubling contradictions and even the immoral behavior attributed to God in its pages began to trouble me. It is hard to be a biblical literalist if one actually reads the Bible.

I became even more active in the affairs of my church, graduating from the boys' choir when my soprano voice began to break to become a member of the acolytes' guild. This obvious advance in status enabled me to stand in the presence of the "holy mysteries" performed at the altar. In time I became the head acolyte with that role's attendant prestige. This church had become quite clearly my second home, the center of my life. I probed within it and within the pages of the scriptures for meaning and for answers. Increasingly the Bible did not respond to my questions. Indeed, when read literally it only began to multiply my questions and my anxieties. My desire was not to bail out, however, but to go deeper and deeper into that Bible and into religion. I was certain that the answers I sought must be there to be found.

This was not an easy time for me or for our family. I soon came to realize that we lived on the edge of our financial resources every week. I delivered the *Charlotte Observer* to supplement the family income. One historical note was that the last home on my paper route belonged to Frank Graham, one of the owners of the Graham Brothers' Dairy. Frank Graham's son, who was about twelve years older than I, was named "Billy," and he was already a local celebrity. World War II was still on. The economics of our family soon forced us to move into a much smaller house in a much poorer neighborhood. It was very different from the house a mile or so outside the city limits where we had lived before my father's death. All of our economic security had disappeared with his death. I always had a job during that period, sometimes coupling my paper route with employment at a laundry after school, both of which isolated me from school activities and cut deeply into my time for study. I had few friends, not for lack of interest but for lack of time, and wearing clothes that revealed our lack of this world's goods, I found my school life to be increasingly difficult. I became in my school what the kids today might call "a marginalized nerd." In my church, however, I was the model young person, the leader, the extolled example. I lived more and more in and through my church and less and less in and through my school. Because of the depth of this church commitment it was not surprising that my church would ultimately provide me with a person who would dominate my life as a powerful role model for at least the next ten years.

World War II finally came to an end in 1945, when I was fourteen, and our servicemen and -women began to return home in great numbers. Among those returning veterans was a former chaplain on an aircraft carrier in the South Pacific. His name was Robert Littlefield Crandall and he came to be the rector of my church.

Before I had met this vibrant, thirty-two-year-old priest, I thought that all clergy were, and of some necessity had to be, very old, very distant and very austere men. The only ones I had ever known were that way. As such they seemed to model the ancient, distant and austere God that I had met in Sunday school and that I had later assumed inhabited the dark, mysterious and holy space inside my new church, where things seemed so quiet, so ordered and so filled with an otherworldly aura. Robert Crandall was a dramatically different kind of person. He made Bing Crosby in the motion picture *Going My Way* look stuffy. He dressed in white buck shoes. He drove a Ford convertible. (I thought clergy drove only hearses!) He escorted his wife, Erin, on his arm. Erin Crandall was perhaps the most beautiful and sophisticated woman I had ever seen or known. She was elegantly dressed, often with a fur wrap around her neck. She sat on her husband's desk after church each Sunday morning, crossing her legs in a very worldly way, while lighting up a cigarette held in a long, golden cigarette holder. She was stunning. Both of these people broke all of my ecclesiastical stereotypes.

Because of Robert Crandall the content of my experience of both church and religion shifted dramatically. God was still a supernatural, external, miracle-working deity, but this God was no longer a moralistic judge ready to punish wayward sinners through all eternity. My new rector was not a Bible-quoter, nor was he bothered about contradictions in the Bible, or those ghastly biblical tales of divine behavior and misbehavior. This was no old-line evangelical. He was worldly-wise, fun to be with and quite confident, not in the Bible, to which he related very tangentially, but in what he regarded as his ultimate authority—namely, what he called "the faith of the church and its historic teaching."

With Robert Crandall I began to move beyond the literal Bible to those "teachings of the church." It was still a kind of fundamentalism, but it offered me much more wiggle room. I walked into this new understanding with relief. The teachings of the church were so much broader, less tightly defined and looser than the inerrant words of the Bible. I was still in that phase of human development in which I needed an ultimate arbiter of truth to keep all of my anxieties in check. "The faith of the church" was a more interactive authority and had a more pleasant feel about it than did those confusing, authoritarian words "the Bible says!"

Robert Crandall talked about what he called "the faith," or "the deposit of faith," as if it were a concise, well-defined body of data that had been handed down from heaven in propositional form, complete with footnotes, for the benefit of believers. I suspect he actually thought it had been. It was not important to him that he wrestle with issues or debate opinions. It was essential only that he remain faithful to "the church's teaching" as an aid in living life. He related to "the faith" as if it were a garment that he could actually put on and wear. All of my questions about God and about death were gathered up in the security of his confidence. He filled a great aching void inside me and so I quickly became a disciple, a devotee, almost a "groupie." He and his wife had no children at this time, so perhaps my teenage devotion met some need in both of them. I will never know. This relationship, however, would clearly be identified by me as life-changing. It was because of Robert Crandall that I wanted to be, indeed was eager to be, a priest like him. It was because of him that I went to the University of North Carolina, where I followed the course of study that he had outlined. It was because of him that I chose the theological center I would attend for my ordination training. It was, of course, the institution from which he had graduated. He would also provide for me the example, the shape and the focus of my early priestly career. Robert Crandall was so certain and so assured about what he believed that he gave me a sense of religious and personal peace that I had never known before. I was quite convinced that though I still had unanswered questions, my faith would, in time, give me those answers. I needed only to be patient. I was eager to be with my mentor and to "put on" this "faith of the church" and to live securely within its tight fit. Robert Crandall came across not just as competent, but also as loving and caring. I admired him openly. My inerrant Bible had been replaced by an inerrant church. I realize now that I was still being driven by my need for security. That is the primary function of religion, after all: providing security. Empowered by this newfound security, I turned my life toward the goal of ordination, eager to spread the security I had found in my new understanding of Christianity. It would carry me for years, but it never really stopped the searching process, which continued even beneath my priestly confidence.

If I were to try to locate this phase of my personal journey on the blueprint of the human journey, I would say that I had moved from that ancient world where nothing was really understood fully into what might have been represented by the thirteenth century in western Europe: the Age of Faith, with its unquestioned, unchallenged propositional understanding of Christianity. That was a time of great religious certainty, a time of pretending that truth could be captured in human forms and that "the true faith" could be our possession. I became a thoroughgoing "Crandallite."

In a quite "monklike" fashion, I regularly buttressed this faith by a series of spiritual disciplines. I used the Episcopal *Book of Common Prayer* as a kind of ecclesiastical corset, adopting the monastic practice of daily prayer at specified times in the morning and again in the evening, together with regular Bible readings and study. My busy university years challenged my adolescent faith, but my seminary years put it back together, I was sure, in a way that would last forever. Forever turned out to be rather brief.

My first congregation was made up of two distinct groups that reflected the church's physical location in Durham, North Carolina. On one side of this church stood the Erwin Cotton Mills, around which the mill community was built, with the mill owning most of the houses. On the other side of this church stood Duke University. The part of the congregation that came from the mill community was generally not well educated or particularly inquisitive. They had no idea why they needed to celebrate the Feast of St. Philip and St. James in May or the Feast of St. Simon and St. Jude in October, but they tolerated my passions. The university portion of the congregation was made up principally of students, both undergraduate and graduate, many on the way to becoming doctors at the medical school of that great university. They kept pressing me to step out of my religious ghetto. They found little appeal in the cloistered halls of theological certainty to which I was still committed. They exhibited no desire to return to the thirteenth century. While I was not yet ready to leave the religious security I had so recently found, I recognized, even if I could not yet admit it, that it was fading away. No one can really engage a university world without being challenged by it. If there was no such thing as the "true faith," then how does one know how to measure truth at all? That was my frightening dilemma.

The Age of Faith did not last past the thirteenth century in human history. At Duke University I too was forced to move on, and more quickly than I wished. Resting places where security was believed to abound become places for shorter and shorter stays. I found myself increasingly trying to proclaim traditional religious solutions while feeling the first waves of what, when it was experienced societally, was called the Enlightenment, which was eroding the presuppositions of all that I was asserting. If God had really been captured and if truth had really been known in the words and phrases of traditional religion, then it was clear to me that both this God and the words and phrases of this God's religion had to be defended. Yet the world into which I was moving seemed to know almost intuitively that no one could ever again remain in or return to the certainties of the past. Such a desire simply dies as a realistic possibility. The question then becomes: Where shall we go? It should surprise no one that the God I thought I had found was now fading. The church's responses to the questions that life increasingly posed for me seemed to be answers no longer. I was left to revisit that ancient trauma that self-consciousness had originally raised in my ancestors. I wondered about many things. Is there any purpose or meaning that can be imposed on the world from outside it? Is that not what religion has always tried to do? Is there any future hope for our lives, which are so clearly bounded by finitude and mortality? If the answer to both or either of these issues is not to be found in religion, is there an answer that can be found *anywhere* or, as we have for so long feared, are we hopeless people who seek so desperately to create hope that we are willing to be deluded? The religious quest was now itself filled with anxiety.

I was at this point in my life a priest just beginning my career. I had to do my ministry with integrity. I had to believe in what I was doing. Yet, even then, I knew that I could no longer play the religious game that I had once embraced so totally. No, God did not die or disappear for me in that moment, but the way I had always defined God began to do so. To me it felt like the same thing. This was the valley that I had to enter and the world through which I had to navigate. I could not ignore it much longer. I had begun, I now realize, to emerge into that period of history we know as the modern world. No, I was not then aware of it, but it seems to me now that I was once again replicating the human journey. I had moved first from the birth of self-consciousness into the religious symbols of certainty. As those symbols began to crack and break apart, I had to move again. But to where? The clue to that will be found only if I now shift back to the human story and bring that once again into our focus. I was about to discover that there was nothing especially unique about the things with which I was grappling.

SIX

LIFE'S DOMINANT DRIVE: SURVIVAL

Man [or woman] is equally incapable of seeing the nothingness from which he [or she] emerges as the infinity in which he [or she] is engulfed.

Blaise Pascal[1]

Man [or woman] is the only animal for whom his [or her] own existence is a problem which he [or she] has to solve.

Erich Fromm[2]

Is there something that all living things have in common? I believe there is, and to know what life is all about, this defining mark must be made clear and understood existentially. Charles Darwin, surveying the sweep and grandeur of biological history, called it "the survival of the fittest."[3] Richard Dawkins, England's outstanding and perhaps most articulate scientist, called it "the selfish gene."[4] The drive to survive seems to be a biological reality in all living things. We can interpret it in a variety of ways, but we cannot deny that all living things, even those with no signs of consciousness, not only resist death, but also appear to participate in what might be called the universal drive for survival. I have already identified the growing awareness of mortality in my own life, and its attendant fear. Now I need to look at that same phenomenon in the history of humankind. The drive to survive seems to motivate human life so deeply that perhaps the time has come to face openly and honestly the question of whether the human hope and yearning for life after death might well turn out to be just one more manifestation of this biologically driven survival desire that is present in all living things. That is a rather uncomfortable idea that cries out to be explored, so our journey will travel on this pathway for at least a short distance. It cannot be denied that this is at least a possibility.

I begin by simply illustrating from the world of nature that the quest to live, the very tenacious survival quality that is self-consciously present in human life, appears also to be present at *every* level of living things. One sees it almost universally in the world of nature. Even plant life, looked at from the outside, appears to be endowed with a will to survive, though perhaps that will is just an innate physical attribute. I know that to state it this way is to read human yearnings into inanimate objects, but the fact remains that plants do stretch their thin leaves toward the sun in a process that we call photosynthesis so that they might survive. Plants have also developed both beautiful blooms and enticing smells to attract other forms of life to them—life forms that in turn spread plant pollen to make it possible for those plants to reproduce themselves. There is a remarkable adaptive quality in plant life that seems to equip each type of flora to survive in the most difficult of environments. The cactus, for example, has developed the ability to retain water, enabling it to thrive in the desert, while plants located in the earth's rain forests have developed the means of shedding excess water. Of course, the plants are not *aware* of these things, but the quest for survival and the adaptability that enables these living things to blend into the circumstances of their location in such a way as to be sustained in life are essential parts of nature's story. At the same time, life in all its forms is so deeply interdependent that some living things survive in order to become the means for the survival of other living things. That is nature's paradox: it is so marvelous and awe-inspiring that it drives us to declare it the gift of God, while also reflecting a violent and certainly relentless tooth-and-claw struggle. I am constantly amazed both by the capacity of living things to survive in the harshest and most demanding of environments and by nature's fierce struggle to maintain life.

Traveling into the interior of central Australia, one comes upon one of the truly great wonders of the world, a place that the aboriginal people of that land regard as "holy ground," calling it by the name Uluru. Westerners, upon discovering it—and characteristically insensitive to its aboriginal history—named it "Ayers Rock," after Sir Henry Ayers, the chief secretary of South Australia. Uluru is a massive outcropping of rock in the middle of nowhere. Measuring 5.8 miles, or 9.4 kilometers, in circumference, it is so large that multiple helicopters, perhaps as many as a hundred, could land simultaneously on its surface in relative safety. It has challenged climbers from all over the world and claimed many of them as its victims. To feel the cold surface of Uluru at night or its warm (over one hundred degrees), but still hard, surface in the heat of the day is to be aware of how inhospitable to life this smooth rock surface is. All rocks, however, including gigantic rock formations like Uluru, have crevices. With the passage of time the wind blows dust into those crevices, and some of it sticks. Next, the wind or perhaps the birds deposit seeds in those dust-filled places, and soon the miracle of life is replicated with tiny sprigs of green sprouting from the crevices. No place on this earth seems either too harsh or too inhospitable for *all* life; there is always at least *some* form of life that can adapt itself to every demanding environment. There appears to be a will to maintain life that is present in all living things, manifesting itself even in primitive environments, even on huge rock outcroppings. This drive to survive is a remarkable fact of life itself.

Australia is the land that also introduced me to what the people there call the "sacrificial leaves" of the mangrove trees. I became aware of this reality while traveling in a boat on a tidal river in northern Queensland, near Cairns. This river, which varied in flow and salinity with the tides, was lined on both sides with mangrove trees. These trees had thick green foliage, and yet there was an occasional orange leaf on their branches. Furthermore, now and again orange leaves could be seen floating on the river. These bright leaves did not reflect the first colors of fall. No, they were specific, isolated bits of orange located intermittently among the massive numbers of green and thriving leaves. This mystery was explained by one of our guides and I offer it as one more illustration of the drive to survive that is apparently a part of nature.

The mangrove tree, she told us, is essentially a fresh-water plant. Because more of the mangrove is below water than above it, it has had to adapt to accommodate those times when the tidal river in which it lives is up to ninety-five percent salt (or ocean) water. First, it developed a thick and complicated hair-like root system that removes most of the salt from the water before it enters the mangrove tree. Even with that elaborate filtration system, however, there is still too much salt that enters the tree, so a second survival technique has been developed. The incoming salt is routed to specific leaves that are some-how designated to receive it. This causes those leaves to turn orange and eventually to drop off the tree and into the river.

They "sacrifice" themselves so that the plant might live and thus are designated "sacrificial leaves." Of course, none of this is conscious. It is all part of nature's incredible adaptive capacity, but it serves to illustrate that deep in all living things there appears to be an innate will to survive. The bias toward life is almost undeniable.

I do not know how aware insects and arachnids are, but the will to live and the drive to survive seems to be present in those forms of life as well. This is certainly not connected with the anticipation or fear of death, for insects are surely not capable of thinking in such a manner. Yet have you ever gone into the bathroom at night and discovered a bug of some description, perhaps a "granddaddy long legs," in the sink? In your eagerness to rid your world of this nocturnal and unwelcome visitor, you turn on the tap, only to observe the instinct of survival at work. The six- or eight-legged creature scurries rapidly around the sink to avoid the rush of water until finally it disappears down the drain. This behavior seems to reflect the same commitment to life and survival that is in all living things; perhaps it is even encoded in the DNA of life.

One observes worms, insects and small animals which burrow into the earth to escape the keen eyes of birds looking for prey. One observes fish diving to escape the skilled fishing beaks of the seagulls. In still higher forms of life, barely aware creatures seem to exhibit what we call the fight-flight syndrome, an instinctual response designed to keep them in life as long as possible. Herds of zebra and of various members of the deer family, for example, flee if they come within the sight or the smell of a natural enemy. There is some safety, however, in the herd's numbers. The predator has no interest in destroying the herd, so the herd flees as one until the predator isolates its prey and pounces for the kill. The others then cease their flight, knowing that the hunger of the predator has now been satisfied and that they no longer need to flee. In effect the herd sacrifices one of its own for the privilege of living another day. The herd returns to graze in contentment until the next predator appears. Each species of living things seems to produce enough of its kind to satisfy those in whose food chain they live and yet to keep the species alive in the wondrous balance of nature.

Even when the fight for life in the world of nature is one on one, the drive to survive is apparent. The weaker creature flees its enemy until cornered or trapped and then it typically turns to face that enemy in one last stand, one final struggle to preserve life. With back arched and teeth bared, it utters whatever sound it is capable of uttering and offers whatever resistance it can before the curtain on its life rings down. Everywhere one looks in the world of nature, life, no matter how conscious or how primitive, seems to be valued. It does whatever it can to make it through another day. Nature might well be the realm of kill or be killed, but within that struggle for life there appears to be a balance that *sustains* life, that *enables* life, that *encourages* life. That drive is not conscious. It does not preoccupy the rudimentary thinking processes of most living things, but it is there. Life in all of its forms is driven by the adaptive power of this innate quest for survival.

The world before self-consciousness entered it did not have to wrestle with mortality, for living things that are not self-conscious do not know either that they are alive or that they will die. They do not know loneliness or separation, for they cannot conceive of themselves as distinct creatures. They are instead simply part of nature. They might know instinctual anxiety in the presence of a natural enemy, but they know no chronic anxiety such as that which marks the self-conscious creature. When life took the dramatic step from consciousness into self-consciousness, it was never to be the same again. The "shock absorbers" of not being aware of either life or death were removed. Now self-conscious beings had to learn to cope in many arenas: They had to cope with the forces of nature that had power over them. They sought and developed ways to win nature's favor, to aid their now self-conscious struggle for survival. They had to cope with what the prayer book of my church calls "the shortness and uncertainty of human life."[5] Non-self-conscious creatures still do not have to cope with that reality. Finally, they had to deal with the knowledge of death as their ultimate destiny, as well as with questions of purpose and meaning. If the species Homo sapiens had not found a way to lower the anxiety that self-consciousness brings and to transform it from chronic trauma into meaning and hope, I am not sure that this step, which we think of as an inevitable part of the evolutionary journey, would have been sustainable. From a survival point of view, it matters not whether that meaning and hope were real or delusional; they were necessary for the maintenance of human life. The dinosaurs did not quake at the moment of their extinction, but we do. If self-conscious creatures had not been able to find a way to address the chronic shaking of the angst that self-consciousness introduced into this world, that evolutionary step would have proved too painful to manage. The drive for survival, apparently present in all forms of life, that adaptive capacity that enables us to change in order to live, had in human life now reached the level of self-consciousness. That step into being human was as big as any other transition that had been made in our entire evolutionary history. It was as significant as the moment when life divided into animate and inanimate things. It was as big as the emergence of consciousness itself. Coping with this tremendous new experience of self-consciousness was a life-and-death matter. In short, there was a compelling need to lower the anxiety to manageable levels if we were to survive.

One of the ways we learned to cope, indeed I would say the *primary* coping device that we developed, was religion. The pattern of turning to religion in order to deal with the anxiety of death, I have discovered, is not unique to me or to those people with whom I have been privileged to interact. An all but universal human practice, it appears to have been born with the moment of self-consciousness itself. That discovery inevitably raises huge theological questions that most of us are loath to face. For example: If God is an entity whose primary purpose is to still our trembling hearts, then can God really be anything other than a creature of our own making? Must this insight not drive us to the conclusion that God can no longer be viewed as anything other than a figment of our imagination, created in our own image for the sole purpose of providing a cushion against the emotional shocks brought on by self-consciousness and the knowledge of our inevitable mortality? No one can look openly at our human beginnings and not wonder in this manner about these things.

If we decide, as many seem to be doing today, that this is really all that God is, then we have to ask another question: Is this definition of God what God is? Or is there, as Paul Tillich once stated, a God behind the gods of men and women—one that can be experienced but not defined, and that makes all of our definitions woefully inadequate?[6] Can we ever escape these human creations of God sufficiently to explore any other option? These become our uniquely human questions as we look at the mutual interrelatedness of all forms of life, including the life of the human race as well as that of your or my individual self. The mystery deepens and the anxiety and fear rise in us all. All meaning in life seems to hang in the balance. We cannot stop here, however; we must continue our journey. The mystery of life will presumably continue to unfold as we walk more and more deeply into it.

SEVEN

RELIGION'S ROLE IN THE FEAR OF DEATH

Old age is always fifteen years older than I am.

Bernard Baruch[1]

Death is the destiny of everything that lives. Nothing ever escapes it. Human beings, however, relate to death differently than every other living thing. We, alone of all the living entities in the world, know that we will die. We anticipate our death, seek to deny it, and even try to avoid it. We fear it, dread it and yet have to endure it knowingly. Human beings are forever seeking to transform death in some way, and most of us search for some means whereby we can transcend it. More than any one of us seems to realize, or is willing to admit, death casts its shadow over our conscious lives, invades our every waking moment and penetrates even our dreams. Only human beings think that what is both natural and normal in the animal world is unnatural and abnormal.

Perhaps that is one of the reasons that human beings try so hard and in such obvious ways to put distance between

ourselves and the animal kingdom. Most of the religious systems of the world have developed myths designed to hide any
close relationship that human beings might have with the
animal world. These myths proclaim just how and why it was
that the creation of human life was different, a special and separate act on the part of some deity or deities. We are, these narratives proclaim, wonderfully and fearfully made in the image
of the holy one. We are the rulers or at least the stewards of all
other living things. Perhaps that is also one of the reasons why
negativity toward the idea of evolution is so fierce among religious people and why we find ourselves resisting the evidence
that links us so firmly to all other living things. Perhaps that
is why we do not cringe as we probably should at slaughter-
houses or complain about the cruel ways that chickens, hogs
and various other animals, including alligators, are farmed and
harvested all over the world. Animals are not of infinite worth,
we say. They are not like us. They do not have souls. It is a comfortable, but not necessarily a true, rationalization.

A few years ago my wife and I, accompanied by a professor from the University of Pretoria named Izak (Sakkie)
Spangenberg,[2] went on a safari to Kruger Park, a giant game
preserve in the eastern part of the Republic of South Africa,
bordering Zimbabwe on the north and Mozambique on the
east. For several days we searched for or watched in astonished
delight a wide assortment of animals, including South Africa's
big five—the lion, the leopard, the elephant, the rhino and the
water buffalo—living in their natural and wild habitat. Our
search was largely successful: we missed seeing only the lion. As-
toundingly, even in the wild we could get as close to them as ten
to twenty yards. We observed those patterns of animal behavior that served the survival needs of various species, including
mating dances. We also came to understand anew something
of nature's pecking order. We saw the laws of nature at work,

the security found in the sheer numbers of the herds, the deep interdependence of all life, the chase of the predator that ends in the kill and even illustrations of recycling on the part of nature. In that animal world ultimate things like birth and death seem so natural, so matter-of-fact. Herds show no ill effects when one of their number becomes dinner for a lion or a leopard. Among the more dramatic sights we came upon was that of a full-grown but dead giraffe. One does not realize just how large a giraffe is until one sees it sprawled out on the ground. Death appeared in this case not to have come from some natural enemy. It was suggested by a park guide that one of the game wardens had put this giraffe down, perhaps because of a broken leg, leaving it on the ground to let nature dispose of it in its own way. By the time we arrived on this scene a row of vultures, perhaps six in number, were already standing on the giraffe's carcass preparing to eat their fill. They were the first step in the natural recycling process. In a very short time a large hyena appeared, soon to be followed by others. In one of the more amazing facts of nature, there are some creatures, hyenas being one of them, who prefer rotting dead meat, and thus they serve as the cannibalistic undertakers of the natural order. Had we been able to return to that same spot the next day, I suspect that little evidence would have remained that this giraffe had ever lived. Nature's recycling power is efficient and complete; nothing is wasted. The other animals, including fellow giraffes, took little notice of this dead giraffe. Non-carnivorous animals simply walked past this carcass without pausing.

Compare that behavior, if you will, with the response to death among human beings, who have crossed the Rubicon that separates conscious life from self-conscious life. Our human uniqueness and our power to think, signs of our grandeur, lie in our self-conscious grasp of reality, but so does our anxiety, much of our fear and the burden of being human.

All are by-products of the same reality. Self-consciousness is thus both our crown of glory and our cross of anxiety. One cannot be human without embracing both aspects of humanity. So it is the nature of human life to press the edges of reality in acts of gigantic courage and at the same time to shiver in our mortal boots as chronically fearful people, wondering if life has any meaning. We know that we are alive and we know that we will die. We cannot have one without the other. That is why human beings alone count their years. That is why human beings alone understand the concept of being an "I." That is why human beings alone seek to overcome or to transform death. That is why we dream of some continued life beyond the limits of this life. That is why death is never far from our conscious minds.

George Carlin, the late world-famous comedian, during the last days of his life thought with some intensity about both life and time. Prior to his death he sent out a widely circulated e-mail in which he shared his thoughts about aging. He suggested first that the human custom of celebrating birthdays is part of the way we deal with mortality. One has only to look at the way we relate to birthdays, he said, to see the rising tide of anxiety about our impending demise. Only children, Carlin noted, appear to want to rush time in their quest to become "grown up" or to reach maturity. My five-year-old twin grandchildren love to tell me: "I am five and a half." I have never known an adult to say: "I am forty-nine and a half." Adults rather try to slow down the invisible time machine. Only adults ever say such things as "I am twenty-nine and holding." Only adults would understand the old Jack Benny comedy routine where he remained thirty-nine forever.[3]

It is only special, youthful and transitional birthdays that are marked with panting anticipation. Our vocabulary reveals that fact when teenagers tell us, "I'm going to be sixteen," as if they can hardly wait. In some states, the sixteenth birthday opens the door to one's driver's license and thus to what teenagers perceive as the emancipation from childhood and parental control. The eighteenth birthday is also anticipated since it brings with it the right to vote and, when the draft is in force, gives the right or privilege of serving in the armed forces of our nation. The words "I will soon be twenty-one" are also spoken with heightened expectations, since achieving that goal opens the door to what many regard as the adult vices. As the years pass, however, the tone changes dramatically as anticipation declines and anxiety rises.

Carlin noted the popular and revealing way that we use verbs in counting our major birthdays. He pointed out that we "turn" thirty, we "push" forty, we "reach" fifty, we "make it" to sixty, and we "hit" seventy. When we get to the eighties and nineties— if we do—he observes, some actually try to go backwards. "I'm *just* ninety-two," he records hearing one person say!

Spending a few minutes in the birthday card aisle of a supermarket or a stationery store reveals similar attitudes toward aging and the passing of years. Aging is obviously a significant source of human anxiety. Birthday cards for those turning thirty reveal the shock that accompanies this fateful step into what teenagers think are the "middle years," perhaps even the obsolescent years of life. Cards for those turning forty or fifty are filled with words of reassurance that the one reaching those lofty heights is still vital, attractive and desirable. There is also a note of hedonism attached to these ages, as birthday cards exhort us to live it up while we still can. Jokes and insults about rising decrepitude, however, come to a screeching halt on birthday cards after age fifty. Reality has now become too painful to be the subject of humor. Cards designed for those reaching sixty, seventy and above reflect dramatically changed tones. Here we find congratulatory notes, praise for longevity and the extolling of the gifts of wisdom that are presumed to accompany the aging process. We also read words of reassurance that the aging one still has a future that can be anticipated, enjoyed and lived. There is clearly present in our vocabulary of aging the awareness that we have only a one-way ticket through life and that the end of the line is just that, the end of the line. It is this aspect of self-consciousness that makes human life both unique and difficult.

The eighteenth-century hymn-writer Isaac Watts captured this anxiety of self-consciousness when he penned the words: "Time, like an ever-rolling stream, bears all its sons [and daughters] away. They fly forgotten as a dream dies at the opening day."[4] The words that constitute the liturgy of birthday cards, combined with Carlin's analysis of the verbs used in reacting to the aging process, reveal the depth of the human struggle for survival and the sense that human beings are constantly aware that the battle against mortality is not only one we are losing, but one that cannot be won.

The multi-million-dollar cosmetic industry is another manifestation of our awareness that we are engaged in a losing battle against the passing of time and that our rendezvous with death cannot be forever postponed. Cosmetics actually start out to be the enhancers of maturity. Kids first use them to make themselves look older. I remember well the occasion in 1978 when I was one of the bishops attending in London the Lambeth Conference of the Anglican bishops of the world and we were to be entertained at high tea by Queen Elizabeth II at Buckingham Palace. The bishops were generally accompanied at this tea by their wives, if they were married. My wife was ill at the time and not able to attend, but my twenty-year-old daughter, Katharine, was in England and so I maneuvered to have her accompany me. Children were not invited, but I hoped to let her use my wife's invitation. She did everything she could do to add years to her looks, since the average age of the bishops and their spouses was somewhere between fifty-five and seventy. At forty-seven I was actually one of the few younger ones. Still, a twenty-year-old university student has a hard time posing realistically as a spouse to someone my age. With her hair upswept in a French twist, a delicate hat on the top of her head and a creative use of mascara, she passed and we entered the private gates of Buckingham Palace. Princess Margaret Rose was the member of the royal family assigned to greet a group of six of us and I suspect she thought that I must be some "dirty old man" with a child bride. It mattered not to me and I suspect not to the princess as well, but Katharine and I enjoyed the queen's tea enormously.[5]

Making one look older rather than younger is, however, not the major agenda of the cosmetics industry. This is the industry that produces face creams to slow down the development of wrinkles and then even more powerful creams to cover up the now fully developed wrinkles. Wrinkles are a sign of the aging process and nothing can ever stop them. The world of cosmetics also produces various tints and dyes to hide the graying effect in human hair, many of these products designed to reverse that effect so slowly that the public "will never know." This industry, however, finally reaches its limits of effectiveness. Then it gives way to surgical procedures that appear to excise wrinkles by tightening the skin of one's well-lined neck, by lifting faces and by propping up and expanding sagging breasts. Next we Botox everything that can be Botoxed. The cosmetics industry, together with its surgical auxiliaries, is part of our massive attempt first to stop, then to slow down and finally to hide the ravages of time, the unmistakable signs that we are coming to the end of life. No one should ever underestimate the threat that mortality brings to self-conscious, time-aware human beings.

Everywhere we look we discover that being human is filled with knowledge of and anxiety about aging and mortality. We human beings live our lives aware every moment of our waking days that the shadow of death walks with us, always waiting, always hovering. We know that it will never go away until it has claimed each of us for its own. That is a heavy emotional load and yet we all must carry it. Bearing that burden is both a heroic task and a universal responsibility.

How do we do it? The search for this answer drives us deeply into the coping devices that human beings have developed to prevent themselves from being overwhelmed by this burden. Coping devices are designed to provide or to create meaning and purpose to counter the specter of living in a meaningless and purposeless world, and they are almost universally directed toward overcoming the fact of our mortality. Perhaps another definition of human life is just that: we are self-conscious animals who have developed coping devices to bank the fires of our own mortality-based anxieties. When we examine these devices, however, there are some serious questions that need to be asked: Do these coping devices really deal with our anxieties or do they simply suppress or drug them? Are they real or are we engaged in a game called "let's pretend"? I would argue, as I began to do in Chapter 6, that the development of religion is the chief and the most powerful coping device that human beings have ever constructed. Human beings are uniquely and almost universally religious creatures.

To understand our own humanity, then, we must also understand the religious systems which we have developed and why they work as they do. Part of our defense against exposing our religious systems as fraudulent is to claim that they are not *human* creations at all; that they were divinely revealed. One cannot really study the meaning of that for which a divine initiative is claimed. Thus one cannot raise the questions that need to be raised until one is able to step outside religion. The problem is, however, that none of us can really step outside religion until we cease to be one of its practitioners. We have to affirm the power of the system before it will support us. A coping device no longer works once it has been recognized as a coping device. That is why I have suggested that before we can talk about life after death we must step beyond religion. One of the great gifts coming to us in a post-religious world is our ability to do just that. So our next step is to find a way to probe religion as an outsider seeking to understand how it has been constructed to give strength and courage to anxiety-filled human beings. This study must, therefore, raise the questions that it is impossible for those who still live inside the boundaries of any or all religions ever to raise. My own spiritual journey has led me to exactly this place. I think the journey of the human race has also come to this same place. We—individuals and society—must both, therefore, be prepared to take the next critical and crucial step. Some will think this is an immobilizing conclusion, but we press on with other questions.

Does religion, as it has been practiced in human history, actually make us more human or less human? Is it possible that religion, rather than transforming reality, enables us to hide from reality, a reality which we are not emotionally equipped to embrace? Is religion in all its forms, as Marx suggested, an opiate for the people?[6] Is the very function of religion calculated to provide us with a believable denial of the angst that accompanies self-consciousness? Beyond those questions is the deeper probe into religion's origins. Was the development of the various religions a human inevitability? Is the anxiety of self-consciousness so great that only the belief in the existence of an external supernatural deity, who has the power to come to our aid, will ever quiet our fears? Is God or is religion itself now revealed as little more than a human creation? These are the tough questions that we must now pursue.

If we can entertain these questions, then we also have to ask: What will happen if our suspicions are validated and this defense shield called religion loses its credibility? What will happen if the external supernatural God of religion dies? Can the human psyche bear the experience of self-consciousness without the narcotic of supernaturalism? Is there another option? Was the development of religion the only choice we had at the dawn of human awareness, or was it just the choice we made?

If there was another choice, and I now believe that there was, then we must ask why it was that we could not see that choice, much less embrace it, until we had exhausted what was clearly the first, almost the universal, choice—namely, to develop a religion which would allow us to "place our hand in the hand of the one who made the mountain." I am not taking us on a side trip when I now say that before we can examine this alternative to religion, we have to examine the history of human religion itself. We also have to accept the conclusion that humans made the choice to create religion because it was the only choice we saw. Whatever the weakness of religion may turn out to be, we again have to admit that religion worked for quite a while, perhaps for as long as two hundred thousand years! If it is beginning to fail us now, as I think it is, does that signal despair or a unique opportunity to allow us to consider the denied alternative that perhaps we could never see until the religious option had run its course? I would go so far as to say that this non-religious, denied choice might still have the ability to redefine God, to lead us to an understanding of what it means to be human and even to open the door on a new way to embrace eternity and our participation in it. That is quite a claim. At this point I do not want to identify this option, which we human beings have failed thus far to take, for I am convinced it cannot be seen as an option until we surrender the coping device of religion. I hint at it now only to give us the courage to trace the development of human religion to its ultimate conclusion, to understand how it worked and why it worked, to recognize its impending demise and to begin to feel the weight of self-consciousness in a religionless world. Only then will the heretofore hidden alternative to religion stand before us and invite us to walk in a dramatically new direction. Religion was always external to the human world. I believe we must now go through the human world to discover the ultimate truth to which religion pointed, but which is beyond religion's domain. When we arrive at this place we will discover that the human journey that I have sought to trace and the personal journey that I have lived will finally come together and a new doorway will open and beckon to us to step inside it. I will return to this when the time is right, but for now I must turn to an analysis of the role religion has played in human development, what needs it met and why it can play that role no longer.

EIGHT

THE FACES OF RELIGION

In the South Sea Islands they call this mysterious force Mana; others experience it as an impersonal power, like a form of radioactivity or electricity—the Latins experience numina (spirits) in sacred groves. Arabs felt the landscape was populated by the jinn, when they personalized the unseen forces and made them gods, associated with the wind, sea, and stars, but possessing human characteristics, they were expressing their sense of affinity with the unseen and with the world around them.

Karen Armstrong[1]

Human religion changes in response to human circumstances. That is a dead giveaway, it seems to me, that despite claims that locate religion in the realm of that which has been divinely revealed, religion is, in fact, a human creation that serves a human need. It is a device designed to enable human beings to bank the fires that the anxieties of self-consciousness ignited. We cover religion with myth and magic to make it easier to pretend that it is about an external power and not about ourselves.

The purpose of religion is to elicit divine protection, to win divine favor and to give divine assurance, all of which served to ease humanity's way in a self-conscious world.

If religion is a human, not a divine, creation, then we need to recognize that it too can die. All human creations, all human institutions, do. If the primary purpose of religion is to keep the anxieties of self-consciousness in check, then the question before us is: What happens to those debilitating anxieties when religion dies? Where then will they go? What will those now untamed anxieties do to human life? I believe that we misunderstand religion when we define it as an activity engaged in a search for truth. *Truth* is not religion's ultimate agenda; *security* is. That insight alone makes sense out of the many rationally absurd claims that religions and religious people make. Among those claims, for starters, I include the infallibility of the pope, which is asserted in the face of historical evidence to the contrary and even in the face of that period of history between 1378 and 1417 when there were *two* "infallible popes," each excommunicating the other. This concept also assumes that there is such a thing as "truth" that is or can be settled forever and for which there are no more questions to be entertained.

Another one of religion's more absurd assertions, which makes sense only when viewed through the perspective of security, is the claim for the inerrancy of the Bible. This claim is still made by many despite the fact that we now know that when both Matthew and Luke incorporated Mark into their gospels they each changed, corrected, edited, deleted from and added to Mark and that this was not done infrequently. How can one do any of these things to "the inerrant word of God"? There are thousands of other illustrations of the ineptitude of biblical literalism, but this will suffice for the moment.[2] Other specific and equally irrational claims made by established religious traditions include the idea that God dictated the Torah and that Allah dictated the Koran. In the East we discover claims that the Divine One revealed truth to the Buddha, wisdom to Confucius and insight to Tao. Every religious system has a segment of adherents within its larger body who proclaim that they have the only true understanding of God or the only true church, and that their tradition alone possesses the pathway to salvation. Again the slightest bit of study renders these claims nonsensical. The doctrine of the immaculate conception, for example, was declared to be undoubted truth in 1854 by Pope Pius IX. It was not, however, an infallible teaching so much as it was a political necessity. One needs to understand that this dogma, proclaiming that Mary was born without the stain of original sin, was created by the church only after scientists had discovered that women produce egg cells, which when fertilized form fifty percent of the genetic code of every person who has ever been born. This meant that women could no longer be viewed as unimportant passive receptacles of a life that the male actually produced. Women now had to be seen as co-creators of life. The problem with that was that since the Catholic Church believed that all people passed on Adam's original sin, then Mary, as the daughter of Adam, would have corrupted Jesus. To provide her with an immaculate and sinless conception took care of that. Theology always adjusts to reality. Unchanging or infallible it is not.

These authoritarian claims and many others like them are not benign. It is in the name of these same irrational claims that religious people go to war to force their religion on others. In the service of these claims, religious people become martyrs, persecute "false believers," burn heretics at the stake and all of the other things that human beings have done to others throughout history in the name of "true religion." Yet even the most casual study of religious history will reveal that, even while these ultimate claims are being made for various religious entities, religion itself is an ever-changing, always-evolving human activity. The change agent is never a "new revelation," but a new human situation, an increase in human knowledge, or a transforming human experience. These are the things that ultimately render the religious understandings of the past unbelievable and thus null and void. "Time," to quote James Russell Lowell, always "makes ancient good uncouth."[3] Briefly, but I trust accurately, this point can be demonstrated with considerable ease simply by studying the history of religion.[4]

The most important and perhaps the first key word in the origin of religion was the word "spirit." It is to this day still a primary word in all religious thought. The word "spirit" is a conveniently vague, necessarily unbounded and undefined word. It thus served well those human beings who had just crossed the boundary from consciousness into self-consciousness, who were dealing with the anxieties of aloneness, separation, meaning, purpose and death. They looked for a power beyond their power, someone or something to whom they could attribute the reasons that things happened the way they did. A plan or purpose was sought in the explanation, which of course required that there be a purposeful planner. They needed a "being" who could not only explain why things are as they are, but could actually control those forces of nature before which they felt so impotent, and one who might come to their aid when they were in distress. This understanding of God would someday produce the religious cliché, "There are no atheists in foxholes."

The word "spirit" met all of these criteria. The early humans then applied the word "spirit" to almost everything that moved and to everything that was alive. Sometimes "spirit" was a single force with many manifestations, but that appears to be a later and more sophisticated stage of development. Originally it appears that human beings believed that there were many, many spirits in a spirit-filled world. They interpreted these spirits in a variety of ways. Some were good and so human beings sought to bask in their favor. Some were evil and so human beings sought to avoid or minimize their wrath. What was common in all of their definitions was that these spirits, unseen but presumed to be real, were external to life and thus were not bound by the laws of this world. They were of a realm that possessed supernatural power. Spirits imposed purpose and meaning on the world from outside the world, and thus accounted for everything that people could not otherwise explain. Spirits inhabited every living thing and even caused nonliving things to move. There was a spirit of the sun that caused it to travel across the heavens each day and a spirit of the moon that enabled it to turn in a regular pattern that could be counted on every thirty days. A spirit inhabited every mountain, every grove of trees, every bush and every bloom. The rivers, creeks and ponds all had spirits, as did the crashing waves of a relentless ocean. It was the spirit of the ocean that bound it within specific tidal limits, unless the spirit of the ocean was angered and expressed its fury in extremely high tides that brought flooding. It was catastrophic divine anger that stood behind and explained a tsunami.

Every kind of bird of the air, fish of the sea and beast of the field had an animating spirit. Totemism captures this theme in a semi-modern form. Even the things that would much later be thought of as the basic ingredients of the world—earth, air, fire and water—were assumed to be spirit-filled. To the best of our knowledge it was this understanding of the world as spirit-filled that formed the basis of the first human religion.

This earliest religion, called animism, was the worship of what was believed to be the animating spirits that appeared under a variety of forms. Human beings, like their animal ancestors from which they had just emerged, were nomadic hunter-gatherers in those days and so this spirit-filled world surrounded them no matter where they went. Of course, these spirits were human-like, but in order to quiet human anxieties the spirit world had to be more than just human. This is how the concept of supernaturalism developed. Human beings needed supernatural beings not to be bound by the limits of our physical world. Our definition of these spirits and of the nature of their unseen world reveals quite clearly that they are human creations. We have throughout human history created gods who were in our image and from whom all human limitations have been removed.

We see in the religious practices of animism the essence of all future religious systems. Religion's initial and primary purpose was to enlist divine assistance to help us to cope with the anxieties of self-consciousness. The way religion did this will be the substance of our next chapter. Suffice it now to say that animism served us well as a religion in the hunter-gatherer phase of human history.

Animism faded when hunter-gatherers turned toward living in agricultural communities. That was an enormous shift in human development and it inevitably required the creation of brand-new religious content and the development of a whole new religious system. While animism declined, however, it did not disappear. No human religious system ever does. When Christians today talk about the Holy Spirit, one can hear the ancient echoes of animism.

Recently my wife and I spent an afternoon with a Native American couple of the Pueblo tribe in their pueblo home in New Mexico. During our conversation we encouraged them to talk about their religion. A rather ornate Roman Catholic church was located in the physical center of their Pueblo community and they guarded it from photo-taking tourists night and day. Clearly this was the dominant institution in the village. When this couple talked about their religious practices, however, it became obvious that Roman Catholicism was little more than a thin veneer spread over their animistic, native religion. These people lived in a spirit-filled world and saw all living things as holy. They saw themselves as part of a natural world, along with dogs, birds, rabbits and plants, and believed that they should relate to their environment with respect. They saw sex as a natural and holy part of life, designed to be celebrated. Sexual repression, so much a part of Western religious thinking, was simply not part of their understanding. Animism had not departed; it had merely been covered over with another layer of civilization. The Pueblo people still thought appropriately in the hunter-gatherer style of their ancestors. As this example illustrates, religious systems are best thought of as cumulative, not as one replacing the other.

As the pattern of human life shifted over many generations from nomadic groups of hunter-gatherers into the settled life of agricultural communities, a transition that occurred only some twelve thousand to fifteen thousand years ago at most, it was inevitable that the content of human religion and its understanding of the divine world would also change. Human beings were drawn into this new lifestyle by the attraction of fertile land that would serve their survival needs by providing a readily available source of food. That is why the first human civilizations developed in what is still very rich and productive land like the Nile River Valley of present-day Egypt and the Fertile Crescent formed by the Tigris and Euphrates Rivers in what is currently Iraq. As the context of human religion made its parallel dramatic shift, it did so as a new garment designed to be placed on an old idea. The basic needs in human life that the concept of God met were still identifiable. God was still "other," still external and still endowed with a supernatural power that human life does not possess. God's favor could still be gained by manipulative or even coercive tactics. God was not bound by mortality, which gave human beings a way to claim that they were not bound either.

In an agricultural community survival was not as dependent on the power of the benevolent, supernatural spirits as it was on the fertility of the soil and the hidden powers of what came to be called Mother Earth. It was inevitable, therefore, that the animistic religion that roaming human beings had created now had to adapt to and accommodate to settled communities engaged in agricultural endeavors that tied them to the soil. To move from the nomadism of hunter-gatherers into a relatively permanent living space seemed to separate human beings even farther from the status of the animals, of which they had once been a constituent part. Animals in the quest for survival were perpetual hunter-gatherers, always in search of food and water. Animals expended no energy today worrying about finding the food they might need tomorrow. They did not plant in the spring in order to harvest in the fall. Animals hunted and gathered to live one more day, or until the time when they became food for others. They had no anxiety about the future, nor did they fret over the reality that they were destined to finish their days as part of another creature's food chain. Thus chronic anxiety and the angst of mortality served to separate the human from the animal by what seemed to be an ever-widening divide.

When human beings began to create settled communities and to depend on the land to produce the food they needed, they were depending on the fertility of the soil of Mother Earth and on receiving the necessary rains from the sky. The human coping system called religion inevitably began to adapt to these new realities. Animism evolved into a religion focused on a deity who was more earth-centered and even a Goddess who encouraged fertility. Now it was not the favor of the animating spirits that human beings needed to solicit; it was the favor of the Earth Goddess out of whose womb the living things that sustained their lives seemed to come. It was this sense of the earth as divinized that brought the feminine principle into human worship for the first time in a conscious way. Human religion turned away from animating spirits and began to see the divine in the feminine, especially the feminine symbol of the fertility of Mother Earth.

The womb of Mother Earth began to be seen as that which brought forth the food needed to sustain life. This in turn caused the status of the female to rise. It also did not escape the notice of these ancient people that it was the female of the animal species that gave birth, causing the flocks to be replenished, and it was the women of the tribe who produced the sons and daughters that kept the tribe alive in a new generation. Suddenly, or perhaps not so suddenly as it now appears, the guarantor of continued life was not the "supernatural" spirits, but the feminine principle. So God began to take a new and more settled form. Mother Earth and Mother Nature are feminine concepts in every language of the world. These words are the vestigial remains of this moment of feminine worship in human history. This was the time in the history of religion when reproduction was glorified, when sex and religion became intimately related and when temple prostitution, both male and female, became a fixture in agricultural-based worship. This is also when child sacrifice became a religious act. People believed that if they offered their firstborn child to the Goddess of fertility they would be blessed with many more children. Even the custom of opening the body of Mother Earth to insert into her womb the bodies of her sons and daughters who had died is a manifestation of this kind of female-oriented religion. The content of this Earth Goddess religion did not last long, but it is part of our religious history. Its decline came primarily because of three things. First, a rising awareness developed of the male's role in reproduction. Previously the nine months between cause and effect

had simply been too long for the first human beings to understand the connection. With that new knowledge the custom
began of coupling the female Goddess with a male consort,
and the gradual masculinizing of the deity became the path
that human religion was destined to follow.

The second factor that hastened the decline of feminine religious content was that the agricultural communities, as they
grew larger and larger, needed to be protected from pillaging
nomads. The military virtues of size, strength and training
thus became necessary for the well-being and the continued
life of the growing community. Males, who generally possessed
greater strength and swiftness and who were never burdened
with either pregnancy or nursing, were the ones upon whom
the protection of the clan rested.

Finally, as agricultural community life became more and
more organized, it had to be governed. A chief then emerged out
of the ranks of the warriors. The job of the tribal chief was to
enhance the survival of the tribe and to provide for its security
and well-being. It was not long before the content of the deity
in whom survival was vested began to look more and more like
a tribal chief and we human beings entered the phase of tribal
religion. This tribal God was clearly male. He had the task of
protecting the tribe that worshipped him. This God in time
began to be identified with the sky out of which came light,
warmth, rain and wind. The tribal deity was believed to live
beyond the sky. The rain falling from the sky began to be understood as the divine semen sent to impregnate Mother Earth
and to cause her womb to reproduce various forms of life.

Like animism before them, the feminine aspects of God
and worship faded, but once again they did not disappear.
Throughout human history there has been a series of Goddess
figures who have kept the feminine religious principle alive. Isis
in Egypt and Diana of Ephesus were two of its ancient forms.

The rise of the cult of the Virgin in the Western world and the labeling of the church as "Mother Church" were two of its medieval forms. Today both the environmental movement and the peace movement are attempts to recover the feminine in worship. As noted previously, human beings do not appear ever to *dismiss* the stages of religious development through which they have moved; they simply bring them back in another form. Perhaps that is something we should never forget.

Despite persistent female elements, in time the masculine deity overwhelmed the feminine principles and the masculine deity of tribal religion became totally dominant. The marks of a tribal deity are certainly visible in the early stories in the Bible. A tribal deity always has a chosen people—namely, the people of the tribe for which this God is God. This tribal God reflects tribal values. This God is jealous and demands loyalty. This God hates everyone the tribe hates. This is the God who sends plagues on Egypt and who stops the sun in the sky so that Joshua will have a longer period of daylight in which to slaughter more of the enemies of the Jews.

As the world grew more interdependent, the various tribal deities competed, just as their respective tribes competed. If a tribe lost a war, its members tended to disappear, taking their tribal God with them. No one today builds an altar to Chemosh, Baal or Marduk.[5] Defeat meant that one tribal deity had been defeated by a more powerful deity. In those circumstances the surviving deity began to grow into a larger presence ruling over a larger and larger part of the world.

As time passed, these deities also began to expand in power and new human qualities were added to their characters. In the Jewish tradition it fell to the role of the prophets to transform the tribal deity of the early Jewish tradition into a larger universal presence that was more abstract and less masculine. It was the prophet Hosea who redefined God as "love."

It was the prophet Amos who redefined God as "justice." It was the prophet Micah who helped people understand that God's focus was not on proper worship, but on effective lives. It was the prophet Malachi who finally stretched the God of the Jews out of its tribal mentality and into a universal presence: "From the rising of the sun to its setting," wrote this voice in the wilderness, "my name is great among the nations [i.e., the Gentiles], and in every place incense is offered to my name" (Mal. 1:11).[6]

We have not yet in our world reached a universal consciousness in human religion, but we are coming closer. The concept of God as "One" is widely recognized throughout the world. The nature of this one God, however, is still much in debate. In the Western world the content of the Judeo-Christian God of the Bible tends to define the universal deity. In the Middle East it is the God of Islam and the Koran and in the Far East it is the God of the Hindu-Buddhist tradition, with its variations of Sikh, Jain, Shinto, Tao and Confucius. Basically, human religion has evolved into three tribal religious groups, each of which claims to represent the one universal God.

We human beings have been through a long journey with God in the years of our self-consciousness and thus in the years of our human history. Though it has never been a static journey, no matter how radically the external forms of religion have changed, three principles have remained intact to meet the original human needs born in self-consciousness and to relieve the attending human anxieties: God had to be external to us. God had to be supernatural and able to come to our aid. God had to be timeless and the guarantor of our hope for immortality.

Religion is thus revealed to be a human creation designed to meet human needs. When we look at religion from this perspective, it is not nearly as noble as we like to pretend, either in its origins or in its practices. Religion is not divinely inspired; it is sometimes quite manipulatively human. Does this sound harsh? Perhaps it is, but that is the way truth is often perceived, and truth can never be dismissed simply because it is inconvenient. So I hope you will read on.

NINE

THE TOOLS OF RELIGIOUS MANIPULATION

Banished after his sin, Adam bound his offspring also with the penalty of death and damnation, that offspring which by sinning he had corrupted in himself, as in a root; so that whatever progeny was born (through carnal concupiscence, by which a fitting retribution for his disobedience was bestowed upon him) from himself and his spouse—who was the cause of his sin and the companion of his damnation—would drag through the ages the burden of Original Sin, by which it would itself be dragged through manifold errors and sorrows, down to that final and never-ending torment with the rebel angels. . . .

. . . So the matter stood; the damned lump of humanity was lying prostrate, no, was wallowing in evil, it was falling headlong from one wickedness to another; and joined to the faction of the angels who had sinned, it was paying the most righteous penalty for its impious reason.

Augustine, Bishop of Hippo[1]

We have now noted the fact that throughout history religious systems adapt in direct response to the changes in the way that human life is organized. This means, of course, that religion is clearly a weapon in the arsenal of human survival. This realization challenges the "objectivity" claims of the religious myths that have served through the ages to define religion as "revealed truth." To think of religion as "revealed truth" is to invest it with the power to compel conformity and to enable nonconformists to be effectively silenced or to be ostracized. That is why excommunication and other forms of shunning have been such terrifying punishments throughout history. Once we embrace this understanding, we can begin to see just why it is that particular religious practices developed the way they did. For even though the particular forms and content of religious beliefs have varied widely across both time and culture, the needs that religion is designed to address are deeply human, and in that humanity they are remarkably similar. Consider, for example, the popular religious idea that God has revealed to a designated religious leader the rules that must govern "our duty toward God" and "our duty toward our neighbor," even inscribing them on "tablets of stone." Variations of these familiar themes are found in almost every religious tradition, which means that any serious study of the meaning of religion in human life must identify these self-serving attempts to build impenetrable defensive walls behind which human beings seek to hide their fear and thus to cope with these threatening realities. If we want to journey beyond religion, we must navigate these barriers. We must see them for what they have always been and finally set them aside. Most of the time human beings are not able to do that, but instead work to keep these realities hidden from our conscious minds.

It was Sigmund Freud who once observed that when religious leaders claim that they possess their mandate from God by way of a divine revelation—which is, of course, not subject to challenge—and when these same authorities claim to be the only ones authorized to interpret these revelations accurately, we must recognize these claims as nothing more than hysteria in search of certainty![2] One would not have to build such irrational protective walls around truth *that was indeed self-evidently true*. One does, however, have to protect truth that one only *pretends* to believe. In our probe into how religion works we must expose pretension and dismiss all such religious claims. That is why it is all but impossible to enter into a study like this until one has stepped outside the emotional claims of religion and is no longer a devotee of that system. Only those who inhabit a post-religious world can go where I am headed, for they must avoid the circular religious arguments that act as sentries to guard that which no longer makes much sense, but which we are loath to relinquish.

Religious practices, when analyzed objectively, make it obvious that their hidden purpose is to manipulate the external supernatural deity so that this deity will bring divine power to bear in the service of frightened human beings. When the myths and fantasies are scraped away, that is what remains as religion's ultimate goal. The first focus of religion, we have already noted, is to secure this life by allowing us to solicit the divine favor of a supernatural power to come to our aid. The second focus of religion is to overcome the fear that accompanies the knowledge of our mortality and to win eternity by having a guarantee that we will be victorious over the awesome power of death that threatens our hold on meaning at every moment. When we accept these insights and go underneath the surface piety of organized religion, the picture we see is not a very pretty one. In this chapter I will examine those twin foci of religious activity, designed as they are to manipulate God so that God will do our will, and thus we might gain for ourselves an advantage in the battle for survival in this life. Only then can I proceed to look at the self-serving dreams that religion has taught us to project onto life after death, which is the subject into which I will move in the next chapter. In both studies religion's dark side inevitably becomes apparent. Reward and punishment are religion's weapons of choice in this life, and they then become the ultimate force in our thoughts about the life to come. Most people think these images of an afterlife reflect only human yearnings, but a closer look reveals that they also reflect human hostility, judgment, rejection and fear. We enter this discussion, therefore, with some apprehension. I begin with a human analogy.

The purpose of the human tactic of flattery is always to manipulate the flattered one. It is a tactic that human beings have used since the dawn of time with authority figures. It is the "apple for the teacher" writ large. It is seen in the titles that human beings have applied to kings and ecclesiastical leaders. Those titles run the gamut from asserting divine status to acknowledging both king and priest as chosen by God and favored by God. Kings are addressed as "Your Excellency," the pope as "Your Holiness," the patriarch of Constantinople as "Your Beatitude," and clergy as "the revered ones," since that is what the title "reverend" means. Human flattery has another, diametric manifestation that religion regularly uses. The flip side of flattery is to state one's own unworthiness to be in the company of the authority figure, whether it be royalty or one who claims to be a representative of the divine. Self-denigration is thus just another name for what might be called the tactic of humble flattery. Whatever it takes to gain a boon, to enlist the help of the authority figure in achieving one's own goals and agenda, becomes our adopted practice. The transition made in religion from the way we relate to human authority figures to the way we relate to God is easy to document.

It begins when God is defined as "other" and is assigned all of the attributes that we believe we ourselves lack. Only then do we seek the means to solicit and to manipulate that power. That is how the activity of flattery became part of the divine-human dialogue. The human origins of religion are once again visible in our assumption that the deity will respond to our flattery in the same way that human authority figures respond. Flattery presupposes that the flattered one can be enticed to do what we wish. So early humans developed liturgical words to be used in worship that are unashamedly designed to flatter the deity, to gain the deity's favor, to win approval and to enlist divine power on our behalf. Today in ecclesiastical circles, we call these words praise, but they are in reality little more than liturgical flattery. Listen with rational ears to what people are doing when they sing the hymn "How Great Thou Art" to God. Try to imagine a deity who needs to hear the words of that song. Observe the flattering titles by which God is addressed in prayer: we call God "almighty," "ever-living," "most gracious," "most loving," with many more superlatives added. Those titles should, we seem to think, get God's attention. We continue by telling God that "the heavens declare God's glory," and that these same heavens cannot contain God's power. In our prayers we find ourselves describing what we hope God is, at least what we hope the God whose help we need is. "Thou art more ready to hear than we to pray," we say. We plead: "If thou, Lord, wilt be extreme to mark what is done amiss, O Lord, who may abide it?" "You have taught us in your holy word that you are slow to anger and of great kindness," we say, reminding God of what God must be. On and on we could go. The God who is "other" has clearly been created in terms of this deity's ability to meet our human need. God cannot be helpful if God is limited. God must, therefore, be mightier than we, capable of dealing with the things with which we do not feel capable of dealing. The

God of religion and religion itself must be able to relieve that human sense of powerlessness that we feel and to deal with whatever it is that we bring to God in prayer. Worship is simply an act of flattery by which we hope to gain God's attention and to force the deity to meet our needs.

Next, examine the posture and demeanor of people in church. We who gather for worship are frequently encouraged to kneel and kiss the ring of the divine representative, to go down upon our knees in the presence of the holy God, or to bow our heads and even to beat our breasts in acts of humility. These behaviors, typical of one who is seeking a favor, are just another form of flattery. Beggars understand this when they go on their knees to importune those who might supply their next meal. Slaves understand this when they go on their knees to implore their masters, who have authority over their very lives, for mercy. Serfs understand this when they go on their knees to gain favor from the lord of the manor. What does it say about our understanding either of God or of ourselves that we think the proper behavior of the worshipper before the deity is the position of kneeling, the same position employed by beggars, slaves, serfs and others who judge themselves in the manipulative process to be inferior and inadequate?

Going one step farther, it is important in human discourse for the subordinate one to recognize in a self-conscious way his or her unworthiness even to be making such demands on, or petitions to, the superior one. That is why beggars state their unworthiness to impinge upon the time of the one being implored. That is why slaves readily confess to whatever charges the master might bring as to their unworthiness for special treatment and serfs remind the lord of the manor that they know their place as the inferior ones. The greatness attributed to the authority figures is apparently maximized by the recognition of the gross inadequacy of the petitioners. The stance of weakness and the seeking of pity are thus also part of the array of manipulative human responses to people in authority. We have borrowed them from the human arena and then we have applied them to God.

Now armed with those insights, look again at the familiar patterns of worship, even contemporary worship, and notice the similarities. We are encouraged liturgically to say dreadful things about ourselves in a tactic designed to win favor, in this case divine favor. In religious liturgies we call ourselves "miserable offenders." We remind God and ourselves that "we have done those things which we ought not to have done and we have not done those things which we ought to have done." As a consequence we tell God that there is "no health [that is, wholeness] in us." We even remind God that we understand that we are not worthy enough even "to gather up the crumbs" from under the divine table. A familiar plea in both ancient and contemporary worship is called the "Kyrie eleison," or "Lord, have mercy." We say it constantly. My church typically uses a "three-fold Kyrie," but when three "have mercies" are not enough, we offer a "nine-fold Kyrie." What, indeed, does it communicate about who we believe God is that our most constant and repeated petition to the embodiment of divinity is "Lord, have mercy"? Is that not the human attempt to gain favor through recognition of our unworthiness? Is that not finally an attempt at divine manipulation?

We also frequently use parent words in our worship to describe both God and those who purport to represent God to us. To refer to the insights of Sigmund Freud once more, the famed psychiatrist suggested that for most people God seemed to be only a parent figure projected into the sky. To call a religious leader "Father" or even "Mother" is to become immediately childlike in religious matters. The use of a parent word like "Father" for God is, he argued, little more than an attempt to return to that level of security we enjoyed when as children we could ascribe infinite power to our parent figures. Remember that when parents are observed from the child's level of comprehension, they appear to possess both unlimited power and infinite knowledge. Children feel secure in the world they think their parents control, so adults yearning for that remembered sense of security create many of the same emotions and invest the same hope in the parental God above the sky, so often called Father. "Our Father, who art in heaven," the prayer attributed, I think incorrectly, to Jesus himself, captures both the parental image of God and the hidden location, above the sky, where the supernatural power that the earth does not possess can be assumed to exist. The motif of flattery in all its forms is a primary aspect of worship, and it is so clearly a human attempt to win divine favor just as in human dialogue flattery is used to gain the approval of earthly authority figures.

The second focus of worship is the pleasing of the deity by the act or acts of obeying the deity's rules. Again the image is rather childlike. Be a good boy or a good girl and you will please God, as you once pleased your parents, and God will reward you just as your parents once did.

Every religious tradition has a code of rules or a sacred text in which the will of God is said to have been spelled out quite clearly. By obeying these rules enjoined to govern behavior, we are thought to guarantee divine favor. God's requirements normally include, first, believing properly and worshipping properly. In the Jewish version of these rules this first component is said to include acknowledging the reality of God, worshipping nothing less than God, honoring God's name and keeping God's day holy with proper liturgical and personal observance. God's requirements include a second component: rules that spell out how we are to behave toward members of the community. Again in the Jewish version of these rules we are told that this means we are to honor our parents and not coincidentally other parent substitutes in the community, and to refrain from killing, committing adultery, stealing, violating the truth and envying. Ask yourself: What is the agenda of the one who seeks to discern the divine will and to obey it? Is it not to enlist the support of the supernatural being on one's own behalf?

Of course there are other dimensions involved in human behavior. Certain laws must be obeyed to allow the community to function and to survive. The primary burden of keeping the law in religious circles has always been, however, to bring divine favor on the tribe and on the individual. Throughout the Bible the idea was expressed that the disobedience of the law of God on the part of an individual, or of the corporate people of Israel, brought the divine wrath not just on one specific offender or even a group of offenders, but on the entire nation. If God is going to be manipulated, the whole nation will either benefit or be punished. Corporate interdependence runs deep. The whole people are to live in such a way as to earn God's approval and not to incur God's wrath. Indeed, there are biblical narratives that enforce this teaching dramatically by suggesting that disobedience brings God's immediate punishment and even death at God's hand. So human survival depends on having God approve the behavior the people have adopted. This, of course, also empowers the community to deal with those who might want to violate the community's understanding of its own vested interests. Because God is always the supernatural "other" with the power to make a difference, the agenda of survival requires that we make this deity serve our needs and that we of necessity must bow to community pressure. In the process we gain as our ally "the parental one" whose limitless power and overt approval are necessary, if we are to keep our anxieties in check. Thus conformity to the adopted standards of community life is just one more tool of our survival arsenal.

This supernatural, theistic God was thus created to be a human coping device, and the human system called religion domesticated this deity, empowered the ruling figures of both king and priest, and spelled out the specific means of coping and indeed of winning. Religion taught us that we could win the struggle for life, the battle for survival now, only by enlisting the help of the supernatural one and by obeying those who claimed for themselves the title of divine representatives. So religion created the framework in which we could sing praises and perform acts of overt flattery designed to cultivate a positive response, while we acted in such a way as to please the all-powerful one. Once again, we are driven to the conclusion that human religion, no matter what its external form or its internal content, was designed to address the primal anxieties born in the trauma experienced when we evolved into self-consciousness. Not surprisingly, then, underneath the variety of religions that human beings have devised, the behavior and practices of all human religious systems are remarkably similar.

Surviving the anxieties we face in the here and now is only part of the struggle. Human beings also yearn to survive the specter of death and the constant threat of nothingness. We turn now to look at the religious content humans created to meet the anxiety of mortality.

TEN

RIDDING RELIGION OF BOTH HEAVEN AND HELL

It is too late to get ready for the past.
**A quotation from a conference called Common
Dreams, held in Sydney, Australia, in 2007[1]**

Can life after death be freed from the ideas of our past, including our Christian past? If it cannot, then the whole idea of seeking a way to talk about and even to believe in life after death is really not worth the effort. The religious barnacles on the old concepts must be scraped away from the original idea before the idea itself can become either believable or inviting. We cannot content ourselves with the task of seeking to revive traditional hopes that are quite frankly based on no longer acceptable presuppositions; we must rather seek and hope to find a new point of entry into this subject. Is there one? That is the question that we will now explore.

The Christian hope, indeed the religious hope, for life beyond the life of this world has heretofore always been dependent on the idea that there is an external deity who watches over us and at our deaths "calls us home." Now we must face the fact that this hope runs counter to everything we see and understand in the observable world. From all that we know about the physical universe itself—and that knowledge is both massive and extensive—there is no hint anywhere that anything in the universe shares in eternity. Even the universe itself had a beginning, which means that the universe itself is finite. We can today speculate in very intelligent ways about how the universe will end and even project an approximate date on which that ending will occur. Things that have beginnings always have endings, no matter how much time expires between the two events. This means that everything is mortal and, therefore, that nothing is eternal. Human life and the giant redwoods of California are both equally finite. The human life span is generally contained within the area of the biblical standard of "threescore years and ten," even though some of us die young and some of us actually pass the century mark. The giant redwoods on the other hand will live an average of seven hundred years. The end result, however, is just the same. All living things exist inside a finite universe and finitude is our common destiny. The question then becomes: Can we find a doorway into infinity through that which is obviously finite? Is there anything eternal in a finite universe, or are such ideas expressions only of our willingness, perhaps even of our yearning, to be deluded?

The claim for the reality of the eternal God is the primary place that human beings have expressed this belief, or should we say this hope, for the promise of eternity. There is, however, certainly no eternity connected with any of the religious systems that we human beings have developed. Those systems inform us about the nature of this God for whom we claim eternity. If the religious system is mortal, then how can the deity worshipped inside that system be immortal? Even in our earlier brief, sketchy history of the development of human religion, it was obvious that every religious system rises and falls, is born and dies, just as every other human creation or institution does. The museums of religious history are filled with the graves of popular deities who were once served with great devotion by significant numbers of people. No one that I know of still serves the deities of our tribal past, or those of Mount Olympus. Even Mithra, the focus of worship in an early mystery religion, is mentioned today only when the rise of Christianity is being studied. Does this mean that these gods were nothing more than figments of their worshippers' imagination? That is certainly a conclusion that it is easy to draw. Yet in those days, when the prayers of the people were addressed to one or another of these gods, all of them promised eternity to those who were the true believers. If these gods were not eternal, then neither were their promises. Is that not a logical conclusion?

It is fascinating to see the standards that religious systems through the ages have imposed on believers as necessary for the people to meet before they can pass through the doorway into a promised eternity. The idea that creedal adherence alone opens the door to eternal life is still present in religious circles today, though it is not nearly as overt as it was just a century ago. In evangelical church circles eternity is reserved for those who have "a personal relationship with the Lord Jesus as savior." Does that rule out, as it seems to do, those who have never heard the name of Jesus? In Roman Catholic circles, heaven is reserved for those obedient to and formed by the faith of the "one true church." Is heaven thus limited to the Catholic faithful? In the more overtly imperialistic and darker days of Catholic history, part of the conversion pressure was the assertion that Jews, Protestants, Unitarians, heretics and those who profess other religions would not be present in heaven. They did not pass the "faith test." The "saved" were a specifically finite number. Aggressive and even hostile conversion tactics were not only encouraged, but were regarded as both loving and acceptable. "We are adopting these tactics," the pious would say, "because our love for these people and their souls compels us to seek by whatever means are available to enroll them in the only faith that guarantees them life with God after death." A professor of mine, Robert O. Kevin,[2] once observed that he could deal with his friends and even with his sworn enemies, but he had great difficulty dealing with those who convinced themselves that the dreadful things they were saying and doing to him were really being done for "his own good." Heaven as a place of reward for proper believing and hell as a place of punishment for improper or false believing are concepts which have lost almost all of their credibility in the marketplace of contemporary ideas. They continue to exist, however, in the shrinking ghettos of "true believers." Eternal life, if it exists, surely cannot really be about these things.

Try to imagine for a moment a deity who would consign to eternal punishment those at the Council of Nicaea in the fourth century (325 CE) who agreed with the argument of Arius that Jesus was of a *similar* substance (in Greek *homoiousian*) with God, while rewarding Athanasius and those who stood with him with eternal bliss because they stated that Jesus was of the *same* substance (in Greek *homoousian*) with God. The differences between heaven's bliss and hell's flames, observed one wag, lay "in a single iota." As strange and distasteful as this idea is and as these conclusions are, they were once the coin of the religious realm. It seemed to help the human sense of insecurity to draw the belief lines very tightly since that is what created the "blessed assurance" that one was destined for the higher ground to which the old evangelical hymn referred. Yet even if we could convince ourselves that God acts this way, who would want to spend eternity in such an environment with such closed theological minds, being abused by those holding these "unchanging" convictions?

Once proper believing was established in early Christianity as the sole doorway to eternal life, then that particular faith community could begin the secondary religious concentration on proper living as the next standard for gaining access to heavenly joy. When one shifts from "proper believing" to "proper living," however, the issues become more complex. It is easy for religious people, once they convince themselves that they alone possess the ultimate truth of God, to condemn lives lived outside their recognizable Christian convictions, but it is quite difficult even for "true believers" to include in the ranks of the condemned those whose lives are by every standard imaginable noble, life-giving and worthy of emulation, yet whose lives are not lived inside the "one saving religious tradition." Because of that difficulty confidence in the power to exclude wavered.

In the early years of Christian history the popular names for consideration in such a discussion were Plato, Socrates and Aristotle. These men were obviously not Christians since they lived well before the time of Jesus. It was, nevertheless, quite difficult to condemn them on the basis of bad behavior, since the church fathers often cited these philosophers as their authorities! In the modern world, Mahatma Gandhi is the human being most often cited to make this same point. People have gone so far as to say of Gandhi that the twentieth-century being who most deeply lived out the Christ principles was, himself, not a believing Christian.

The next bit of reality that tempered Christianity's harsh claims was the problem of babies who died before they had been baptized. The "original sin" into which they were said to have been born, the church asserted, had not been washed away. They were therefore still in "the sin of Adam" and were thus disqualified from entering heaven and sharing in the presence of God. The more religious people defined who qualified for eternal life, the more unbelievable the whole concept became, until the sensitivities of even the most fervent believers no longer found it tolerable. For God to pour out divine wrath on these categories of apparently innocent people became simply unimaginable. When "unquenchable flames" became the expression of that wrath, which the church was asserting that these "sinners" had to endure, it became morally repugnant. Because such thoughts violated common sense, to say nothing of divine justice, they served to force the church ultimately to modify its concepts of the afterlife until they began to look like a house built by a committee! First, church leaders created various intermediate states, like limbo and purgatory. Limbo became the destiny of the "noble pagans" and the unbaptized infants. It was conceived of as a benign place in which neither the pain of eternal suffering nor the bliss of heavenly joy was available. Its primary purpose was to make the dreadful theology of judgment less guilt-producing for those who administered it. Its secondary purpose, however, was to keep the bar of judgment high enough to continue to build the authority of that religious system. Limbo itself, in our generation, has fallen into limbo in Catholic theology, primarily because of the status of aborted fetuses and the pastoral sensitivity that went with that debate. Limbo, says the Vatican, will now die a natural death, moving over the centuries from neglect to oblivion. That is the way many outdated Catholic claims have been allowed to die.

Purgatory on the other hand was created, as its name suggests, to be a place of purging. As such this option offered everyone a potential way out of the eternal punishment that was said to be the price that our own misdeeds required us to pay. Now, instead of eternal punishment that would cause us eternal agony, purgatory offered time-limited suffering and thus "commuted" sentences. Once we had suffered long enough and thus were thought to have paid the price that our evil lives deserved, we could escape the torture and be welcomed into heaven as purged (or cleansed) and obviously repentant people. While the specifics varied, these ideas of reward and punishment afflicted both Catholic and Protestant versions of Christianity. The threat of hell and the promise of heaven were both real and constituted the teachings of traditional Christianity for centuries. One will never understand the power of the Inquisition in Catholic Christianity or the power of revivalist preaching in Protestant America without understanding the power and the fear connected with both heaven and hell.

When heaven and hell were understood in this way, they were not really so much about our perceived eternal destiny, though that was certainly a part of it, as they were about establishing the ability of religious institutions to control behavior in this life. Vivid images of both afterlife destinations were therefore little more than power tools utilized to build earthly ecclesiastical authority. When that awareness began to dawn, helped I'm sure by the church's greed in selling "indulgences" to shorten time in purgatory, these images began a steady decline. They are today more memory than reality, hanging around the edges of religious institutions like huge deflated balloons, possessing little power except in the lives of relatively neurotic people. The decline of these images was a step in the emancipation of the human spirit, and I believe most people rejoice in that.

When one removes reward and punishment, however, from the conversation about life after death, that concept itself has little further content for most people, so deeply have these images infected their concept of eternity. That leads me to my first, and I hope obvious, conclusion. Ideas that have nothing to do with life after death, but everything to do with controlling human behavior in the here and now, are simply not worthy of human beings, religious or otherwise. No one becomes holy through fear. No one becomes whole by a promised reward for good behavior. We therefore must jettison from further consideration of life after death all concepts of reward and punishment, dismissing them as crude, debilitating, hostile and, finally, unbelievable. The secular world has long since done just that. It is time for religious voices to do the same, and to do it emphatically.[3]

If the enhancement of life is the goal of all religion, then we need to recognize that the promised rewards and the threatened punishments of religion will never accomplish that. Behavior-controlling tactics always suppress life. They are never about becoming human or whole; they are always about becoming or being religious, about gaining an advantage. The emphasis is all wrong. That understanding of life after death is little more than one more aspect of the driving human need for survival. The fact is that if you and I live our lives motivated by our desire to gain paradise or to avoid eternal punishment, then we have not escaped the basic self-centeredness of life that is so natural to survival-oriented, self-conscious creatures. There is nothing worthy in that understanding of life after death. It must be abandoned and the personalistic God of reward and punishment, in whatever form we have been led to understand that deity, must be abandoned with it. It is the product of a childish religion continuing to live in an immature humanity. This mentality has produced a religion that has nothing about it that I can salute or that I desire to preserve. Its harm has been enormous. Its fruit has been minimal. Heaven and hell, as we have been taught to understand them, have got to go!

Throughout Western history we have supplemented our behavior-controlling definitions of the afterlife with a variety of secondary "fulfillment images." That is, we have created our content of the afterlife based upon our perceived human needs. The things human beings experienced as lacking in life became the things that our images of heaven were designed to supply. That is still, please recognize, an exercise in self-centeredness and is always motivated by the drive to survive. I will mention only three of these fulfillment images, just enough to illustrate the point.

The earliest image of heaven, "a land flowing with milk and honey," was a Christian adaptation of an idea born in early Jewish history. The Jews, wandering in the wilderness after escaping slavery in Egypt and wondering whether or not they would find sufficient food to last another day, yearned according to this ancient biblical narrative for what they called "the promised land" in which food was abundant. This land was located geographically, they said, just "across the Jordan." Christianity adapted this Jewish image to its circumstances and needs. Christians too conceived of themselves in the early years of the first century as escaping from the reality of persecution in this life, so they also dreamed of crossing the Jordan and entering the promised land, which they now called heaven. "Milk and honey" was originally a literal fulfillment dream for the hungry children of Israel, but for the Christians it was a fulfillment symbol. Milk and honey may well sound to us like a limited diet, but it met the Jewish yearning for survival. The Christians simply deliteralized this symbol first and then magnified it until it became a symbol of eternity. Heaven was the place where human need was transformed and human fulfillment became possible.

The second popular fulfillment image that gave new content to the word "heaven" was that it would be a place where there would be "no sorrow, no sadness, no separation and no death." This image grew primarily, at least in Christian history, out of the period of persecution, but it had then as it has now a deep human appeal. Death and separation, while part of all life, were daily traumas in the days of Christian persecution, when families were separated, loved ones imprisoned and even executed. This image, however, endured well beyond the times of persecution, since one does not live long before becoming aware that no life ever escapes having sadness, sorrow and death. If one does die early, he or she does not live long enough to know much suffering, but early death is itself viewed as a sign of a tragically unfulfilled life and those left behind must grieve deeply. If one dies late, he or she has lived long enough to have buried those one has loved best, and thus has known great suffering. Deeply loving relationships turn into aching voids. It is not being negative to say that all self-conscious life is by its very nature ultimately tragic. Mother Nature in the last analysis annihilates all of her children.

The aging process is for many an experience of increasing powerlessness, debilitation, irrelevance, and weakness. A friend of mine asserted that he had reached the stage of life where he now had a doctor for every organ! One deals in old age with diseases that are either chronic or fatal. Someone described life as the process through which we go from diapers to diapers. This is not to denigrate life's sweetness, to minimize life's moments of incredible joy, or even to fail to acknowledge life's transforming relationships. It is to say, however, that this sweetness, this joy and these relationships are always lived out in the context of a trajectory that is ultimately fragile, finite and painful. Loneliness, a reality of self-consciousness, is a uniquely human experience. We temper that loneliness with pledges of ultimate caring even as we state that this love is "till death do us part." It is quite natural, then, that human beings dream of a heavenly realm in which we will be reunited with our fathers, our mothers, our brothers and sisters, our spouses and our friends. Heaven is, we assert, that place of reunion, that place of being eternally with those whose love has brought us fulfillment. It is an image that rises out of our sense of separation, yet it is dictated by different experiences of this life more than by our knowledge of eternity.

The third popular image of heaven that fills religious history is that of "an eternal Sabbath of rest." This image rose out of the feudal period of the Middle Ages, when the peasants had to work at backbreaking toil from sunup until sundown, six days a week. The Sabbath, which they mistakenly identified with Sunday, "The Lord's Day," rather than with Saturday, the seventh day of Jewish observance, became their symbol of that fulfillment. As "rest from their labors" became the desired goal of eternity, the end of life became analogous with the day of rest. In the context of that feudal world the eternal Sabbath was thus a powerful symbol, and it still might maintain a portion of that power in some of the world's underdeveloped nations. It is less so today in the forty-hour–work week modern world, with scattered holidays creating three-day weekends almost once a month and vacation time off in the summer and perhaps also at Christmas. To offer people in today's context the hope for an eternal Sabbath of rest at the end of life might sound in our affluent society more like five hundred thousand years of playing shuffleboard in a retirement community, so its power does not translate nearly so well as it once did.

The lesson we learn from these three images is that people in the context of their history yearn for wholeness, for completion, and that this yearning expresses itself in fulfillment dreams. These images are then frozen in time and literalized until they are so far removed from our current reality as to be nonsensical.

That is what has happened to all of our former life after death images. They have lost their meaning. They are barely translatable. They assume things we cannot assume. They use space-time language—which is, of course, the only language we have—to describe something that, if it is real at all, is not bound by either space or time. All of these heavenly images assume a deity outside ourselves to whom we can relate. They assume a world beyond this world to which we somehow have access. They assume an extension of time beyond all time boundaries that we can know. It is no wonder that talk of heaven, hell and life after death has lost its meaning.

Had we lived at the time these images were developed, we might well have made the same choices that early believers did. Human images, however, become irrelevant and ultimately die as circumstances change and knowledge expands. When we literalize these images, they do not quite die when their time to die has come. They rather linger to become intellectually and spiritually embarrassing. Almost all of our life after death vocabulary has done just that. Does that mean that the concept of an afterlife has also died? Not completely, but its content has, so it has become a content-less concept, the shelf life of which is historically quite brief. It finally must be cleared out. That is happening today. What, if anything, will replace it becomes the issue to which we must turn next.

ELEVEN

PUTTING AWAY CHILDISH THINGS: THE DEATH OF RELIGION

The church is like a swimming pool. Most of the noise comes from the shallow end.
Quoted by Professor Sarah Coakley, Harvard Divinity School[1]

Jesus is always betrayed by those who profess to love him.
Pastor Gretta Vosper, United Church of Canada[2]

We come now to the critical turning point in our quest. Why does it matter whether or not traditional religion fades and the external God of traditional religion dies? It matters because we would once more be alone facing realities that threaten us deeply. It matters because we have invested in this deity our sense of purpose, our sense of meaning and our hopes for eternal life. All of these things die if this God dies, or at least that is the common wisdom. When these issues are stated outside their usual "stained-glass" setting, their strangeness becomes apparent. It becomes clear that we believe these things not because we are convinced that they are true, but because we have a deep need for them to be true. We do not seem to recognize that our need for something to be true does not affect what *is;* it only manifests our willingness to be delusional. In order to support and to shore up our believing, we human beings have tended to resist every new insight into how the world operates over the last five hundred years or so, if it was perceived as challenging our religious presuppositions. The heart, however, cannot finally worship what the mind rejects, so in the struggle between faith and knowledge, knowledge always wins.

Religion begins its slow retreat when we first discover that we cannot reconcile human tragedy with a benevolent deity who has supernatural power. We utilize various convoluted explanations to save the integrity of this deity, but none of them work. It is nonsensical to explain tragedy as deserved punishment, as many believers have done for as long as religion has existed. In several recent examples, popular evangelical leaders suggested that the terrorist attacks on September 11, 2001, were caused by America's involvement in the feminist movement, the gay rights movement or the work of the American Civil Liberties Union; and that a hurricane struck a particular city because it was the birthplace of a comedian who happened to be a lesbian. These strange explanations of tragedy do little more than provide fodder for the routines of late-night television shows, where they are lampooned and ridiculed. Neither does it work to attribute tragedy to a divine plan that we do not understand, but hopefully will someday. That is called denial or pious hope.

Religion retreats further still when we discover that the physical universe acts quite independently of a presumed manipulative deity above the sky. Over the past five hundred years our world has begun to explain in a new way without any recourse to religion the things religion once attempted to explain. Each intellectual breakthrough drove another nail into the coffin of yesterday's religious understanding. Each new insight into almost any aspect of life challenged the reality of those things I have previously identified as the core principles of all religious systems: God defined as an external being who helps us explain what we do not understand; God perceived as supernatural in power and thus not limited as we are; and God viewed as being capable of coming to our aid in time of need or trouble.

It was in the power and timelessness of this deity that we also traditionally invested our hopes for eternal life. Under a variety of names and guises we built religious systems to make the world we live in and the life we live make sense. All around us today, however, we see this kind of supernaturalism dying a natural death, the victim of new and better understandings of the world and of ourselves. All of this knowledge seems to point to a conclusion that we are loath to face, much less to entertain, but the quest on which I have launched myself in this book cannot be continued unless these realities can be engaged. I begin this chapter, therefore, with a series of simple, declarative statements of what I believe is reality. Listen carefully, for if we do not recognize and accept—yes, even feel—the death of religion we will continue our futile search for answers from this arena from whence they will never again be forthcoming.

There is no supernatural God who lives above the sky or beyond the universe. There is no supernatural God who can be understood as animating spirit, Earth Mother, masculine tribal deity or external monotheistic being. There is no parental deity watching over us from whom we can expect help. There is no deity whom we can flatter into acting favorably or manipulate by being good. There are no record books and no heavenly judge keeping them to serve as the basis on which human beings will be rewarded or punished. There is also no way that life can be made to be fair or that a divine figure can be blamed for its unfairness. Heaven and hell are human constructs designed to make fair in some ultimate way the unfairness of life. The idea that in an afterlife the unfairness of this world will be rectified is a pious dream, a toe dip into unreality. Life is lived at the whim of luck and chance, and no one can earn the good fortune of luck and chance.

I recoil even now to write these words, for this traditional definition of God has been my companion from the earliest days of my life. When I state that this God is no more, I know that many will hear or read these words as saying things that are quite different from what these words mean to me. I cannot and will not deny the reality of my God-experience. The fact that the way we thought of God in our past has died does not mean that God has died or that there is *no* God. That is a distinction that, in my experience, many people are not able to make. Even I find myself deeply and emotionally conflicted to state these conclusions, so incredibly powerful is the impact of these words. It is to these very conclusions, however, that my study has led me, so I must press on beyond this sense of dis-ease.

To feel the full, stretching and painful weight of these words, I need to state that the understanding of God that I have just dismissed as no longer viable is the primary way in which the God of the Bible is portrayed in the vast majority of that sacred text. Only if one assumes that there is a deity above the sky do so many of the biblical stories make any sense at all. How else, for example, can the raised Jesus come out of the sky to give the "Great Commission" (Matt. 28:16–20)? How could anyone conceive of building the Tower of Babel so high that it could reach God in the heavens (Gen. 11:1–9)? Those narratives are incomprehensible in any other context. How could

God pour down manna from heaven on the children of Israel in the wilderness unless God operated upon the earth from the heavenly realm (Exod. 16:14–36)? Why was a mountaintop chosen as the place where God and Moses would meet for conversation, if that did not represent a halfway point between the God above the sky and Moses down below (Exod. 19:3)?

It is also this external God living above the sky who is invoked in the gospels as the key to the understanding of the Jesus story. Jesus is traditionally portrayed as God's agent of salvation, sent from the God above the sky to carry out the rescue of the fallen and thus earth-bound mortals. God is portrayed as invading human history in the person of Jesus through the miracle of the virgin birth (Matt. 1, 2 and Luke 1, 2), and then to have triumphed over death and the grave in the miracle of the resurrection (Mark 16, Matt. 28, Luke 24, and John 20, 21). To complete this divine round-trip Jesus is portrayed as returning to the God above the sky in the miracle of the ascension (Acts 1). Next, out of that same heavenly dwelling place above the sky, the biblical narrative says Jesus poured the Holy Spirit "down" on the gathered disciples in the miracle of Pentecost (Acts 2). Finally, to wrap up this mythology, it was said that it would be the destiny of this Jesus to return someday from that same sky at the end of time in the miracle of the second coming.

Can we all now understand, given the presuppositions that lie behind these texts, just why it was that Galileo was such a tremendous threat to religious belief? Galileo was condemned to be burned at the stake. Fortunately, because of his age and infirmity, and the fact that Galileo had friends in high places, that harsh sentence was reduced via a plea-bargaining process. The compromise was that Galileo would publicly deny his own conclusions, accept the penalty of house arrest for the balance of his life and pledge never again to publish his scientific findings. Truth, however, does not cease to be truth just because it is either troubling or repressed. Even the Vatican finally made peace with Galileo and, not coincidentally, with reality, when in December of 1991 the curia issued a paper declaring that they now believed that Galileo was correct. By that time space travel had been inaugurated, which, of course, would not have been possible if Galileo had not been correct! No one paid much attention to this too little and too late proclamation.

Most people in Galileo's day were not literate, so it took centuries before Galileo's insights would trickle down to the common mind. During that time organized religion, trying to relate to Galileo, sought to develop one new defense line after another. God is not "up there," religious spokespersons began to say, but "*out* there." That was not a significant advance. It sounded credible only because we had not yet fully embraced the vastness of space. Where is "out there"? Is it beyond our single galaxy, which contains some two hundred billion to four hundred billion stars and is so large that light, traveling at the approximate speed of one hundred eighty-six thousand miles per second, takes over one hundred thousand years to go from one end of our galaxy to the other? It was not until recently that we learned that there are stars in our galaxy that are actually larger than the earth's orbit around the sun![3]

Is "out there" beyond the universe itself? Well, the universe has within it somewhere between one hundred billion and one trillion other galaxies and more are being formed as these words are being read. The closest galaxy to our Milky Way is Andromeda, a mere two million light-years away. Our minds boggle at the immensity of space. When we talk about God "out there," we have no idea where "out there" is. It is inevitable in the light of this knowledge that God understood as a supernatural being who watches over the world has begun to fade from our view and the frightful loneliness in the human soul once more becomes overwhelming. The religious stakes in this debate have been rising for years. At the beginning of this revolution in thinking we asked "where" God is, expecting some answer to be forthcoming. Now we wonder "if" God is. Galileo, and all of the space-thought that flowed from him, has rendered God homeless. That was, however, but the first of three scientific body blows directed at religion as we have created it, which together have brought about its demise.

In the same year that Galileo died in Italy (1642) a man named Isaac Newton was born in Lincolnshire, England. This man, building on the foundations of Galileo, would continue to dismantle the system of thought called religion, in which human beings had sought security since the beginning of self-consciousness. Although Galileo had inaugurated the debate on God's locality, the duties which that God was traditionally assumed to perform were thought not to have changed significantly. That comfort zone, however, was powerfully disturbed when Isaac Newton published his major work, *The Principia*, in 1687. If Galileo had rendered God homeless, then Isaac Newton was destined to render God unemployed. Everything that we once attributed to this supernatural God and to God's power Isaac Newton explained without any reference to God at all. He showed us a mathematically precise universe that functioned according to something that came to be called natural law. To this threatening reality religion and religious leaders all but turned a deaf ear. They did not want to embrace the threat that confronted them when the realm of miracle and magic, the claim of supernatural intervention, the power of prayer to bring God to our aid, and the protective qualities we once attributed to the deity were all swept away. There is no need to flatter or to obey an impotent God who is not capable of doing the things we once assumed God could do. After Newton we no longer understood who God was or how God acted. The result of this provocative insight was once again to magnify that vast and existential human feeling of loneliness. Human life also experienced the loss of its sense of purpose and meaning, which had once been invested in the external deity, and with that loss human beings were bereft of any sense that they might somehow possess eternal worth. The response to this intellectual breakthrough was the rise of what came to be called deism, which involved the idea that God in the creation of the universe played only the role of a clockmaker who started the universe in the big bang, but who now allowed it to run without any divine interference. This was just one more of religion's inadequate attempts to adjust to these new insights. It satisfied no one.

In his private papers Isaac Newton indicated that he knew exactly what his new thought had done to Christianity when he entered the ancient debate on Christology inaugurated at the Council of Nicaea in 325 CE. Newton came down on the side of the losing argument. Whatever Jesus was, said Newton, he was not the incarnation of the supernatural deity who lived above the sky. That idea, he said, was no longer conceivable. No religion, primitive or modern, could, after Newton, still assert with credibility that God acted in supernatural ways as an external force on our physical world. There was no place in Newton's world for an uncaused cause or even for a divinely caused cause that was outside natural boundaries.

In Newton's world, therefore, one could not, as the Bible assumes, cast oneself off the pinnacle of the temple and expect to be rescued. There is no way that the laws of the universe can be set aside to enable five loaves to expand to feed five thousand men, plus women and children, or to allow someone to walk on water or to enable a virgin to conceive. These things are not possible in the world that we inhabit, not even for one defined as an intervening supernatural being, said Newton. If one insists on postulating a God who can actually do these things, then we are left, not with an ordered world, but with a chaotic one in which the rules of nature can be and are set aside for miracles. Such ideas might have been comforting to primitive human life, but they are hardly comforting to contemporary people.

If God has the power and the ability to intervene in human history, then God is rightly blamed when God does not act to stop such things as the holocaust, tornadoes, hurricanes and tsunamis that randomly destroy. A supernatural God in charge of the universe would surely have the power to prevent these natural and human disasters, but since God does not do so, the proper rational conclusion is that God must have *chosen* not to do so. Then by every known measure God would have to be judged as immoral. Beyond that, all of us would then have to live at risk from so capricious a deity. Yet many of these things are the precise assumptions of prayer, of religion and of those who believe in an external deity. Religion as we know it thus becomes unraveled, its premises systematically dismissed by the advance of knowledge.

A friend of mine named Michael Donald Goulder, a New Testament scholar and former priest in the Church of England, faced this disillusionment with traditional religious concepts in the last quarter of the twentieth century and gave up his religion quite publicly. When asked what had led him to this decision, he responded, "God no longer has any work to do!"[4] That is, I believe, the conclusion to which the work of Isaac Newton drives us, since that work calls into question the possibility that there is an external power who is the source of our meaning, the one in whom purpose is invested and who can and will deliver us from the insecurity and insensitivity of this world, as well as from our inevitable destiny in death and extermination.

The religious establishment, slow to comprehend the challenge of Isaac Newton, first simply blinked and then retreated to yet another presumed defense line. Human life is so complex, so unique, so capable of self-transcendence, we said, that something of what we once called "the divine" must reside inside human beings. So religious spokespersons began to talk of the "divine spark" within, and the modus operandi of religion was to cultivate the inner self where communion with God was thought to be possible.

Then along came Charles Robert Darwin to deliver the third scientific body blow to religion. Prior to Darwin our human self-understanding was that we were just a little lower than the angels. Darwin challenged that understanding authoritatively, and when the dust of that debate finally settled, we were forced to accept the new definition: that we were just a little higher than the apes. That is a very different perspective!

Religious reaction to Darwin started immediately with the publication of his book *On the Origin of Species by Means of Natural Selection* in 1859. Before the ink was dry on the initial press run of that volume, the Anglican bishop of Oxford, Samuel Wilberforce, launched the ecclesiastical counterattack in a debate with Thomas Huxley before an audience at the British Association for the Advancement of Science at Oxford. In that debate Bishop Wilberforce resorted to ridicule, a sure sign that he knew that his case was weak and that he was wrong.

In the early years of the twentieth century American evangelical leaders, organized around the ultra-conservative Princeton Theological Seminary in New Jersey, launched an offensive with the worldwide publication of a series of tracts designed to defend the basic tenets of Christianity from what they clearly understood as the attack on Christianity's jugular by Charles Darwin. These tracts, funded interestingly enough by the Union Oil Company of California (Unocal), were called

"The Fundamentals" and gave rise to the familiar words "fundamentalism" and "fundamentalists," used today to describe biblical literalists. It would not be the last time that big oil money would be used to defend right-wing religion.

By 1925 the religious attack on Darwin was focused on the trial of John Scopes in Dayton, Tennessee. The charge against this young biology teacher was that he had been "teaching in the classroom of the State of Tennessee, something contrary to the word of God in Scripture." This trial was a media event unlike anything seen before, as it attracted the nation's press, the world's press and the infant industry of radio, to say nothing of nationally known lawyers in the persons of Clarence Darrow and William Jennings Bryan. *Time* magazine referred to it as "the fantastic cross between a circus and a holy war."[5] John Scopes was convicted, but his fine of $100 was never paid and everyone soon saw that it was a Pyrrhic victory, as any attempt to suppress truth always is.

This was not religion's only response to Darwin in the field of education. Many teachers and school districts took religion's side, first with "creation science" and later with "intelligent design." Both were finally recognized for what they were and were declared to be violations of America's constitutionally mandated separation of church and state by the Supreme Court of this nation. (On that court it is important to note that, among the nine justices, seven were appointed by conservative Republican presidents.) Religion was simply no longer in tune with reality. This quick survey reveals, however, just how deeply the thought of Darwin threatened the traditional tenets of religion. Religion's political power would still be visible and even appear to gain strength for decades longer, but its hold on reality was damaged beyond repair. In 2008 the Republican Party in America, seeking to mollify its declining religious base, would still nominate for the vice-presidency a candidate who favored teaching "creation science" in our public schools. In every confrontation between new knowledge and religious assumptions, however, it is a fact that religion has lost to the power of expanding knowledge.

More than anything had done thus far, the insights of Charles Darwin changed the way religion thought about and proclaimed its conviction concerning life after death. Human beings had never attributed to animal life a sense of eternal worth. We had never invested animals with immortal souls. We had always defined human life as unique, a special creation, made, according to the biblical story, in the image of God. So different were we from animals that God was quoted in the book of Genesis as giving to human life domination over all other living things. Animals existed, we believed, for our benefit. The idea that we human beings were, in fact, animals was repulsive, and from Darwin's first announcement of that relationship people reacted strongly. Elliot Engel, an English professor at North Carolina State University in Raleigh, even argued that the religious reaction to Darwin was responsible for the development of two things that most people do not see as related: the puritanical, sexually repressed Victorian mentality found in the development of a genre of literature called the Victorian novel, and the creation of what we know as English table manners. Both, Professor Engel claimed, had as their purpose to increase the distance between human life and animal life that Darwin had narrowed. This was accomplished, Professor Engel suggested, by taking the two things human beings appeared to have in common with animals—sex and eating—and repressing one while refining the other. Sex was repressed in Victorian England so deeply that sexually titillating words were never to be spoken in public. That was the time when we began to describe the parts of a chicken as "white meat," "dark meat," "drumsticks" and "second joints," so that we never had to say words like "leg," "thigh" or "breast" at the dinner table. That was also, he continued, why silver cutlery began to be laid out at each place setting in the Victorian home in the order of its usage at a meal, when separate dishes appeared for salad, bread and desserts, when special glasses for water and for red and white wine entered the scene and when the formal style of dining by candlelight emerged. These things served, Professor Engel maintained, to rebuild the separation between human life and animal life that Darwin's thought had diminished.[6]

We human beings are nothing but animals with bigger brains, Darwin contended. We have the same identical organs as all other mammals. We have the same number of vertebrae in our necks that, say, a giraffe has. We share, it was later discovered, the same DNA found in all living things. We clearly evolved out of a common background. Religion in all of its forms, but Christianity as the dominant religious system in the Western world in particular, was built on a very different premise. Thus if Darwin was right, then Christianity is wrong. Few people today regard Darwin as wrong.

One can track the decline of religion and the decline in the conviction about life after death in the Western world to the following developing human understandings of how the world and life operate: First, the size of the universe challenged our worldview and God's place within it. Second, our knowledge of how the world operates destroyed our dependency on a supernatural power. Third, new understandings of human origins forced us to recast our myth about human uniqueness and with it our sense of possessing eternal worth. These understandings reflect the direction in which we are walking today. God, as we have traditionally understood God, has died or is in the process of dying, and with that demise we are watching those things that religion once was thought to provide slip away. The external meaning and purpose for life are gone. There is no agreed-upon basis for human ethics. There is no realistic hope of life after death, at least as that idea has been traditionally understood. That is where we are. No, not everyone is there, but that is the way that we are going and few doubt that as a culture we will all finally arrive at these conclusions.

Now the issues and the questions are clear. Where do we go from here? Some will inevitably try to respirate artificially the old symbols. We call those people fundamentalists. They create more heat than light. They always attack in the public arena, seeking to stop or at least slow down the changing consciousness that erodes the old convictions. They oppose the emancipation of women not just in the church, but in everything from the right to equal education in state-supported universities,[7] to the right to vote,[8] to making birth control and family planning available, to the legality of abortion,[9] to careers in business and even to ordination and equality in the churches.[10] They seek to erect statues of the Ten Commandments in their courtrooms, so that the old verities will not disappear.[11] They condemn the rising consciousness about homosexuality and especially gay marriage, even seeking to enshrine their prejudices in constitutional amendments.[12] They fight furiously, but history reveals that they always lose. When defeat comes they retreat once more into religious ghettos, where they sing their hymns, read their scriptures, say their prayers and reinforce their prejudices by citing traditional authority-claims. The fact is, however, that fewer and fewer people listen and fewer and fewer people care what the fundamentalists think. They typically become splinter movements within their churches, so that, by withdrawing from the mainstream of life, they can continue to pretend that the world has not changed.

There are others, those who are not and cannot be fundamentalists, who respond to the mismatch between traditional religion's worldview and today's scientific understanding by simply walking away from religion. They enter what Harvard's Harvey Cox called "The Secular City,"[13] or what I call the "Church Alumni Association." At first they miss the supernatural God on whom they once relied, but gradually that sense of loss fades—as God has faded—and they set about living as religionless people in a religionless world.

One of the early signs of the demise of traditional ideas concerning the afterlife is seen in the rise in the Western world of what might be called liberal politics. Liberal politics has as its primary agenda to make fair an unfair world. Please note that this was not a passion in the Western world so long as we were convinced that fairness could be accomplished in an afterlife. If God was believed to redress in another realm the obvious inequities found in human life, then there was no need for us to address those inequities here and now. We could thus tolerate a world in which the good die young and the charlatans live to a ripe old age, a world in which a harsh disease like the bubonic plague strikes sinner and saint alike. In that earlier time we could abide a world in which natural phenomena punished the good and the bad equally. Few listen any longer to claims that worldly unfairness need not be redressed in *this* life. Ours is a world in which both food and wealth are so unequally distributed that some diet while others starve and some live in luxurious comfort while others live in the squalor of poverty. When fairness was believed to come in life after death, there was no great pressure for us to address these issues in the here and now. When confidence in an afterlife faded, pressure began to rise to address the fairness issue in the one world we do have and about which there is certainty. So from the late nineteenth through the twentieth century we saw the rise in the Western world, especially in Europe, of things like labor parties, liberal parties, socialist parties, Christian socialist parties and even communist parties. In America we saw movements and emphases like the Square Deal, the New Deal, the Fair Deal, the Great Society, the War on Poverty, the New Frontier and other attempts to make fairer the unfair world. I believe the motive for these phenomena was an unspoken doubt about the reality of a future life and the growing conviction that this life is the only life we have.

This shift in conviction was visible even in our religious institutions. A century ago Christian funerals asserted the ability of God to overcome the power of death. Today Christian funerals are more likely to be memorial services intended to remember and to extol the virtues and the example of the deceased.

Two centuries ago the concept of hell had sufficient power to ignite what we called in America the Great Awakening. When Jonathan Edwards described God as dangling sinners by the singed hairs of their heads over the flames of hell, people responded in mass conversions and with tears of repentance. Today the concept of hell is so empty that one can actually hear it said: "It is cold as hell today." Today the word "heaven," once the symbol of ultimate hope of those who knew themselves to be both finite and mortal, has become only the name of the sky, as in "my blue heaven." In romantic ballads it is identified with being in love. In its adjectival form it is used to describe everything from a dress to lemon meringue pie! Increasingly there are recognized Christian leaders who state publicly that they do not believe in life after death. I meet them everywhere I go. They are less and less predisposed to deny the conclusion to which they have arrived. I think of such people as Don Cupitt in England, Lloyd Geering in New Zealand and Robert Funk and Schubert Ogden in America.[14] Other religious leaders learn to fudge their words and thus to avoid perjury without expressing conviction.

To arrive at this point of admitting that the content of religion is dying is for many to reach the end of the journey. God has died, and while some of us can do nothing about it except to gather around the divine grave to weep,[15] others are beginning to enter joyfully a religionless world. Neither of those options, however, is where I am. I regard this place at which our study has arrived to be not the end of the journey, but only the end of the search for life's meaning inside the realm of religion. It is that religious journey, I believe, that has now come to an end. The premises upon which religion was built are now revealed to be null and void. The God who was understood as an intervening supernatural deity living above the sky is no longer believable, and Job's question about whether there is life after death finally receives here a firm no. As these new realities are recognized, the intellectual conflict that has troubled people as they tried to hold on to the security blanket of religion is finally eased. As a result, however, we now experience bankruptcy in the search for meaning and purpose. A new starting point in that quest must be found or the search must be ended.

I am of the opinion that in the analysis of the things that have brought traditional religion to its knees, the clues are present to find a new approach to meaning, purpose, God and life after death. At this point my narrative moves beyond my spiritual autobiography to the biography of humanity itself, or perhaps it would be more accurate to say that the two begin to come together.

So to that part of the journey I now turn again, as my dance with death continues and my rejoicing in life actually intensifies. I will seek God apart from religion.

TWELVE

THE SHIFT OF THE RELIGIOUS PARADIGM

Envoi
God within me, God without,
How shall I ever be in doubt?
There is no place where I may go
And not there see God's face, not know
I am God's vision and God's ears
So through the harvest of my years
I am the Sower and the Sown
God's self unfolding and God's own.

From a tenth-century gravestone,
St. Lars Church, Linköping, Sweden[1]

Enabling people to turn around in the way they think about and conceptualize God in order to embrace new possibilities is not unlike trying to turn the great ship *Titanic* around in a small pond. It is not impossible, but it feels that way. There are many who say it cannot be done. Perhaps there are many more who do not want it to be done. Yet turn we must.

My personal journey has carried me through the arena of religion to what I now see as its bankruptcy. The human journey into God has reached a similar destination. God-talk still fills the world, but it is no longer believable in the way that it once was. Secularism is on the rise everywhere—perhaps more obviously in the West than in the rest of the world, but that is not because the West is decadent, as our critics in the Third World like to say, but because the West has engaged the intellectual revolution more deeply than any other part of the world. There will be no turning back on the insights of Galileo, Newton and Darwin, at which we have looked far too briefly in these pages. The old verities simply are not holding, nor will they, no matter how desperately we wish for them to do so. No one today really thinks that the religions of miracle and magic and of supernatural beings who manipulate the world of cause and effect for some ulterior purpose will long enjoy the confidence of the people of the present and coming generations. There is little remaining trust in such a deity. We continue to talk about this God, but there is no conviction in the way we live that there is an external supernatural deity who stands ready to intervene, to provide purpose or to guarantee eternity. Human life is in the process of adjusting to the death of this God.

It is not as if we have not had time to adjust. This God's demise was first announced in the nineteenth century by Friedrich Nietzsche in a book entitled *Thus Spake Zarathustra*.[2] It was not an announcement that was welcome. The response of the generally religious population of the Western world was predictable. First Nietzsche was attacked as mentally ill and called a madman, and when that failed he was subjected to biting ridicule and was dismissed with "cuteness." A popular quotation, used so often that its original author has been lost in the shadows of time, reads:

God is dead! —Nietzsche
Nietzsche is dead! —God

Those were the tactics employed by the religiously threatened. It was also in the nineteenth century that a similar recognition of the demise of religion as it had been practiced for centuries arose, surprisingly enough, from within the heart of the religious world of academia. For the first time biblical scholars admitted publicly that the claims of popular religion were no longer sustainable in the light of their current studies. Slowly the dated and increasingly uninformed literal jackets in which we had hidden our claims for scriptural or theological authority were riddled with holes and inconsistencies that could no longer be kept from public notice. It was a twenty-seven-year-old German New Testament scholar named David Friedrich Strauss who blew the first trumpet that allowed this knowledge to move into the public awareness. He published a book entitled *The Life of Jesus Critically Examined*[3] in 1834. The response of both the religious public and the public at large was swift, immediate and predictably hostile. Strauss was dismissed from the faculty of the University of Tübingen and was blackballed from other teaching positions in every university across Europe. He never taught New Testament again and his brilliant potential was lost in his own increasing bitterness. His work was translated in the 1850s into English by George Eliot, the pen name of Mary Ann Evans, the iconoclastic author of *Silas Marner*. As a woman who felt deeply oppressed by Victorian religion, Evans identified with Strauss' struggle against both ecclesiastical and political repression. It was neither by accident nor by chance that she became the one through whom Strauss' work entered the English-speaking world. This book represented the first public awareness that the old religious formulas—including the image of a supernatural, external deity to whom we could look for meaning, the claim that the truth of this deity had been captured in a divinely written book and the hope for eternal life that was said to rest on these in- errant scriptures—were passing from the scene. A chill set in among the established religious leaders, and the suppression of this book and all that it represented became the response of choice from almost every ecclesiastical institution. As the work of Strauss was driven underground, the religious world tried to pretend that he had never lived, much less written. His book, amazing as it seems, is never referred to, even today, in most denominational theological seminaries.

More than a century would pass before these irrepressible thoughts, which continued to bubble beneath the notice of insti- tutional religious leaders, would break forth once more into the public arena. This time its protagonists were Christian theolo- gians, academics more than pastors, who were no longer able to make sense of the traditional religious symbols. They were called the "God Is Dead" theologians. While many people were in- volved in this movement, the four who seem to me to have made the greatest impact were Thomas J. J. Altizer of Emory Univer- sity, William Hamilton of Colgate Rochester Divinity School, Gabriel Vahanian of Syracuse University and Paul Van Buren of Temple University. On April 6, 1966, *Time* magazine made this movement its cover story, entitling the piece "Is God Dead?" This debut of radical theology into popular culture stirred a debate for which neither the public nor the Christian church was well prepared. The result was not profound and the movement withered under clichés that avoided the real questions that these theologians were raising. Reaction degenerated into a popular bumper-sticker message which read:

My God is alive!
Sorry about yours.

In that same decade two Anglican bishops, each calling for a move beyond the now discredited traditional religious thinking, also raised their prophetic voices within the Christian church, one in England, the other in America. In 1963 John Arthur Thomas Robinson, the English bishop of Woolwich, an area of the Diocese of Southwark (London south of the Thames), published a book entitled *Honest to God* that set off shock waves around the Christian world. This man took the writings of three premier Christian academics, well known and respected inside the walls of the world's leading theological colleges, and made their thought accessible to the population at large, thus leaping over the filter of the denominational training schools. The three were Rudolf Bultmann, probably the leading New Testament scholar in his generation; Paul Tillich, probably the best-known and most widely read theologian in the twentieth century; and Dietrich Bonhoeffer, the German Lutheran pastor who had been part of the underground anti-Nazi resistance movement and who had been hanged at a prison camp in Flossenburg by the Hitler government in April of 1945 just before the war in Europe came to a conclusion. Bultmann referred to the scriptures as "mythology" that needed to be "demythologized," since its message had been framed and thus captured in the presuppositions of an ancient world that no longer existed. Tillich suggested that God could no longer be conceived of through the analogy of a person and he developed a transpersonal theology in which God was perceived as "the Ground of All Being." Bonhoeffer called for the development of "religionless Christianity." In one of his letters from prison to his friend Eberhard Bethge he argued that just as Christianity in the first century could not be contained within Judaism, so in our day Christianity can no longer be contained within religion. *Honest to God* sold more copies than any religious book since John Bunyan's *Pilgrim's Progress* and set off a debate that the English press encouraged with no great comprehension, but with much heat. The masses of people recognized in Robinson's words the articulation of things that they had long felt, but did not know how to express. The religious establishment, however, went into "damage control" mode. The archbishop of Canterbury, Michael Ramsey, condemned Robinson,[4] and Robinson's career, both as an English bishop and as an academic, was marginalized. First, Robinson was forced by the Anglican Church to remain an assistant bishop, and was never allowed to have his own diocese, until he finally resigned to return to the teaching career he had exercised at Cambridge prior to his appointment as a bishop. Second, at Cambridge the long arm of cultural fear and negativity was still operative. His former position as a university lecturer was never restored to him; he finished his career as the dean of Trinity College, a relatively junior position usually held by a promising, but recently ordained young cleric. Robinson died in 1983, somewhat disillusioned. The fact is, however, that he opened the doors to the future and to exactly the themes that I seek to develop in this book. That is not a coincidence, for this man was my mentor, my friend and my role model.

The second person was the American Episcopal bishop of California, James Albert Pike, who entered this debate through the publication of two books, *A Time for Christian Candor,* 1964, and *If This Be Heresy,* 1967,[5] both of which ignited furious controversies in American Christianity. Pike suffered a fate similar to that of Robinson. He was threatened by his fellow bishops with a trial for heresy and was encouraged to resign. He did just that, and after moving to a think tank and experimenting with the world of séances and the use of a medium to make contact with the dead, he gradually faded from the scene. He died in 1969 in a desert in Israel.

The world was even then still not ready to hear the message that the image of God into which we human beings had invested so many of our security needs for so long was no longer believable. The debate was out of the ecclesiastical closet, however, and while it would go through backing and filling operations for generations, it would never again disappear, until it finally began to be dealt with openly. That is the course followed by every radical new consciousness shift. Some, who catch just a glimpse of what this shift means, become so frightened that they retreat into an irrelevant version of the deceased thinking of the past. That never works. One cannot restore life by doing a facelift on a corpse. Others, who see farther, decide to give up on all ultimate issues and all God-talk and content themselves with seeking to live the good life and to make the most of what this life offers now. Some, however, are able to see still farther; they are the ones who begin to build a new paradigm and to walk into whatever direction that paradigm leads them. It is into this path of unknowing that we must now be prepared to journey.

The first step is to let go of the religious paradigm of yesterday and allow it to die. It will not die quietly or easily, but it will die. The rattles of rigor mortis can be heard even now. This is the place to which my journey of a lifetime has led me. It also seems to be the place to which the human journey has led or is leading all people. None of us can turn things around to make the viewpoint of yesterday live again. I no longer have a desire to do so, and what I sense is that there is a diminishing desire in the world at large to resuscitate this now deceased body of religious thinking, allowing its noble death to be accomplished and accepted. The only question is: "Where do we go from here?"

I am ready now to explore the dimensions of what our word "God" represented in our long human quest for identity and self-definition. What aspect of human life was the word "God" used to define? I am ready to pose new questions that have not and probably could not have been imagined in the paradigm of yesterday's religious thinking. Recognizing that "the divine" and "the holy" are human concepts, where must we look for them? Surely it must be in life, not in some realm apart from life. So I will search for them only in the midst of the human, the known and the mundane. Religion in the past was a search for security, but security is something that I no longer recognize as a virtue. I must seek to embrace *insecurity* as one of the essential marks of our humanity and strive to help people understand that it is no longer a vice, but a doorway into a new understanding of our humanity. The religion of the past sought to locate meaning and purpose in an external deity. That effort succeeded only in robbing life here and now of its own intrinsic worth, meaning and purpose. The religion of the past sought an answer to the unique human awareness of death by postulating a realm in which death is overcome. I seek to find a doorway into the eternal by going deeply into this life. My search for "heaven" will cause me to turn to this life, to its very depths, for that is the only place where I now believe we can hear the echoes of eternity. In that search, I believe, we will discover that the word "heaven" points not to something external to us, but to something that is part of us.

I will seek to understand what our deep and natural interdependence is with all of life and indeed with the entire universe. I will look into how we can be so small and so insignificant when compared to the vastness of the universe, but can at the same time be the only living creature that can with a finite mind embrace, contemplate and interact with the vastness of space. Do these dual realities make us too small to be of any ultimate worth or so incredibly wondrous and mysterious as to cause us to believe that we were made for eternity?

The time has come, I believe, for us to turn our spiritual telescopes around so that we no longer look outward for meaning or God, but begin to look inward. That is not to walk away from God, as the fearful will scream; it is, I now believe, to walk into God. The path is internal not external, for it is identical with a walk into ourselves, and that is a journey that we must never refuse to take.

I do not want to walk away from religion so much as I want to walk through religion and then beyond it. I want to walk into things that religion has never known. I do not want to abandon the wisdom of the past, but neither do I want to be bound by that wisdom, since wisdom is itself ever-changing. The turn from the deity above to the deity within is an enormous shift. It is, however, the only pathway open to us. We enter it with new, and shall we say great, expectations.

THIRTEEN

WHO AM I? WHAT IS GOD?

O Light that none can name, for
  it is altogether nameless.
O light with many names, for it is
  at work in all things . . .
How do you mingle yourself with grass?

How, while continuing unchanged,
  altogether inaccessible,
Do you preserve the nature of grass unconsumed?

Symeon, an early Byzantine mystic,
from *Hymns of Divine Love*[1]

The world of science, which has concentrated its increasingly powerful gaze on the here and now, the seen rather than the unseen, has in the process come up with some fascinating insights that form the basis for the inquiry to which I now turn. Instead of speculating in a metaphysical direction about who or what God is, the focus of modern science has been on human life and what scientists can learn about who we are. Some of their discoveries have forced us to entertain thoughts that previous generations could never have contemplated.

How many of us are aware, for example, that the same laws that govern life on this planet earth also appear to govern life in the entire universe? There is no distinction. The same dust that makes up the stars of our universe constitutes the substance of our human bodies and perhaps our minds. In fact, we now know that all matter within our universe, from the farthest star to the content of your body and mine, is interconnected. Such a sense of interdependency has, before our time, never even been imagined. Human life is kin not just to the great apes but to the cabbages and indeed even to the plankton in the sea. A common DNA flows through all living things. These are just some of the physical insights at which our generation has arrived. This sense of a unified oneness stands in sharp contrast to the sense of separation that we human beings have experienced as our reality from the moment we entered the realm of self-consciousness. That insight leads to the conclusion that while separation may have been our perception, it is not the law of the universe. A deep interrelated unity is.

From such an insight is it not possible to postulate that consciousness is also a single whole, which emerged within the universe, and which can be accessed on a variety of levels by creatures of varying capacities? From this perspective, while the genesis of self-consciousness gave the human creature a sense of having broken into an entirely new understanding of life—that is, a new awareness—that awareness was certainly not a new *reality*. We have always been part of that which is greater than we are. Is it not, therefore, reasonable to assume that we just might always have been a component of that greater reality? What would it do to our self-definition if we were to become convinced that we have always been part of a whole and are not separate from that which is "other" than ourselves?

We note, for example, that even though the world, which is our home, is bound by both time and space, the human mind,

which seems similarly bound, and which surely has no independent existence apart from the physical brain, can nonetheless
transcend both time and space. We are able somewhere within
ourselves to store the past and to remember it, even to recall it
into the present. Sometimes we can even have the intense experience of reliving it as if it had escaped the past and reentered
the present. We are also able to anticipate the future, to plan for
it, even to enjoy it before it arrives. I have both practiced and
watched the results that come from giving elderly or terminally
ill patients something in the future to anticipate and have seen
them, in response, live against all odds to reach that goal. In
that sense we seem to have some control over our own destiny.
Experiences like this help me to suggest, perhaps even to realize, that maybe it is actually the *present* that does not exist for
us human beings. The present appears to be little more than
that non-real instant through which the future passes on its
journey into the past. So there is something about human life
that escapes time's boundaries and experiences timelessness.

Like time, space also appears not to be as binding on us as
we once believed. In our thoughts, imaginations and dreams
we can actually transport ourselves to different places. With
nostalgia we can recall vividly places in our childhood, as if
we were somehow there again. I can still see the field where I
played baseball as a child and the ditch that made right field
so hazardous to play. We generally assigned that low-status,
right-field post to the last person chosen and thus the one assumed to be the least talented player among us. My sister qualified for this position regularly. I can still see the cherry tree
I climbed and from which, on more than one occasion, I removed the ladder my little brother had used to enable him to
get up that tree, thereby capturing him until he was willing to
jump, which usually took a long time and many tears. I can see
the muscadine grape arbor (some people insist on calling them

scuppernongs), where he and I climbed to taste the sweet flavor of its fruit in the summertime and, not coincidentally, to be stung by the bees with whom we competed for the grapes. I can recreate the dairy barn with its smells from the first job I had at age twelve, stripping the cows after the electric milkers had done their best. When the milking was complete we poured the fresh milk, not yet either homogenized or pasteurized, through a coiled cooling system that chilled this creamy substance to a temperature that caused slivers of ice to appear in it. One of the perks of this job was that we were allowed to drink all the milk we wanted. When I took a glass and filled it with this icy beverage and drank it, there was nothing like its taste. To this day I still pour my milk over ice cubes, frequently surprising, sometimes appalling, those who look on. It is my effort, in a vain but nonetheless close attempt, to recapture and to relive that childhood moment.

Whenever I have gone through one of life's major transitions, whether it was my first day in public school, my graduation from the university, my ordination as a priest and later as a bishop, one of the many professional transitions that took me to new places and responsibilities, and even that penultimate transition into retirement, I have always been able to imagine myself in that new place or in that new situation long before the day of the move actually arrived. While I am clearly a creature who lives in a specific time and who occupies a particular place, I am not like the plants of the field or the beasts of the forest. I am not bound in the same way that they are bound by either time or space. With my mind I can move back into the past and forward into the future. I can even transport myself to places different from the one I presently occupy. So I experience something about my life that is both limitless and timeless.

While not having been trained as a scientist, I have done what only a self-conscious human being can do. I have studied science extensively. I have read deeply about our human origins. I have recently completed a ninety-six-lecture course on the origins of the universe taught by a professor of astrophysics at the University of California, Berkeley.[2] A wondrous place this universe is! This course has heightened my knowledge, but more importantly, it has increased my sense of awe and mystery in the world that is at once so vast and so humble. I have been fascinated to embrace in the smallness of my finite mind both the dimensions and the interdependence of the universe. This course also raised for me very existential questions about my place in it. My experience is that the more I have read and studied these things, the more mysterious life seems to become. We have noted earlier that this universe began between thirteen billion and fourteen billion years ago when, as one scientist wrote, "the singularity of an enigmatic force generated a universe and ultimately the prerequisite conditions for life on this planet earth."[3] This was the moment of the so-called big bang! By tracing the scientific footprints of energy, matter, physics, chemistry, biology and molecular biogenetics back through billions of years, the human mind can recreate with amazing accuracy the birth of the universe. That in turn brings us to the realization that all energy and matter within our universe ultimately derive from that big bang moment. Yet only relatively recently, within the past fifty thousand to two hundred thousand years, to give the spread in current thinking, with the emergence of the living and thinking human mind has it been possible for such a concept to become part of the awareness of any living thing. How does one who discovers this ability process such information regarding the meaning of the time and space that appears to bind us? What kind of creature is this self-conscious human being? How does one define the human brain or its more mysterious component, the human mind?

Some nine billion years after the birth of the universe this planet earth was formed out of a clump of cosmic dust spinning about the thermonuclear core of one of the stars in one of the galaxies within that vast universe. That star was destined to become our sun. At that time this planet earth was devoid of water and was composed of nitrogen, carbon and silicon with liquid iron at its core. Oxygen would appear later as the essential element that would sustain and balance carbon-based life. The surface of the earth was extremely hot. It was unprotected from ultraviolet solar radiation, and for the first five hundred million years or so of its existence, like so many other heavenly bodies, it was constantly bombarded by the flying debris that littered the universe. Yet in the next two hundred million years, or at some point prior to about three billion, eight hundred million years ago, the unique reality of life appeared in an apparently spontaneous way on this planet. From micro-fossil remains we have discovered it was quite primitive, limited in form to a single cell, but its potential we now know was unlimited. This is to state and even to embrace the fact that life—the complex, cellular, self-replicating biochemical process known as DNA—emerged out of material that was available within the atmosphere of this earth. Life's origins are still shrouded in mystery, though there are many explanatory theories. The deeper we search into the center of life, however, the more we see that it is made up of those same things found in other regions of the universe where there is no such thing as life. Yet in this tiny corner of that universe, a lifeless atmosphere was changed into a biosphere conducive to life, and so it was that living things emerged here.

I do not want or intend to fall back into that old religious trick and offer the supernatural, external deity as the only possible answer to this mystery. A gap-filler God, used to explain that for which there is not yet a known explanation, lasts only so long as knowledge remains static. That, as we have noted, has been the fate of our theistic explanations of the past. What I do want to assert is that life is mysterious and that there is not yet a full explanation for its emergence, for its massive proliferation or for the fact that early cells of life ultimately added oxygen to our biosphere, which made the evolution of other life forms possible. What a magnificent picture of interdependence! Finally, just as there is no explanation about how living things could emerge out of inert matter, so there is also no explanation for how consciousness could emerge out of unconscious living things, and no explanation about how self-consciousness could emerge out of consciousness, as it appears to have done relatively recently in history.

While we can surely study the past, even becoming expert paleontologists and anthropologists, we have no way of predicting or even anticipating what the next stage in life's development will be. Will we human beings become clairvoyant? Will we evolve beyond self-consciousness into something not yet imagined? Or will some other form of life that we do not yet recognize be the pool out of which a whole new aspect of life will emerge, as has happened so often in the past? I suspect that Neanderthal people once thought, as we do, that they were the source of the future. The time has come for human life to remove the blinders imposed by humanity itself and to think in very different ways. The "parent" god in the sky who comes to rescue us is an image from the childhood of our humanity. My friend Don Cupitt, with whom I disagree at the core but not on the periphery, has entitled his newest book *Above Us Only Sky*.[4] He is correct in seeing no deity above us, but he draws a very different conclusion from that fact than I do.

The advent of quantum physics forced the scientific world, even including people like the brilliant Albert Einstein, into embracing concepts that defy intuition and logic. That is why it has been called "quantum weirdness" by some. Quantum physics evolved from the discovery that atoms, previously considered to be the basic building blocks of nature, could be split into particles. Furthermore, these subatomic particles were observed to act in unpredictable ways. They could emit discrete bundles of light, which are quantified packages of energy that can spontaneously transform into physical waves of measurable energy. The discoveries from this new world of quantum physics heralded the modern era of nuclear science. It is now evident that such subatomic particles are prevalent within the outer spaces of our universe. These particles energize the interconnecting fabric of the entire cosmos. It is this knowledge that introduced us to a new awareness that we are not now and never have been separate or alone, as the experience of self-consciousness caused us to imagine that we were. That was a crucial assumption in human development. Around that assumption we organized self-conscious human life to deal with that sense of separation, making the presuppositions of religion, in regard to an external deity and our separation from this deity, our working hypotheses. Now we are beginning to suspect that this sense of separation, by which we were quite frankly overwhelmed, may itself be a delusion through which we had to live before its falseness could be revealed. It appears increasingly clear that we are now awakening to a sense of oneness with all that is; indeed, we are more connected than our minds can yet embrace. Self-consciousness begins to look like just one more stage in our development that will finally bring us to an awareness of our essential oneness with the universe, a oneness that binds together the material and immaterial things, and even our bodies and our minds, perhaps as a universal consciousness.

In a paper entitled "Cosmos to Consciousness: The Ascent of Humanity," Daniel Gregory, a physician, a research scientist, a seeker and a friend, wrote:

The highly developed architecture of the human brain provides humans with a multi-sensory and multi-perceptual awareness of the surrounding world. It is composed of more than twenty billion interconnecting neurons, and thirty thousand genes which provide a communication network and an integrated information center within the human body that receives stimuli from the complex electromagnetic and sub-atomic forces of the universe through a common energy system that can be traced back first to the big bang and later to the emergence of life on planet earth. A functioning brain has endowed humans with the capacity for creativity, genius, insight, inspiration and emotions such as love and desire. Humans have the capacity to judge good from evil, sort out potential outcomes, anticipate and plan for the future and generally to optimize their survival. As the human brain evolved with these powers of perceptual awareness, it also assumed the ability to perceive its own existence as a functional and independent human being with an inner, personal, cognitive and emotional self.[5]

My friend Milton LeRoy, in one of his many letters to me while he thought he was facing his own death, wrote: "If whatever attracts atoms and molecules to each other could also be called 'Love' then the source and creator of all could be called love. Dare we be so simple?"

In the light of these insights, and so many more, which are still trickling down from the world of the scholars to the workings of our common minds, the issue for me is the necessity to expand tremendously or even to rethink totally what it is we mean when we say the word "God." The problem with and the limitations of language become acute at this point. Words are symbols, not only shaped by our experience but bound by time and space. "God" is a word we use to seek to give expression to a concept beyond our experience and bound by neither time nor space. Is such a word inevitably unreal? Is such a realm nothing more than a human fantasy? What are we saying when we utter the word "God"?

In attempting to address this question we discover that the only language by which humans have been able to package their conceptions of the deity involve analogy and metaphor. We must face these limitations as we seek to understand God-talk. Traditional religion has always conceived of God in some kind of personalistic way: God is spoken of as if God were a "great big human being" who somehow is able to escape our limits. It is the world of human reality that always and inevitably shapes the divine definition.

Is there any way that we can get beyond these ideas and this frame of reference? Martin Buber, the great twentieth-century Jewish philosopher-theologian, sought to move us in that direction when he suggested that the God-human relationship should be viewed as "I-Thou."[6] "I" and "Thou" are both human words, but they signify movement toward a new dimension. To call ourselves "I," as we have noted, is to say something about self-consciousness. To call God "Thou" is to make God holy, but it does not escape the idea of God as an external "other." It still implies separation, but it enables us to see that it is a separation that must be transcended before the language can move to a new place. How do we move beyond this separation that appears to have come with and be a mark of self-consciousness? Can we understand selfhood without the kind of separation that in self-consciousness brought to us all of the anxieties that still plague human life?

The clue for me is to try to think outside the parameters of the concepts that we have used for all the years that definable human life has existed. Perhaps the personhood we have ascribed to God is really our own, projected onto God. God might then be conceived not as a being, but as the process that calls us into being; not as a person, but as the process that calls personhood into being. That would open us to consider the idea that the birth of self-consciousness meant a birth into an identity with the power of life that flows through the universe in billions of forms but reaches awareness only in the penetration through the barrier that turned conscious life into self-conscious life. The goal of that process, we have always assumed, was to carry us into personhood. Personhood, however, is also separation. Perhaps the real goal was to carry us through the separation of personhood and then beyond it to new possibilities.

What could lie beyond personhood? Is that not the highest thing we know? I do not think so. Individuation is just another step in the creation of a wholeness that enables the individuated one to be unique and part of the whole simultaneously. It is our recognition of the fact that only through the process of the individuation of the separated whole can that whole even be perceived. We stretch and groan against the limitations of language. We run the risk of having our words sound like nonsensical gobbledygook to some, while we seek to crack through our limits in order to reach or find a new perception of all that is. When we travel this road, will we come to see this journey as an invitation to walk into a state of awareness which eternally is and to which we ultimately belong? Are these just convoluted words, or have we finally reached a perspective from which we can raise in a proper way the questions of life after death and eternal life? I think we have.

Human beings need to understand that we must reconcile the biological drive to survive, which is present in every living thing but achieves self-consciousness only in human life, with the creative thought, emotional feelings, and ability to love others even at the sacrifice of ourselves which are the things that self-conscious creatures alone can choose to do or to have. That is the challenge of humanity. It is in the recognition and reconciliation of this tension that we discover that the way to what human beings have traditionally called God is not through some external projection of our needs, but through entering the depth dimensions of the human experience. The divine we have always sought turns out to be a dimension of the human. Religion ultimately becomes not an activity in which we explore the meaning of God, but an activity through which we explore the meaning of the human. Religion is not a journey into an external deity, but a journey into the heart of our humanity, where we break out of our separation fears and enter the meaning of transcendence, oneness, timelessness and, finally, eternity. Perhaps God is that presence in whom, to use another personal word, or in *which*, to stretch our language substantially, "we live and move and have our being," as Paul is made to say in a sermon in the book of Acts (17:28).

A new line of vision thus opens into the meaning of the word "God." "God" is not an external being apart from us, to which we must relate as powerless ones to the all-powerful one. "God" is more a glimpse into the meaning of the totality of human experiences, where we recognize that we are part of an ultimate grasping after a universal consciousness with which we are one and in which we are whole. This universal consciousness was, however, hidden from us until we exhausted the possibilities of religion in which God was always perceived as other. "God" is present whenever a person transcends human boundaries and sees the portrait of unity, not separation. "God" is the journey beyond the fear of loneliness into a new wholeness, a new sense of what reality actually is. Suddenly everything in both the religious landscape and the human landscape begins to shift and to be reconfigured in newly incredible ways. It is as if someone had turned the theological kaleidoscope and now the task before us in the post-religious world is to embrace the new vision, stare at the new configuration and learn to speak of the holy in a new way, a way that becomes not the domain of religion, but the domain of life.

So our journey carries us beyond any place that we have ever imagined. We have reached a position similar to that of Moses, who climbed the mountain so that he could look into the "promised land" (Deut. 34:1–4). All Moses did, according to this story, was to stare at that future vision. We cannot stop with just a view; we must enter it.

FOURTEEN

THE APPROACH OF
THE MYSTICS

When we needed the outer form of a
savior You were there for us.
When our conscious mind matures we turn within
rather than without to find You there, not separate
or apart but one in the same with ourselves.
We are moving toward Christ consciousness.

Maureen Ramsay Hughes[1]

Are the mystics simply crazy? They might well be! They frequently say strange and weird things. A fourteenth-century Christian mystic named Meister Eckhart once said: "God's being is my being and is the being of all beings. My me is God."[2] I have known patients confined to mental institutions to say similar things. On another occasion, Eckhart observed: "Between a person and God there is no distinction. They are one. Their knowing is with God's knowing. Their activity is with God's activity, their understanding with God's understanding. The same eye with which I look at God is the eye with which

God looks at me." I doubt if these are lines that would communicate much either to our secular world or to the members of the typical Sunday morning congregation. Mystics appear to be those strange people in whom all boundaries have been removed. This would be particularly true of those boundaries that human beings once perceived that separated them from the external God. Indeed, when mystics talk about God, they appear to be talking about an unbounded presence, a timeless reality or even what Paul Tillich called "the Eternal Now."[3] Eckhart appears to have understood as long ago as the fourteenth century that relating to a supernatural, external deity is finally a violation of the oneness of the universe and of the expanded consciousness of human life, suggesting that perhaps we have finally reached the place where we no longer have need for that hypothesis.

Eckhart was, however, a Christian, even a priest, perhaps the first post-religious Christian. He stood inside an understanding of God that was not and could not for him have been bounded by creeds, forms, doctrines and dogmas. He was not popular with those ecclesiastical leaders who felt it was their duty to monitor behavior and to enforce conformity in belief. He seemed to be aware that the goal of religion had become little more than seeking to control life in the here and now in the service of a personal security. Religion's weapons of choice in this struggle were guilt and fear. Religion made life in this world something to be governed by either the eternal reward of heaven or the eternal punishment of hell. The mystics through the ages have always stood against this mentality, which also means that the mystics have always threatened the established religion. Perhaps that is why we ought to look again at the mystics: they might turn out to be the means through which the essence of yesterday's religion can be transformed into tomorrow's spiritual understanding. Enter with me then into an examination of the mystical experience, for this seems to be the place that beckons to me now as the next step to take on this journey.

For years now, it has been difficult for me to use traditional religious language. I have, therefore, tried to talk about the holy, the divine, the "other"—that which most people call God—without using either the traditional symbols of the realm of the unknown and unknowable, or those religious concepts that seem totally bound to the here and now. No matter how hard I tried to force myself to accept those images and theological concepts, they had no reality for me. I always found them to be limiting, falsifying and inadequate. I did not, however, know how to get beyond them. They were all bound by a finite frame of reference while they sought to comment on the infinite. My struggle was not helped by the realization that the people I was trying to serve as a priest, even when my motive was to illumine them, found my approach less than satisfying, to say the least. I did not affirm the language that they knew they no longer believed and yet they could not admit, even to themselves, their inability to believe. As fearful people wrestling with the trauma of insecurity, they much preferred the anthropomorphic images of finding themselves embraced by "the everlasting arms" or invited to suckle at the breasts of the all-enveloping "divine Mother." I have reached the place where I do not hold these images in contempt so much as I recognize that we needed them in the loneliness of what now looks like the "childhood of our humanity." The supernatural parent figure in the sky who could take care of us had great appeal, especially if we could continue to believe what religious leaders regularly asserted—namely, that it was a virtue to dwell in a childlike dependency forever. Churches seem to prefer childlike members. That is why churches so frequently exhort their people to be "born again." The hidden agenda of born-again theology is that when one is "born again," childhood becomes renewed, and a constantly renewed childhood quickly turns into a perpetual childhood. In many ways human beings have for some time been moving away from that mentality and into a new understanding of what it means to be human. Far from needing to be born again into perpetual childishness, we need to grow up, to embrace the new dimensions of human maturity. I think, therefore, that the time has arrived when we need to stop forever the human attempt to see God as the supernatural or divine parent figure, to acknowledge that this is a religious drive for security and that we now need to embrace a new possibility. Perhaps the mystical dimension of recognizing that we are part of who God is and what God is, and that God is part of who we are and what we are, is the place to begin. The human ability to claim our God-consciousness and to act on it slowly emerges as the essence of what it means to be human. A new starting place thus appears.

When I step into this new place, I see God in non-personal ways. Please note that *non*-personal does not mean *im*personal. It means that the holy cannot be bound by the personal. "Personal" is a human category. Only by transcending personal terms entirely can we open ourselves to the recognition that there is a source of life that flows through all living things but comes to self-consciousness in human life alone. That source of life is now, for me at least, a part of who God is. This means that the more deeply I live, the more God becomes identified with my life.

The power of love flows through all forms of life, but it ceases to be instinctual and comes to self-consciousness only in human beings. That power of love is also part of who God is for me. This means that the more deeply I am able to love, the more God becomes part of me. This is why no religion can in the last analysis ever really be about proper beliefs and proper practices. Those are only the artifacts of religious power. Religion has to be about the enhancement of life through love. Religious rules are sacred only if they serve to enhance life. That is the point Jesus was depicted as making when he declared that human life was not made to fit into the Sabbath day rules, but that the Sabbath day rules were created to enhance human life. Suddenly the essence of ethics is seen not as something about good and evil, or even about justice and injustice; and it is certainly not about a code of rules or laws that is inscribed in a holy text or cut into tablets of stone. No, ethics are always designed to assist in the expansion of life. Every act, whether it be individual or corporate, must be judged as right or wrong based solely on whether it enhances or diminishes the life of another. If my action diminishes another, it also diminishes me. A diminished life is never the place where holiness will be found. Diminished lives will never be loving lives.

Again and again we are driven back to the task of trying to process our time-warped and space-bound experience with that which appears not to be warped by time or bound by space. I experience God under the category that I call "being." If God is the "Ground of All Being," the phrase I attribute principally to my shaping theological thinker Paul Tillich, then my "being" not only is part of but participates in the "being" of God. This means that true worship has little to do with saying words of praise, but is rather identical with having the courage to be all that I can be. True worship is a process that suggests and celebrates the fact that the more deeply and fully I can be who I am, the more I will make God, understood as being itself, visible. This God then becomes not a separate entity, but the depth dimension of being itself, which is present in every living thing but comes to self-consciousness only in the human life.

I experience God as expanded consciousness. Life is ever-unfolding. Consciousness is ever-rising. We see that in the growing human awareness of those who are different from the majority. We see it in our increasing sensitivity to, and in the enhanced sense of our responsibility for, the life of our world. All of these things, I believe, are the result of a new awareness of what it means to be human. In expanded consciousness, the barriers we erect and behind which we hide in our search for security actually serve to cut us off from the meaning of life. That is the great sin of organized religion. Organized religion seeks to turn us inward upon ourselves. It binds us into a world marked by enormous limitations. Organized religion always divides the world into warring camps. It separates the followers of "true religion" from the followers of that which it judges to be false religion. It separates true believers from heretics, the clean from the unclean, the saved from the unsaved, the baptized from the unbaptized, and the circumcised from the uncircumcised. These markers, however, cannot be part of the God experienced as life, love, being and consciousness. Whereas God's qualities cannot be categorized, branded or judged by external standards, religious markers such as being saved or being baptized can; the latter are nothing more than the manifestations of the supernatural tribal deity who builds the power of one people by diminishing the power of another. It is only in the expansion of human life and the expansion of self-consciousness that we find the ability to cross barriers and to transcend boundaries. It is this expansion of life and consciousness that invites us into a new understanding of what it means to be human. Finally, it is this expansion of life and consciousness that links us, I believe, with eternity, with timelessness. It is this expansion of life and consciousness that I now think I can say links us with God. We have moved beyond religion, meaning that even God can no longer be a religious concept.

Can we then learn to live without religion? I think we can. Even more important, I think we *must*. When all religions based on an external being die, only then will the mystical union with all that is finally be perceptible. It is the Fourth Gospel more than any or all of the other three that ultimately made this clear to me. This gospel links the human Jesus so deeply to the meaning of God that there appears to be no separation at all.

Yet John has been traditionally interpreted to mean that the human flesh of Jesus has been taken over and folded into the divine life of God. Classical Christianity has leaned on John's Gospel for such doctrines as the Incarnation and the Holy Trinity far more dramatically than any of the others. Jesus, undergirded by the traditional reading of John's Gospel, has been portrayed as a divine invader, a deity who put on human flesh.

The logic of this exalted claim was impeccable. As Christianity developed along incarnational and trinitarian lines, Jesus was more and more portrayed as the savior of the sinner, the rescuer of the lost and the redeemer of the fallen. None of these functions—saving, rescuing and redeeming—was possible unless the traditional definition of human life was accepted. Human beings were the sinners, the lost and the fallen. The implication was that only a sinless one—that is, God—could save the sinful. A human life, which is by definition lost, *cannot* rescue the lost. A human life, which by definition is fallen, *cannot* redeem the fallen. Jesus, this theology proclaimed, could and did perform these functions, but only because he was "God in human form." In Jesus, "the Word became flesh and dwelt among us . . . ; we have beheld his glory, glory as of the only son from the Father" (John 1:14). The portrait of Jesus drawn by John has traditionally been used to deny his humanity, to establish him as a supernatural invader into the fallen world. The human Jesus who cries out in agony from the cross in the Gospel of Mark, "My God, my God, why have you forsaken me?" (15:33, NRSV), has disappeared in the

Fourth Gospel. No human pain could be experienced in the divine Christ by the time John wrote. John's Jesus dies on the cross in triumph, not in despair. His final words according to John are "It is finished" (John 19:30). John's prologue to his gospel, in chapter 1, has the opening verses parallel the opening words of Genesis, and thus the Torah. The opening chapter of Genesis walks through the divine actions of the six-day creation story. When the work of creation was complete, the book of Genesis says, God, looking out on all that God had made, declared it to be good, complete and finished. Only then did God enter into the Sabbath, bless it and hallow it.

In the traditional explanation Jesus, as John has been interpreted, replicated the creative work of God in what he believed was a second creation and in the process he completed the work of salvation. So John has Jesus claim that his work, and indeed God's work, is now complete. "It is finished," Jesus says, only in John. The work of salvation is now accomplished and Jesus, like the God he was assumed to be, was ready to enter into the Sabbath of his rest in the tomb before emerging on the first day of the week in a glorified and eternal form that enabled people to see who, John said, he always was. That culmination was quite different from "My God, my God, why have you forsaken me?"

We need to recognize how deeply the worship images of the Jews impacted John's portrayal of the crucifixion and resurrection. Only in John's Gospel is death on the cross hastened by breaking the legs of the other crucified victims (19:32). Jesus, we are told, was spared this bone-breaking experience because he was already dead. This meant that the familiar Jewish image of the liturgical Lamb of God, sacrificed on the Day of Atonement, Yom Kippur, could now be identified with Jesus. Both were the initiators of salvation. It was the blood of this sacrificial lamb spread on the mercy seat of God in the temple's Holy of Holies that was believed to have covered the sins of the people, thus enabling them to become one with God. Jesus was also sacrificed and his blood covered the sins of the people and made them acceptable to God. In this manner the death of Jesus was transformed. It was not a purposeless tragedy, but the price required to inaugurate the plan of salvation that only God could accomplish. The sacrificial lamb of Yom Kippur had to be physically perfect, young, male (it *was* a patriarchal culture) and physically whole with no broken bones, so Jesus was portrayed as young, male and physically whole with no broken bones. John does have a soldier hurl a gratuitous spear into Jesus' dead body so that he could also identify Jesus with the shepherd king of Israel in the book of II Zechariah,[4] who was handed over for thirty pieces of silver, pierced as Jesus was pierced, and mourned as one mourns for the only son. The culprits in II Zechariah were those who bought and sold animals in the temple. Salvation is accomplished for John when, after Jesus dies, the sun goes down in the west and the arrival of the Sabbath is announced. Then John has Jesus placed in the tomb for the Sabbath rest only to emerge at dawn of the first day of the week when the Sabbath was over and the new creation was to begin. John, in effect, has Jesus relive symbolically the very life of God in the act of creation.

I was never drawn to the traditional understanding of John's Gospel because it assumed the external supernatural invasive deity, the God who came from heaven to bring salvation to a fallen race of human beings. I find incarnational thinking to be bizarre in a post-Darwinian world. It pretends, in the pre-Darwinian fashion, that there was a perfect creation which preceded the fall into sin, which in turn necessitated the rescue that only the God from beyond the world could accomplish. In other words, that kind of thinking transforms Jesus into God's divine rescue operation.

Post-Darwinian thinking, on the other hand, suggests that human life has never been perfect and thus could never have fallen and, in fact, requires no rescue. Human life for Darwin was in the process of *becoming*. Post-Darwinists share that view, seeing human life as celebrating its being in the act of living. The traditional view of John's Gospel does not speak to the reality of our humanity. There is, however, another way to read John's Gospel. It can be read through the eyes of a mystic or be viewed through the eyes of mysticism, and when it is, it becomes a powerful narrative about the divine potential that is in all of life. Whereas the traditional way of reading John has long had decreasing appeal for me, the mystical way of reading John's Gospel offers me a whole new perspective on both God and Jesus. While the mystical conclusion and the conclusions of Christian orthodoxy might sound identical—that is, in both God is identified with Jesus—the way one gets to that conclusion and the meaning found in that conclusion for all life are profoundly different.

Through a mystical lens I can now view John's Gospel as the story not of a divine life invading the world, but of a human life named Jesus of Nazareth. Yet the gospel portrays this Jesus as revealing a deeper and freer self-consciousness that is so profound that the usual human barriers disappeared: John portrays Jesus as having a relationship with the holy that is of indistinguishable identity. Jesus is not absorbed into the holy. Jesus is rather alive with the holy. Jesus, for John, is the life through which the voice of God is heard speaking, the being through which the Ground of Being is experienced as present. God from outside does not enter the human Jesus, as Mark suggests happened at baptism and as Matthew and Luke say occurred at the moment of conception. There is rather in this gospel a kind of intrinsic, inseparable unity, the result of which does not make Jesus more than human, but it does make him fully human and thus fully one with all that God is. That is why

John's Jesus can identify himself with God. When Philip, one of Jesus' disciples, asks Jesus in John's Gospel to "show us the Father," Jesus responds that if Philip has seen Jesus, he has seen God, for "I am in the Father and the Father is in me" (14:8–10). Jesus is interpreted by John to be inviting the disciples to enter him as he has entered God. When they do so, they will know the oneness that is present in the whole universe (14:20). Jesus is made to claim in this gospel that the words he speaks are not his words but God's words (14:24). These remarks might be nothing more than the manifestations of megalomania, but I do not think so. I see them as the words of a new humanity that no longer thinks of God as an external, supernatural deity, but rather sees God as part of who he or she is. When the theistic understanding of God is recognized as a symbol of the human search for security, it becomes a search that will never end in finding, for this God does not exist. We will never achieve human maturity until we let go and take leave of this parent substitute. Jesus is not to God what Clark Kent was to Superman. Jesus was a human life so deeply lived, a human life through which love flowed without barrier or interception, a being so courageously present that he was open to the ultimate ground of all being. He had stepped from self-consciousness into a universal consciousness that brings us into a profound oneness with all there is. He had become one with God.

Reading further into this gospel we come across a series of sayings that are known as the "I am" sayings. "I am" is the name of God revealed to Moses in the story of the burning bush in the Hebrew scriptures (Exod. 3:14). The "I am" formula is placed on Jesus' lips by the author of John again and again. "I am the bread of life," he says (John 6:35). Does that mean that there is something in Jesus that satisfies the deepest hunger and yearning that we have for God? John has Jesus say, "I am the vine, you are the branches" (John 15:5). Does this mean that Jesus' followers found in Jesus such a sense of being opened to and united with what human life can be that he fed their lives in the same way that the vine pours vitality into its branches? He is made to say, "I am the good shepherd" (John 10:11). Does that mean he has the capacity to love the members of the flock more deeply than he loves himself? He is made to say, "I am the way, and the truth, and the life," which he then describes as the only pathway to God (14:6). Does that mean that in his life the door opens, as it has never before been observed to do, to transcendence, to life, to being? These are the things that constitute the only way to God.

John's Gospel has Jesus make this claim to be beyond time: "Before Abraham was, I am, he says" (8:58). Is this a reference to a timelessness that comes to those who refuse to be bound by human limitations? When this gospel sums up Jesus' purpose, the words it has Jesus speak are: "I came that they may have life, and have it abundantly" (10:10). Note that the purpose of Jesus here is not to make people religious, moral, righteous or even true believers. All of those traits are ego trips that insecure people take as part of their strategy of survival. Jesus' gift was the gift of wholeness, and it was lived out so deeply as to be experienced as his very meaning, part of the God-presence that he has entered.

Sam Harris, the author of *The End of Faith,* is as critical of religion as I am. He is, however, quite sensitive to and supportive of mysticism, though he is not able to make the connection that I think John's Gospel seeks to make. Harris says of Christianity, for example: "It is not enough [for Christianity] that Jesus was a man who transformed himself to such a degree that the Sermon on the Mount could be his heart's confession. He also had to be the Son of God, born of a virgin and destined to return to earth trailing clouds of glory."[5] There is no doubt that in the New Testament excessive language is used to convey the Christ-experience as the work of the external God. That was because the experience did not lend itself to the language with which the earliest Christians had to work. By the time John's Gospel was written near the end of the first century, however, I am suggesting, the language of mysticism, of human oneness in the divine, of a life that knew no boundaries, had transformed the earlier language of miracle and magic, of angels that sing and stars that wander. When John relates the account of the feeding of the five thousand it has ceased to be a miracle story and has become a symbolic eucharistic meal in which Jesus becomes the infinite Lamb of God whose life can feed all the lives of the world that hunger for meaning. Is that what the introduction of miracle stories into the life of Jesus was all about, but John alone was the gospel writer who saw it?

In John there is no account of a miraculous birth, no narrative of an ascension into heaven, and all miracles have become signs pointing to an inner reality. Even the story of the crucifixion, as told by John, is the story of the transforming gift that comes when one lives in the face of rejection and gives life to those who think they are taking it away. The ability to give oneself away is the mark of having touched the transcendent. It is the mark of God. Wholeness comes to the world when one's life is given away freely to others. That is when one escapes the basic drive for survival and becomes capable of giving life to "the least of these," one's brothers and sisters. Finally, resurrection in John is not about convincing supernatural acts. If we read chapter 20 of John, the supernatural acts of seeing his risen body, even examining the wounds of crucifixion on his hands, feet and side, do not apparently change anyone's life. In John 21 the disciples simply return to their fishing trade in Galilee as if nothing of eternal significance has occurred. In Galilee, however, the risen Christ is said to appear again, but this time to call them, perhaps to empower them "to feed my sheep," to be agents of life, love, and a way of being that will enable a deeper, universal, consciousness to appear in all the people of the world, a consciousness that is seen as the life of God within them.

As God has life in God's self, says John, so God has given to the son to have life in himself (John 5:26). John's mystical approach to Jesus shouts the reality that we share in the life of God, just as Jesus did. We share in the being of God, just as Jesus did. Does that mean that our consciousness shares in the consciousness of God? I think it does, and as we become more deeply and fully conscious, we move from the being of survival to the being of love and we participate in and reveal the reality of God. One of the hymns of the Christian church captures this mystical oneness as few of them do, when it says of God: "In all life thou livest, the true life of all."[6] What the mystics seem to grasp almost intuitively is that God is not a being external to life that we must woo and flatter to gain divine protection and ultimate triumph over the demons that beset us as we seek meaning, purpose and a stake in eternity. Running counter to this principle of our dying religious past is the mystical perception, more experienced than believed, more intuitive than doctrinal, that God is the ultimate being in which our being shares. The time has come to look once again at what it means to be human and what it means to be one in whom the life of God lives, the love of God loves, and the being of God is made manifest. That is the doorway into freedom, into maturity, into, as the epistle to the Ephesians says, "mature manhood [and womanhood] . . . the measure of the stature of the fullness of Christ" where we will "no longer be children, tossed to and fro. . . . We are to grow up in every way into him who is the head" (4:13–16). It is the mystics who seem to know that this is the potential that human life seeks. This is our destiny as self-consciousness enters the universal consciousness.

When I arrive at this point, I am ready to look again at the meaning of death and the hope of eternal life, and they both look very different from this perspective. We go there next.

FIFTEEN

RESURRECTION:
A SYMBOL AND A REALITY

Religion is no more—
Fragmenting humankind
with doctrine, creed
and narrowness of heart.
Not darkly through a glass
Truth stands at length
in beauty unaffected
A prospect indivisible
Love is her only name.

David Stevenson[1]

Deepak Chopra, in his book *Life After Death*,[2] approaches the subject of the afterlife through the lens and experience of his Eastern religious background. He does it well and powerfully. I admire his work and share in many of his conclusions. I, however, as a child of the West, cannot walk his path any more than he can walk mine. Both of us must arrive at the truth we seek by way of the religious system of our origins, not by rejecting or denying that system, but by transcending it. This means that I must go through my faith tradition to its center, its core and its depth, and only then move beyond it. I cannot start from a place where I have never been, but must set out from the place where I *am*. All of us are like St. Paul, who, when confronting ultimate truth, confessed that he could see only dimly, as though through a dark glass. That is the nature of what it means to be human and to experience more than any of us can process. Deepak Chopra and I may well arrive at a similar place, because truth is bigger than any of us and bigger than any cultural understanding. That is why I have to turn in this chapter to explore my own religious heritage and to examine the essence of the Jesus story from this new perspective. This is the place where I find those clues that might be helpful not to guide me into a religious conviction that life is indeed eternal, but to enable me to move beyond all religion into a universal understanding of what it means to be human, and what it means to touch eternity. That is now my goal.

I begin, therefore, with questions that are designed to open this Jesus story to the new dimensions that I have sought to reveal in this study about human life and human consciousness. Was Jesus raised from death by the intervention of an external supernatural being? Is resurrection to be explained by the assertion that Jesus, since he was himself divine, was therefore endowed with the gift of immortality, traditionally limited only to divine beings? Or is it possible that Jesus was perceived as triumphant over death only because he was so deeply and profoundly human that his life opened to that which we call divine, but which is always present at the depth of the human? Did Jesus transcend the barrier of death because he transcended the boundaries of self-consciousness and entered the timelessness of a universal consciousness? Traditional religious forms have always insisted on the former explanation, portraying Jesus as divinely resurrected and as possessing intrinsic immortality. I now want to suggest that the latter explanation, namely that resurrection into full consciousness and humanity is more profoundly true and even more biblically accurate. I start with the Bible, which I regard as the world's most misunderstood book with most of the misunderstanding coming from traditional believers.

I sometimes wonder how it is that anyone could read the story of Jesus' life as the canonical gospels portray it and ever think that the gospel writers intended their words to be understood literally. They were not writing history or biography. They were trying to interpret a life-changing experience that had been very real to them, but all they had to use were limited human words. The gospel writers signaled this weakness of vocabulary to their readers by exaggerating their language to the point where their words became literally absurd. People do not seem to notice that every scene in the gospel story is told in language that has been broken open in the attempt to convey an experience which the authors were convinced was real, but which language was simply unable to convey. The entire gospel narrative is illustrative of this, but it reaches a crescendo in the stories of Jesus' birth and the stories of his death. None of the details can be read literally, since they are so lacking in rational credibility. As a result many believers simply ignore these details. In doing so, however, they miss the clues that reveal the intentions of the gospel writers. These first-century authors were not people devoid of common sense, nor were they lacking in the gifts of imagination. So I examine now quite briefly the way Jesus' life story is told, beginning with his birth and culminating in the accounts of his death and resurrection to try to escape for a moment the common misconception that the authors intended these narratives to be read as a description of literal or objective history.[3]

Symbolic language is obviously present in the very familiar story of Jesus' birth. Do virgins really conceive? Do angels sing to hillside shepherds? Do stars announce events that happen in human history? Do stars wander through the sky so slowly that magi can follow them, stopping along the way at the palace of the king, then at a home in Bethlehem, to guide their human travelers? Would any Eastern sage set out on a journey to follow this magical star in order to pay homage to a newborn king in a foreign land? Would literal "wise men" travel with symbolic interpretive gifts for that newborn: gold for a king, frankincense for a deity and myrrh to be a sign of what that baby's eventual death would actually accomplish? Would a king use these odd-looking foreigners to be his Central Intelligence Agency, to bring him reports on this potential threat to his throne? Is no one aware that Matthew will tell us later that this regal child was in fact the son of a carpenter (Matt. 13:55)? Even in the first century, would these things not be recognized by all who heard them as the very stuff of fairy tales, not unlike narratives of those who seek a pot of gold at the end of the rainbow? Why have any of us ever literalized them?

The gospel narratives then go on to relate fantastic tales of Jesus doing such things as walking on water, transforming five loaves of bread into enough food to feed multitudes, healing numerous people of their physical and mental illnesses and even raising people from the dead. The narratives then culminate in fanciful tales describing the final events in Jesus' life. Were any of these ever meant to be literal stories even in the first century, or is there something else going on in these narratives that we miss because we have for so long been taught to read them as historical vignettes?

Look with particular care at the accounts that surround the death and resurrection of Jesus and you will see the same kind of "stretched beyond credibility" language being employed. Did the sun literally go dark over all the earth while Jesus lingered on his cross from twelve noon to three in the afternoon, as the gospels not only imply but plainly state (Mark 15:33, Matt. 27:45, Luke 23:44)? Does anyone really think that the gospel writers truly believed that it was a literal darkness that everyone endured, some eclipse of the sun, perhaps? Did the veil in the temple that separated the "holy place" from the "holy of holies" actually split from top to bottom at the moment of Jesus' death, so that access to God, who was believed to dwell in the "holy of holies," could be forever open (Mark 15:38, Matt. 27:51, Luke 23:45)? Did an objective earthquake accompany his death, as Matthew states so overtly (Matt. 27:51–52)? Was the story of Jesus' tomb real? Would a convicted and executed felon be given a dignified and gracious burial in the garden of a rich man who was a ruler of the Jews (Matt. 27:57–61)? Would a temple guard be placed around such a tomb (Matt. 27:62–66)? Did the removal of the great stone, which the gospel writers suggest covered the mouth of the tomb, really require an inter- vening angelic being who came out of the sky (Matt. 28:1–3)? Were the graves of the "saints in Jerusalem" really opened by Jesus' death so that the bodies of these long-deceased ones could rise up, be resuscitated and walk the streets of that holy city in the sight of many (Matt. 27:52)?

Did the risen Jesus miraculously appear out of thin air to the two people on the road from Jerusalem to Emmaus and then just as miraculously disappear into thin air after they had recognized him in the sacrament of the broken bread (Luke 24:13ff.)? Did the risen Jesus walk through locked doors and barred windows to get into that upper room to join his dis- ciples at the time of the evening meal on the first day of the week following the crucifixion (John 20:19ff.)? If people really believed that Jesus could do that, why would the stone in front of the tomb have been a problem and thus why was angelic help needed to remove it? What clothes was the risen Jesus wear- ing? Read the Bible literally and you will discover that the gospels tell us that the soldiers divided his only clothing among themselves (Mark 15:24, Matt. 27:35, and Luke 23:34) when he was being crucified, and the Easter story says that the burial clothes in which his deceased body was wrapped were left in the tomb at the time of his resurrection (John 20:6–7). Was it a nude Jesus that the women saw at dawn on that first Easter day? Surely that puts a whole new meaning into Jesus' words to Mary Magdalene, recorded only in the Fourth Gospel (John 20:17): "Do not hold me, for I have not yet ascended to the Father!" Finally, did Jesus actually defy gravity to return to the God who lives above the sky of a three-tiered universe (Acts 1:9)?

It is in narratives filled with these kinds of extravagant details that we read about Jesus walking literally and physically out of his tomb three days after his crucifixion with the nail-prints on his hands and feet still intact. Does that not give us a clue that these gospel writers were trying to say something that ordinary human language was not equipped to say, so they stretched that language beyond its normal limits? Surely these gospel writers were quite aware that they were using words and images this way in an effort to describe in limited, everyday human language—which was all that they had to use, after all—an internal, profoundly real and reorienting psychic and mystical experience that had altered human consciousness and, therefore, human history forever. Should we expend our time looking for proofs of the literalness of these resurrection details so that we can, first, convince ourselves that they are true and then, second, convince others that the story in which we have invested our hope of life beyond death for centuries might make it into another generation? Is it not time for even those of us who stand inside religious communities to begin to look into these stories for another kind of truth? Can our fear of death ever be transcended by these literalistic games of smoke and mirrors, by closing our minds to reality and by living in the fantasy of self-delusion? In each of the above-cited narrative instances I would argue that the words were not, and were never intended to be, literal descriptions of real happenings and that for anyone to treat them as if they were is to distort them consistently and thoroughly. That, I submit, is never the way that religious language was meant to be read, but that is the way that most people read it.

Everything we know about how Jesus *literally* died points to the fact that his death and his burial were anything but dignified. Crucifixion is a public act of terror designed to intimidate onlookers. There was, quite obviously, no tomb in a lovely garden into which the body of Jesus was laid by his disciples. Indeed, the earliest gospel tells us of the complete apostolic abandonment at the time of Jesus' arrest (Mark 14:50). That source even validates this abandonment by having Jesus tell the disciples in advance that they were destined to do this in order to "fulfill the scriptures." Do people retrospectively seek to justify behavior that never occurred? Jesus died alone. That is literal history.

In that cruel world of harsh political repression victims of execution were normally dumped unceremoniously into a common grave and quickly covered over. The natural processes of decay worked quickly in that climate, unless the scavenging of wild dogs made nature's recycling process even quicker, more efficient and more routine. The empty tomb, so romanticized in our Easter stories, probably never existed. What does it do to our literal-thinking minds to realize that if there was in fact no literal tomb, then a literal body could not have walked out of it on a literal third day? There was also no literal rich man named Joseph of Arimathea who provided for Jesus as a secret disciple. There were no earthquakes to mark his death. There was no eclipse, no darkness at noon that lasted for three hours, no angelic messengers who announced his victory over death. At any rate, these things did not occupy space in the world of cause and effect, of life and death, of blood and tears. I find it both naïve and amazing that religious people today are unable to admit the reality of spiritual truth and psychic breakthrough to a new consciousness unless they can convince themselves that the biblical resurrection details were physical realities that occurred in an objective history that was bounded by time and space. Such resurrection understandings are artifacts of the idea that God is a supernatural being who lives external to this world, invading it miraculously from time to time to rescue us from peril, from meaninglessness or from the reality of death. No, the Easter story is more than that, far more, not less than that. In fact, it is not that at all.

Ask yourself, if you are still trapped in that external sense of the supernatural, just why it was that though the Christian community attached great weight to the resurrection, no two accounts of it were alike? Indeed, there is hardly a detail in any New Testament narrative of Jesus' resurrection that is not actually contradicted in another narrative. The New Testament writers do not agree that there was a tomb to which the women went at dawn on the first day of the week; they do not agree on who the women were that constituted the group of early morning visitors or on whether these women actually saw the raised Jesus on that occasion; they do not agree on where the disciples were when whatever the experience of Easter was first dawned on them or within them as the case might be and they do not agree on who among them was the first of the disciples to "see," whatever it was that "see" meant, when referring to the Easter moment. They do not even agree as to whether the resurrection was a physical thing! The earliest accounts suggest that the event was *not* physical, but it becomes more and more physical with the passing of time. Was the original account of the resurrection of Jesus a narrative seeking to describe the mystical, but real, experience of Jesus being raised into the eternity of God, or was it a narrative in which he was raised back into the life of this world, from which much later he had to be extricated? Since he could not die again, which is the way that people normally get out of this world, his physically resurrected body had to be miraculously lifted from the life of this world into the life of God, who was conceived of as living above the sky. This is what the ascension accomplishes. It is exactly this attempt to use human language to describe a reality that the early followers of Jesus were not able to doubt or dismiss that makes us suspect that all of the resurrection narratives are in fact late additions to the developing tradition. Why were they late? Because the original Easter moment, wherever it was and to whomever it occurred, was so powerful an experience of a living Jesus that no explanation was necessary. Later generations of Christians would be the ones who needed explanations to make sense out of the way they understood God as something other than what they were, something up there or out there. So given the radically contradictory accounts of this solitary, crucial moment in the Jesus story, our task becomes that of going beneath the explanations to try to define the experience.

Please note also the private nature of the resurrection appearance stories as the New Testament tells them. None of them is a public or a temple event. The events are not, as John's account of Lazarus being called forth from his grave was, conducted in a public assembly. Remember that when Lazarus supposedly came forth from his grave, he was bound in grave clothes that presumably everyone in this assembled group of mourners, loved ones, friends and even the enemies of Jesus could literally see and from which his friends would finally free him. The earliest stories about seeing the raised Jesus are centered in rural Galilee.

The later ones have been moved to Jerusalem. The earlier Galilean stories are vague and mysterious. Paul gives us no narrative details, saying only that Peter was the first to see the resurrected Jesus and that, at least on his own list, he himself was the last to see Jesus (I Cor. 15:1–8). Whatever Paul's seeing was, he claimed that it was no different from anybody else's seeing. Yet scholars date Paul's conversion one to six years after the crucifixion, far too long for his seeing of the raised Jesus to be a physical seeing of a resuscitated body. Paul had to be speaking about a different kind of seeing, but what was it? Was Paul saying that he had had a vision that, while it might later have seemed objective to others, was in fact subjective to Paul? Was his seeing actual *sight* or *insight*? Or was it second sight? Was it yet a different kind of seeing from any of these? Paul leaves the answer to this query in the realm of the unexplained, even though he was the writer closest to the resurrection moment in time, having done his writing between twenty and thirty-four years after the crucifixion or some sixteen to eighteen years before the first gospel was written. We have no sources closer than that. The farther removed the resurrection writings are in time from whatever the experience of resurrection was, the more the mystery and wonder have been replaced by objective tales and physical proofs. Mark, writing in the early 70s, has Jesus appear to no one; rather, a messenger informs the disciples that Jesus is alive and will go before them into Galilee and there, in their homes, they will "see" him. Matthew, writing in the early 80s, says that the disciples did see Jesus in Galilee, but what they saw was not a resuscitated Jesus but a glorified being who came out of the sky, traveling on the clouds, clad in the symbols of the mythical "Son of man" and spelling out the mission that the disciples must embrace in the words that we now call the Great Commission.

Luke, writing in the late 80s or early 90s, and John, writing in the late 90s, make the resurrected Jesus so physical that they portray him as eating, walking, talking, teaching, interpreting scripture and offering his body for inspection to demonstrate its physical, resuscitated nature. These are also the two gospels that separate the resurrection from the ascension, but even here they do not agree on the length of the separation. Luke says it was forty days; John separates them only by hours (compare Acts 1:3–11 with John 20:17). It is easy to understand how the stories grew, becoming more supernatural and miraculous, more physical and objective. That is the nature of the human yearning to locate certainty in history by postulating the invasion of the human by the external supernatural being in whom human beings, since the birth of self-consciousness, have invested their need for security. As always, however, these are explanations cast in the language of objectivity, trying to make sense of an experience of transforming consciousness. Our question is not, Did Jesus rise from the dead? but, What was it that these gospel writers were trying to convey? What did "experiencing Jesus alive" mean to them?

We can never penetrate this curtain of mystery for certain, but we can rather accurately trace the effects that occurred in these disciples as they lived into the meaning of what they were trying to describe. We know that something happened to their understanding of God. We know that something happened to their understanding of Jesus. We know that something happened to the disciples' understanding of themselves. These changes were the things that were objective and real and that had distinct and recognizable consequences. Their *experience* of the raised Jesus, if not the raised Jesus himself, was an event that did occur in time and in history and that demands an accounting even if we are reduced to using words like "an experience of psychic consciousness." Jesus had been raised, but into what? Was he raised into their understanding of God so that nothing was able ever to be the same? Skeptics might well call that mass hallucination, because they regard anything that is not objective, or that does not occur in time and space, as unreal. Yet the reality of this shift in consciousness was measurable, undeniable and quite easy to document. The meaning of God was forever altered because Jesus, by the sheer force of his being, had imprinted his humanity onto the definition of the divine. The external God had been discovered at the heart of the human. God was now experienced "through the filter of Jesus."[4] Resurrection was an event of inner history at the levels of consciousness where fundamental shifts occur. The disciples, who had localized the God-experience in Jesus, found in his death that this God-experience was no longer localized. The presence of the holy that they had found in Jesus they now discovered in themselves. It was as if they saw that what it was that they had met in Jesus had now taken up residence in their lives and hearts. This is what John was trying to say when he had the raised Jesus breathe on the disciples in the evening of the first Easter so that they were filled with what later Christians would call the Holy Spirit (John 20:22), but which I believe was originally known as the spirit of Jesus, himself. I have called that presence "Christpower."[5]

The Jesus-experience, which I believe was an empowering call to live, to love and to be, and which had seemed to be unique to Jesus, was now located at the center of their own being. The power of Jesus had entered them just as, they began to say, Jesus had in his resurrection entered into the very being of God. Jesus had in his death stepped aside to let the meaning of self-consciousness, which was at its deepest and fullest in him, expand their consciousness and become both the dominating force and the obvious power of their lives. The spirit that was present in Jesus was the power of his life calling them into a newly expanded consciousness, which expressed itself in the fuller humanity that was now working in them. Jesus had forced them to move away from the fear of life and the need to be dominated by an external God, to recognize that the divine and the human were not separate, but that the human was the vessel in which the divine lived. Paul had even said in Galatians (1:16) that God had been revealed "in" him, but the translators, still in the grip of theism with its external deity, translated the Greek word *ev* not as "in," as it is normally translated, but with the word "to," so that the revelation could come to him from the external, outside deity instead of being "in" him, as all consciousness-shifts are inevitably located. Paul (or perhaps the disciple of Paul whom many believe to be the author of Colossians) had also exhorted his readers, long before any gospel was written, to "seek the things that are above, where Christ is, seated at the right hand of God" (Col. 3:1). I remind my readers that Paul saw the resurrection as Jesus having been raised from death into the life of God in one symbolic action, not raised back into the life of this world in one step and then later lifted from earth to the heavenly realm of God. No story of a separate ascension would come into the Christian tradition for about forty years after these words in Colossians were written. We must learn to read Paul in the light of Paul, not in the light of the much later books of Luke, Acts or John, as we tend to do.

Jesus the man, the fully human one, had not been able to loose his spirit until he died. It was only when that Jesus spirit entered the disciples that the world was turned upside down. In Jesus the values born in our quest for security, values that so deeply shape human religion, were reversed. If the truly human, which was experienced in Jesus, is the content of what we mean by the word "divine" and is met not *beyond* life but at the *heart* of life, then the pathway into the divine is to become human and the pathway into eternity is to accept death as natural and to go so deeply into life that all limits are transcended and both timelessness and God are entered. The human quest for life after death is thus not based in any sense on the claim that my life or anyone else's is immortal; it is based on a new awareness that self-conscious human life shares in the eternity of God and that, to the degree that I am in communion with that ever-expanding life force, that life-enhancing power of love and that inexhaustible Ground of Being, I will live, love and be a part of who God is, bound not by my mortality but by God's eternity.

It is not enough to know the truth of this mystical path; it is essential that we actually begin to walk it. Erich Fromm, a German-American psychologist and author, reminds us that "people never think their way into new ways of acting, they always act their way into new ways of thinking."[6] The ascension of Jesus into God is thus not a spatial idea that must be believed or embraced; it is rather a pathway that each of us must undertake to walk. The task of religion then becomes that of no longer clinging to creeds and doctrines that are based on a dated worldview bound to an external, theistic deity. In the New Testament our definition of God was shaped in terms of the time-bound thought forms of the first century. In the creeds, doctrines and dogmas of the developing Christian church, our definition of God was expressed in the time-bound thought forms of the fourth century. To believe dated concepts with the human brain is not a sign of orthodoxy; it is a sign of being spiritually dead. The task of religion is not to turn us into proper believers; it is to deepen the personal within us, to embrace the power of life, to expand our consciousness, in order that we might see things that eyes do not normally see. It is to seek a humanity that is not governed by the need for security, but is expressed in the ability to give ourselves away. It is to live not frightened by death, but rather called by the reality of death to go into our humanity so deeply and so passionately that even death is transcended. That is the call of the fully human one, the Jesus of the transformed consciousness. To walk the Christ-path will take us beyond theism, but not beyond God; beyond incarnation, but not beyond discovering the divine at the heart of the human; beyond the death of every particular living thing, but not beyond meaning and purpose, because eternity has entered the particular in the self-conscious ones.

With that understanding of Jesus, one thing more remains for me to do. I must enter the Jesus-consciousness and walk into the timelessness of God. That is what I have done, but to describe it and to give it content I must return to my personal and spiritual autobiography. I do so in the hope that it will illumine and even replicate the spiritual autobiographies of both my readers and the human journey of which we are each a part.

I close this stage of my probe with two quotations. One comes once again from Meister Eckhart, who said that the highest parting comes to human life when "for God's sake we take leave of God."[7] I understand that task as moving from an understanding of God as an external being to the recognition, first, that we are part of who God is and, second, that this is what it means to enter into eternity. I do not know what that will look like, but I do experience it to be real. The other comes from Milton LeRoy, one of the two friends who agreed to write me their thoughts while they lived through what both believed were terminal illnesses. He said that this book should be just two words: "God is." I know what he means, but I need more. Because God is, I am. Because I am, God is. I think they mean the same thing. Thank you, Milton, for pointing me in this direction.

SIXTEEN

HIDING—THINKING—BEING

Have we ever faced the possibility that to abandon such an idol [the external, supernatural God of theistic religion] may in the future be the only way of making Christianity meaningful?

John A. T. Robinson[1]

We dance round in a ring and suppose,
But the secret sits in the middle and knows.

Robert Frost[2]

We have traveled a long pathway. We have looked at the journey of human life from consciousness to self-consciousness, into religion in its various forms and then finally beyond religion into modern forms of secularity. I have sought to parallel that human journey with my own personal trek through life as I too walked first into self-consciousness, then into religion and finally beyond it. My walk, however, deviated at this point from the human story, for I journeyed farther, going beyond the new secularization, into an expanded consciousness, a new realm of the mystical, and a new understanding of what it means to be human. With the hope that my personal journey makes contact with the journeys of my readers, I have suggested that part of the process of living is to travel this path, which means that religion is inevitably part of our human trek. Religion is not, as it so often claims to be, the final goal of life. Religion is rather nothing other than one more intermediate stop for us all, whether we are describing corporate humanity or individual humanity. I now want to pull together the human story and my own individual story so that we might see both their similarities and the crucial differences. My hope is that each of my readers will see his or her own journey somewhere in this broad new context. It is always dangerous to reveal that which is so deeply personal, but I hope to avoid the dangers by telling this personal story inside the framework of three words: "hiding," "thinking" and "being."

I have always been a religious seeker. I think that all human beings are. This does not mean that I find all my ultimate answers in religion, for I am not sure that those answers are actually there to be found. It is, however, the nature of human life to seek that which is ultimate, and that seeking is what people now call religion. I have been quite aware of this activity in my own life. On many occasions during the course of my life I even convinced myself that I had found the secrets for which I was searching. While that never really turned out to be the case, it did feel good sometimes just to pretend. Religion certainly allowed pretending to continue in my life. Inside religion I could hide from both reality and the complexity of truth. I did not know it at the time, but helping us to pretend has always been one of religion's major functions in the unfolding drama of self-conscious human history.

So incredible has been the power of religion through the ages that it has forced conformity on the tribe, the nation and the people. When people stepped outside of a particular prescribed religious box, whatever religious box was favored by their area and their era, they suffered dire consequences. That punishment came first in the form of being ostracized, sometimes called excommunication. If that were not sufficient to bring the deviant one to heel, then death became the option of choice. That was clearly the fate of those defined as heretics through the centuries. Few people were eager in the heyday of religious power to abandon what they were told was the "faith of our fathers (and mothers)" or to venture outside the security that religion offered. That is why religion operated with such authority, and in order to maintain that authority, religion had to make excessive claims that it possessed the ultimate truth. The hysterical nature of such claims is quite revelatory since unchallenged and unquestioned truth can never finally be true. Even to this day both truth and the pursuit of truth are frequently viewed as the enemies of "true religion."

As I entered the realm of the self-conscious, there were many reasons why I found it essential to follow this human path of seeking security in religion. The power of religion was very real in the culture of my upbringing. The region into which I was born was called the Bible Belt. A religious veneer lay heavily over every aspect of life. So thick was this veneer that it even relativized moral principles. It amazes me still today to realize that this, the most overtly religious part of my country and the place in which the Bible was actually read and attendance at church was almost required by social pressure, was also the region that practiced slavery, segregation and lynching. It supported the Ku Klux Klan with both money and the religious service of the ordained that they called "Khaplains." When I was born it had been only sixty-six years since the Civil War had ended this "unique" institution's legal reign, but in the Bible Belt intimidation and dehumanization of the descendants of the slaves continued unabated. The fact is that there is hardly a pure-blooded African left in the South today, a testament to the fact that while black men were constantly emasculated, black women were forced to become convenient sexual objects for churchgoing southern white men from Thomas Jefferson to Strom Thurmond. A desire to protect that systematized human institution of constant degradation was the primary cause of the Civil War. That war in turn was the single most powerful force shaping southern religion.

The southern family, almost without exception, had lost one or more of its loved ones in that bloodiest war in our history and the South's defeat had brought massive dislocation to its way of life. If one examines the content of what are called the old-time gospel hymns, still very popular in some circles, one discovers that most of them were written in the aftermath of that war and include as primary themes death, fear, lostness and alienation.

My world, my life and my religion were all products of that history. My small family was deeply unstable, marked by alcoholism, lack of education, early death and poverty. Religion that focuses on security thrives in such a setting. I knew no one in my upbringing who was not religious; indeed, I knew no one until I was well into my school years who was not both evangelical and Protestant.

As I have already chronicled in this book, I was brought into a profound and deep religious awareness as I walked through death experiences and searched for answers, but the only place I knew to search was within the frame of reference that I called religion. I needed the security that that familiar setting promised. I had no desire to abandon religion or even to step outside it in order to examine its claims. That was certainly also true of my human ancestors for most of human history. We were walking parallel courses. It was not until the world entered that period we now call the Enlightenment that it became acceptable for anyone to question religion. Even though that was a sixteenth-century phenomenon, it takes ideas a long time to trickle down to the common mind and perhaps even longer to trickle down to the uneducated masses of which my parents were representative. So I would live inside a religious frame of reference well past the time of the historical Enlightenment and would experience religion very much the way my ancestors did, as a warm and secure place in which to hide from fear, for a very long time. I was not alone in this.

Hiding was a comfortable way to live for me, just as it apparently was for my ancestors. Convinced as I was that I had the truth, there was no great need to ask questions, other than in the service of clarifying the truth that I already possessed. If one lives in a very narrow, circumscribed world, there is no driving passion to explore unexplored terrain. In the world of my upbringing people moved within a very short radius out of the physical environment in which they were born and they raised no issues with which they were not capable of dealing. In such an environment people tended in conversations only to share, and thus to reinforce, the prejudices of the region. Television, to say nothing of the Internet, did not yet exist to force us into a vision of a wider world. Like our ancestors of old, few of us were allowed to roam beyond the boundaries of our tribe, so I could sing with gusto the reassuring and deeply familiar evangelical hymns, even those that encouraged me to "bathe in the blood of Jesus," though that idea has never been an appealing one to me. Hymns like "Sweet Hour of Prayer" and "What a Friend We Have in Jesus" filled me with assurance. To this day I can sing these hymns by heart, including all verses.

Religion, I now recognize, was for me, just as it was for most of human history, always childlike and by definition authoritarian. It was, to be specific, a primary activity of the childhood of our humanity as a species, as well as the activity of my own childhood. With the overt encouragement of the religious institution itself, my spiritual childhood was destined to last until relatively late in my life, as it had done with my ancestors. Hiding in religion, however, is not likely to be successful on a long-term basis since no human system endures forever.

From somewhere I, like all human beings, was endowed with an intellectual curiosity that could not be suppressed. I think it started for me because my religion in its zeal encouraged me to read the Bible and so I did. I read it all. I read it over and over and in that process I read things that I simply could not believe. Biblical fundamentalism has never survived a genuine study of the Bible. My curiosity developed into an insatiable quest for knowledge. Such a quest, which human life also has exhibited, does not bode well for the religious enterprise. Increasing knowledge destroyed animism, but it did not cause religion itself to die. It only precipitated the need for new religious development. The gods of Mount Olympus were finally done in by the rise of the Greek philosophers. Recall that Socrates was required to drink hemlock because he was convicted of being an atheist and corrupting the minds and the morals of young people. Yet even the logical thinking of Socrates and his fellow philosophers and the deaths of Zeus, Jupiter, Neptune and Cupid, just to name a few of the inhabitants of Mount Olympus, did not lead to the death of religion, but rather to another form of religion. It was first the mystery cults and then the rise of Christianity.

Those new religious systems, but most especially Christianity, dominated the Western world for centuries. Christianity undergirded the institutions of control—the papacy, the "divine right of kings" and the concept of the one true church—that held the keys to heaven and hell. It fought off vigorous threats from Islam with the Crusades. It resisted the challenges of science for far too long because it controlled education. It silenced critical thinkers by banishing them or killing them. Recall that a hundred years before Galileo, Giordano Bruno was burned at the stake by Christian leaders for suggesting that the earth was not the center of the universe. Galileo survived him to establish that truth, but the threat that people like Bruno and Galileo represented was the first crack in the authority of Western religion. This crack, however, was destined for the first time in history to lead not to a new religious expression, though the Protestant Reformation was a step in that direction, but finally to the abandonment of religion itself. I too would share in and perhaps replicate this phase in the human religious journey. My move from hiding in religion to beginning to think critically about religion was not an easy step for me. History reveals that it was not easy for the human race either.

I was not born to intellectually curious parents. My father, who finished only high school, and my mother, who did not finish the ninth grade, read nothing that I ever observed other than the local daily newspaper, which shaped and reinforced local views. Perhaps my mother also read a monthly women's magazine like *Good Housekeeping*. That magazine was filled with "feel good" stories, some recipes and a few helpful household tips. It certainly did not encourage intellectual curiosity and neither did my family.

I was probably an above-average student in grammar school, but certainly not a star. In junior high school (grades seven to nine) I made the honor society and must have exhibited some ability, but it quickly disappeared under the social and economic pressures I faced in high school. In the tenth and eleventh grades I was a ne'er-do-well, C-average student at best. I was not an athlete and was too poor to dress well or to drive a car. Economic realities made my engaging in extracurricular activities impossible. I found high school a rejecting and demoralizing experience. With two other of my ne'er-do-well classmates I even contemplated quitting school in the eleventh grade, with the three of us planning to join the Navy. Why we picked the Navy I do not know. I could not even swim! One wonders what my life would have been like if I had actually done that. I now see that idea as a temptation not to grow, and even to call a halt to my progress in the human journey.

My life turned around in the twelfth grade. To the shock of my teachers and to my own amazement, I made straight A's in my senior year, and the possibility of going to a university opened up to me for the first time. My ability to enter the critical world of thinking was the positive result, but the loss of my sense of certainty would be a casualty. My teachers wondered out loud what had happened, but it was no mystery to me. Three things had happened to enable that transition to occur. First, I had found a purpose for my life in my church. It was quite obviously a *religious* purpose, but it was a purpose nonetheless, and one that would ultimately take me beyond the limits of the religious world in which I had been reared, into a world of thought that I did not yet know existed. The second factor was that I had found a role model in my priest, a life I wanted to emulate. The third factor was that I had a girlfriend. Her name was Cynthia.[3] No girl had ever wanted to spend much time with me before. I was looked upon as a chronic loser. Cynthia, however, gave me a sense of self-worth, for which I will be forever grateful. Propelled by these three forces, I discovered that I possessed an intense intellectual curiosity and began a lifelong pursuit of knowledge. Learning has, from that day to this, been one of my most pleasurable activities. I had moved, as the human race had previously done, from hiding into thinking. It was a huge step.

The religious momentum of my early life then combined with this discovery of who I was as a thinking person to carry me into my first step toward the priesthood, the world of a university. My intellectual curiosity was fresh and real. I dove into the life of that university and my work there placed me near the top of my class academically. So did my work in the theological graduate school that I next attended. I was eager to master the studies that would equip me professionally. Both the university and my graduate work in theology, as exciting as they were, still seemed only to scratch the surface of knowledge. Both served only to make me intellectually hungrier and hungrier. I always wanted more and continued to seek it. As I grew older, even as an established priest and bishop, I wanted to go outside my field into subjects that most clergy never seem to entertain. The world of science had been opened to me by a university professor named Claiborne Jones. I walked through that door always as an amateur, but always eager to know more. It wasn't enough for me just to discuss evolution; I had to read the firsthand sources. I read in its entirety Darwin's *On the Origin of Species by Means of Natural Selection*[4] and the extensive notes from his *Diary from the Voyage of the Beagle.*[5] I also read the work of Robert Fitzroy, who captained that trip of the *Beagle* and who violently opposed the growing and challenging insights at which Darwin was arriving. When much later in my life my youngest daughter began her doctoral work in physics at Stanford, I began to read physics, grateful that there were some physicists, among them Heinz Pagels[6] and Paul Davies,[7] who wrote in such a way that I could actually comprehend what they were saying, lacking though I was in scientific training. I read Isaac Newton's *Principia,*[8] Einstein's *Relativity: The Special and the General Theory*[9] and Stephen Hawking's *A Brief History of Time.*[10]

Two other university professors, William H. Poteat and Maynard Adams, had opened me to the world of philosophy, so over the years I have read John Locke, David Hume, Baruch

Spinoza, René Descartes, John Stuart Mill and Blaise Pascal, among many others.

I have always been intrigued by music and how it interprets life. In my childhood the only music I ever encountered was in my mother's devotion to country and western. The Briarhoppers were her favorite singing group. Then there was my older sister's devotion to Frank Sinatra, which knew no bounds. From my university days on, however, I began to embrace Bach, Haydn, Beethoven, Verdi, Wagner, Mozart and Mahler. I was intrigued by how a piece of music or art both reflected the age of its composition or painting and interpreted the timeless inner human struggle.[11] I devoured studies in the field of astronomy and marveled at the size and breadth of the universe, distances in light-years that my mind could not even imagine.[12] I turned to the world of Renaissance art to see the human struggle with religion and out of religion.[13]

While these new studies enchanted me, I also studied the Bible, both constantly and deeply. I read this book on differing levels at different stages of my life. I read it as a fundamentalist, I read it as a scholar, I read it as a believer and as a critic and I read it as a skeptic. I read the great commentaries of my century. The Bible was to me like the God-figure in Francis Thompson's poem "The Hound of Heaven."[14] It would not let me go. I was entering my own age of enlightenment, and belief would become for me, just as it was for the human family, increasingly complex.

Meanwhile my priestly career developed in deeply fulfilling ways. It opened new doors for me to enter and new areas of responsibility through which I could grow. Above all I relished the opportunity that the priesthood offered me to learn and pursue truth "come whence it may, cost what it will," as the motto of my theological school proclaimed.[15]

During my priestly career I had the chance to engage undergraduates, graduate students and faculty members at Duke

University, Randolph-Macon Woman's College and the Medical College of Virginia. I began to interpret my priestly career primarily on the model of a teacher and to see my congregation as filled with people who wanted to learn. I was moving out of religion's security into what even to me seemed like bold and scary places. In two of my congregations, one in Lynchburg and the other in Richmond—both in Virginia—I insisted on teaching an adult Bible class for an hour each Sunday morning before the major church services. I taught this class the way a university course on the Bible would be taught, examining the text's sources, observing its contradictions and probing far beneath its literal words. There was no safe harbor in these classes for traditional believers. Yet I was amazed at how popular the Bible could be with modern men and women. In that fourteen-year process of nine to ten months a year, I clearly mastered my craft and honed my credentials as a biblical scholar. It was this critical study of the Bible and the Bible's truth interacting with truth from many other fields that began to push me, as knowledge had pushed the whole human enterprise, out to the edges of both religion itself and the church. I wondered just how far the church would be able to move in this direction before critical choices for the future would open up. I knew, however, that I would have to follow this path wherever it led me.

Invitations for me to lecture widely began to pour in, inspired first by my being a summer conference leader at a place called Kanuga in the mountains of western North Carolina, and later by the books that I began to write. Slowly I identified my audience and began to approach that audience with single-minded intensity. I would someday name the members of that audience as "believers in exile." I am quite sure now that I was also included in that group. Most of us in the clergy do actually preach to ourselves.

When I was elected bishop of Newark, New Jersey, I specifically stated my intention to be a "teaching bishop." This seemed to scare no one, probably because my colleagues thought of that as a bishop who would clarify the Bible, the doctrines and the practices of the church. My intention, however, was to stand on the cusp between traditional religion and the knowledge giving rise to the tide of secularity and to force the two into dialogue. As the bishop, I organized a series of public lectures every year in the Diocese of Newark as part of what we called the New Dimensions Lecture Series. I always did one of these lecture series each year and then brought two or three other lecturers into the diocese annually to do the others. These lecturers were theologians of world rank, such as Hans Küng, John Polkinghorne, Mortimer Adler, Keith Ward, Rosemary Radford Ruether and Roger Shinn. They were Bible scholars such as Raymond Brown, Robert Funk, James Forbes and Elaine Pagels. They were scientists such as Arthur Peacock, Paul Davies and Timothy Ferris. I gathered a community of scientists from within the diocese who were still at least tangentially part of the church and began dialogues, both public and private, with them on a wide range of subjects. I helped to develop an annual lectureship dedicated to the memory of John Elbridge Hines, the great church leader of my tradition in the twentieth century, which focused on the interface of science and theology. I began to pursue further study at places like Union Theological Seminary in New York, Yale and Harvard in this country, and Oxford, Cambridge and Edinburgh in the United Kingdom. I became a member of the Jesus Seminar and was thus involved with its two hundred to three hundred fellows in constant inquiries into the Bible. I wrote more books and accepted invitations to lecture across this nation and ultimately all over the world.

I developed a passion for reading books on tape. This was before the days of iPods. While driving around the diocese, I was always listening to a book via my tape-player. I managed in this way to read some eighty books a year during my twenty-four-year career as bishop. Almost none of these books were novels, which appealed to me almost not at all. They were rather history, biography, science, political science, economics and psychology.

When I retired, this education continued in remarkable ways. I was invited to teach at Harvard; the Graduate Theological Union in Berkeley, California; the University of the Pacific in Stockton, California; and Drew University in Madison, New Jersey. I found I could exercise on my treadmill each day for an hour while a recorded book, or even a university DVD course, was educating me through my television screen. I attended in this way classes of teachers at America's greatest universities. All of this intellectual activity was designed to force the inner dialogue between the faith that I represented and the explosion of knowledge that I was engaging, much of which challenged deeply the presuppositions of the faith I was professing. The tension between security and truth became palpable inside me.

Sometimes, to the dismay of my more traditional brothers and sisters in the Christian church, it became obvious that I had moved more and more to the edges of church life. What I claimed to believe had to make sense to me. I was not interested in ghettoized religion. I wanted worldly religion where faith and knowledge had to collide. The choice to write this particular book was deliberately made to force faith and knowledge to come together. I decided to see whether or not I really still believed in life after death. No other question posed the issue of faith quite so powerfully as this one seemed to do for me. It was the hardest study and writing adventure that I have ever undertaken. I was determined, however, not to give up until I had brought the ultimate religious question of life after this life under the onslaught of contemporary knowledge, to see whether or not it could continue to stand as an article of faith that could be believed with integrity by a citizen of the twenty-first century, including me.

It was in this process that I discovered another amazing shift taking place within me. It felt like an ultimate shift. I wondered whether it would be the final shift. I had first moved from hiding within the security of religion to thinking critically about religion. While thinking was and continues to be terribly important to me, something else was emerging that was more important. I discovered that beyond thinking there is "being," and that "being" is an even deeper dimension of life. It was being, not thinking, that finally led me into my conviction that life was eternal. I could not reach this level, however, by walking outside my faith tradition; I had to walk through it and then beyond it. That is why I had to look again at Jesus, that central icon of my faith tradition, in the way that I did in the previous chapter. My journey into God had to go through a new understanding of who I was. The Jesus story awakened me to that.

The process I went through was quite simple, and yet it seemed to me to be profound. I recognized first that I am a product of hundreds of relationships that have helped to create and recreate me. In strange ways these relationships called me into a new understanding of being. My shaping theological teacher, Paul Tillich, called this the "new being."[16] I cannot separate myself from these gifts of being which caused me to recognize how deeply interdependent human life is in general and how deeply interdependent my life is in particular.

Of course I can name the crucial and vital relationships that helped to develop and to give to me my being. They are parents and mentors, friends and colleagues. Above all were those who lived with me inside the most complete and intimate relationship of marriage. I was blessed with two wonderful wives, one of whom died after thirty-seven years of marriage. The second one remains today more precious to me than life itself. When one lives inside the bonds of a transforming love that is so whole, so free and so life-giving, one enters dimensions of life that are both transcendent and life-changing. When one is loved without boundary or merit, one finds life emerging into new dimensions never before contemplated. Like Richard Bach's fictional character Jonathan Livingston Seagull,[17] I found I could break barriers, transcend limits and live in a way I had never before thought possible. Life expanded. It was out of the experience of married love that I began to interpret Christianity in terms of the fullness of life, created by the power of love. I began to see the Jesus message through this lens. His call to me was to a life that was abundant. That did not mean the gospel of success, as some of our popular evangelists seem to suggest.[18] It meant discovering the wholeness and the freedom that allowed me to give my own life away both in love and in the service of another. Answering Jesus' call to an abundant life enabled me to escape my survival mentality. The more I gave, the more I seemed to have to give. Perhaps that is what St. Paul meant when he called us to live in "the glorious liberty of the children of God" (Rom. 8:21) and what the author of Colossians meant when he wrote that we are to be partakers of "the inheritance of the saints in light" (Col. 1:12).

It was the experience of being loved that opened my eyes to see the love that is all around me, something that I had never been able to see before. It was the presence of love that empowered me to be able to receive love and then required me to give it away. Love expanded my life to new dimensions. Love enabled me to risk, to be vulnerable, to cross boundaries, to interact and to grow to the point where I could actually be free of those survival fears that caused me to victimize those who are defined as "different." Those fears, so deeply rooted in the survival mentality from our evolutionary history, must be transcended lest our own humanity be truncated. Again, Paul seemed to be grasped by this same vision when he wrote that inside the Christ-experience, which surely is an experience of the unbounded love of God, there is neither Jew nor Greek, bond nor free, male nor female (Gal. 3:28). A new humanity is always the product of love, and that new humanity then grows into an even deeper humanity, an unbounded humanity, even a transcendent humanity. The more I was privileged to live inside the acceptance of an unmerited gift of love, the less I needed to relate to the theistic images of my religious past. So the realm of the supernatural faded while the experience of love as the ultimate dimension of the divine began to grow.

Those aspects of the supernatural had also been rather thoroughly destroyed by the advent of knowledge. The church, however, has not even yet been able to come to grips with the demise of the supernatural. So I began to feel more and more alienated from traditional church life, which was not pursuing the things that consumed me. Increasingly I saw the church as an organization for the spiritually immature, as a body of children vying for the affirmation of the heavenly parent. I saw the church engaged in a medieval attempt at the manipulation of the divine, and all for our benefit. I saw it increasingly turning into a retreat into unreality. Worship became not communion with the power of life and love, but a drama in which the clergy starred. God was addressed in the chanted language of the Middle Ages, language that enhanced little more than the clergy's desire to perform. Church life seemed more and more dedicated to behavior control, and church politics was always about who is out and who is in. I do not want to be part of any faith community that says that the color of one's skin, the ethnicity of one's ancestors, the gender of one's body or the sexual orientation of one's brain determines a person's worth, holiness or access to being part of who God is. How can an institution make such statements and still claim to be in the service of one whose purpose was intended to be that of bringing life abundantly, to all of us (John 10:10)? I find myself increasingly unable to tolerate an ecclesiastical hierarchy that pretends to speak for that which is holy in order to diminish that which is human. I care not whether that spokesperson is the pope who defines some lives as "inherently flawed" because they are different from the majority, the archbishop of Canterbury who dares to elevate ecclesiastical unity above justice and truth, or one of the popular evangelists who uses the Bible to condemn that which is a normal part of the variety of human life, but which threatens him or her.

I came to the realization that I would never want to leave the church, yet I was also aware that I fitted less and less comfortably into its traditional boundaries. I then dedicated my energy to opening the life of the church to new possibilities. I wanted to reform the institutions of religion to make them serve the purpose for which I believed they were created. That purpose was not to hide from reality, but to engage it. It was not to run from truth, but to be in dialogue with it. It was not to become something, but to be something.

My life was once again stepping into the same place where I believe the whole of human life has been journeying. I perceive a spirituality abroad today that is deeper then we have ever witnessed. At the same time I sense that the popularity of religious institutions, which are supposed to be the encouragers of this spirituality, continue to decline. The whole of human life has journeyed, just as I have done, from consciousness to self-consciousness, then into the security of religion, then beyond religion into life and ultimately into the recognition that we are part of God and God is part of us. The task of faith has become therefore not the task of believing the unbelievable, but the task of living, loving and being. The mission of faith is no longer to *convert:* it is to *transform* the world so that every life will have a better chance to live fully and thus to commune with the source of life; to love wastefully and thus to commune with the source of love, and to find "the courage to be"[19] and thus to commune with the Ground of Being. The task of the church is not to make us religious, but to make us human, to make us whole, to free us to be able to escape our survival mentality, and to give our lives away. That is the "new being" to which we are called. That is what I believe Christianity must evolve into becoming. That is also what I now see as the meaning of Jesus.

A friend of mine named Edgar Bronfman, a philanthropist and a committed follower of Judaism, has written a book entitled *Hope, Not Fear: A Path to Jewish Renaissance,*[20] in which he calls on Judaism to move out of its past, out of fear, and into its future, into hope. The mission of Judaism, he suggests, is not to preserve Judaism, but to build the human community. Jews can do that, he continues, not by nursing the wounds of their frequently bitter history, but by taking their experience of suffering and allowing it to work in a positive way by coming to the aid of anyone who suffers at the hands of others for what they believe or for who they are. Edgar has caught the vision of what every religious group must do, beginning with the Abrahamic faiths of Judaism, Christianity and Islam, but spreading into a sense of oneness with the whole human family and finally into a sense of oneness with the whole created universe. The goal of all religion is not to prepare us to enter the next life; it is a call to live now, to love now, to be now and in that way to taste what it means to be part of a life that is eternal, a love that is barrier-free and the being of a fully self-conscious humanity. That is the doorway into a universal consciousness that is part of what the word "God" now means to me. This then becomes my pathway and, I now believe, the universal pathway into the meaning of life that is eternal. It starts when we step beyond our hiding place in religion into thinking and finally into being. It involves stepping beyond boundaries into wholeness, beyond a limited consciousness into a universal consciousness, beyond a God who is other into a God who is all. That is the final step in this process. It is what that means to which I turn next.

SEVENTEEN

I BELIEVE IN
LIFE BEYOND DEATH

Perhaps ultimately, with the fulfillment of the creative process, finite personality will have served its purpose and become one with the eternal reality, but we do not at present need to know that final future. What we need to know is how to live now. This is the way of love, witnessed by the saints and mystics of all the great traditions.

John Hick[1]

The time has come to state my conclusions clearly. The attempt to place the issue of eternal life into a new context has been accomplished. I have walked through religion as the arena in which the human family has long sought answers. I have dismissed religion's two primary premises: first, that God is other, a supernatural being who can do for me that which I cannot do for myself, a formulation that necessitated my gaining God's favor; and second, that self-conscious human life is alienated from the supernatural being and that overcoming this alienation with some form of atonement is necessary. In these two premises we, both as individuals and as a species, invested our hope that life had ultimate meaning, clear purpose and the possibility of eternity. These premises, however, could not be sustained as our knowledge expanded. The alternatives for human life were stark. We could refuse to admit that the premises underlying our religious systems were fatally flawed and live in denial. That pathway is always present in the world of religion. Failing that, we could acknowledge that religion has always been delusional, more about a search for security than a search for truth, and thus be willing to give it up, face the consequences and deal with the fact that we are no more than accidental creatures in an accidental universe. We then must enter the religionless world of a new humanity. That is when we are forced to conclude that purpose is what we give to life, meaning is what we invest in life and the hope of something beyond the grave is only the pious dream of the childhood of our humanity, a dream that we now must abandon in our new maturity. Many regard these working hypotheses as the only real alternative to the mindless, irrational denials contained in fundamentalism.

I have sought to sketch out a new possibility. It involves a paradigm shift of gargantuan proportions. It acknowledges both the grandeur and the potential of humanity. Ultimately it drives us to a new definition of what life is and a redefinition of almost everything that we have ever assumed about God. I arrived at these new concepts not by abandoning my religious convictions of yesterday, but by transcending them. I began to see God in a radically different way: as part of the universal consciousness in which I shared.

The journey I have taken to reach this point is, I believe, the journey we all must take. I hope I have charted it accurately. It is the uniquely human gift of knowledge and the incredible human power to think about and to explore the meaning of life that allow us to walk into these places where few of us have walked before, to transcend the limits of our humanity and, finally, to touch that which is eternal. I can say that, at least for me, it was only when I began to see this journey simply as the next step in a human journey, a journey that began when consciousness finally broke into self-consciousness, that I could begin to embrace the idea that religion was and is just a stage through which we had to pass. Our real delusion as human beings was not the content of religion; it was our assumption that in any religious tradition we could arrive at life's final answers. We had to walk through the fear that abandoning that delusion produced before we could discover the clues that issued in a new human self-understanding. Our ultimate destiny was never to be religious human beings, as we once thought; it was simply to be fully and totally human. Religion, that human activity to which we once entrusted our destiny, is now revealed only as a stage of life that had to be transcended before we could discover our destiny. Humanity is not alone, as we once thought, separated from God and thus in need of rescue. We are increasingly aware that we are part of what God is and we are at one with all that God is. Suddenly it made sense to me that the ancient name of God found in the Hebrew scriptures was part of the verb "to be." God, the great "I Am," blends with the "I am" affirmations that each of us must make on our journey into self-understanding.

It has been the human destiny to walk through the fearful and the limiting in order to discover the transcendent and the infinitely real. We had to walk through self-consciousness to discover the universal consciousness. We had to walk through the time-bound to discover the timeless. That was necessary before we could claim our identity as part of who God is.

It is only here that we sense that finitude finally fades into infinity, that earth is the doorway to heaven and that the human is and can be transformed into the divine. It is also here that all religious symbols begin to fade away, necessary no longer. Religion was simply the arena in which the hidden part of my humanity was struggling to be born. I denigrate that arena no longer. Religion is to me something similar to what Paul said the law was to him, a teacher that led him into becoming and being something more. I now know that not only did I have to walk the religious walk, but those excessive claims that we so often made for our religious "truth" ultimately had to be broken open for our sakes—dare I say for God's sake. That breaking was the prelude to a new awareness.

That was when I began to look anew at that unique life called Jesus of Nazareth and to see things in him I had never seen before. Jesus was not the human form of an external deity who invaded this world to masquerade as a human being, as we have been lulled into believing for so long. We thought these claims elevated him when they actually denigrated him. Jesus was the life in whom a new consciousness appeared. His consciousness called, beckoned and empowered us to be something we could not then even dream of being. Jesus was a human being who was so whole, so free and so loving that he transcended all human limits, and that transcendence helped us to understand and even to declare that we had met God in him. That is what the story of the resurrection was all about. Every human limit, including the limit of death, faded in front of Jesus. So he opens a door for me to walk into the final arena and to walk past the ultimate boundary. I can see in him what I can be—a life at one with God, at one with myself and a part of eternity. That is my stunning conclusion. The Christ-path becomes for me a path that is always opening to something more. It is a human path that all people in all times and in all places can walk, regardless of the name by which they call it. The Christ is no longer a religious symbol and the Christ-path is no longer a religious path. Christ is the fully human one and the Christ-path is above all else a human path, the sign that the doorway into God is always the same as the doorway into our own humanity. The oneness of God held so deeply by the people of the East thus merges with the individualism so deeply valued by the people of the West. Individuation within the oneness of God enables us to transcend all the human boundaries of tribe, race, gender, sexual orientation and even religion. No separation is eternal and no difference can finally be permanent. For God is ultimately one, and that means that each of us is part of that oneness. "My me is indeed God." The mystics are right. They are people of a deeper consciousness. There is one consciousness, but self-conscious people alone can know it. I am finite, but I share in infinity. I am mortal, but I share in immortality. I am a being, but I share in being itself.

So I now have reached the point in my journey where I, like St. Francis before me, can welcome death as my brother. I live in the appreciation that it is the presence of death that actually makes my life precious, since it calls me to live each day fully, and it is by living fully that I enter the timelessness of life.

Three other issues need to be addressed briefly, filing them almost by title, before this book concludes:

First, is this vision of our participation in eternity assuring enough to free those people who live with the vicissitudes and the tragedies of existence to trust the journey? I believe it is—at least it is for me.

Second, is the life beyond this life sufficiently personal— so personal as to be *real,* as close friends of mine seem to demand—or will people now reject these ideas as worth little more than a good intellectual exercise? For me the answer again is yes. I do not see the religious quest for security, coming as it does from an outside deity to a personal center of consciousness, as anything more than a delusion. If that is what my eternal destiny depends on, then I am ready, like many before me, to dismiss it as one more, somewhat pitiful expression of the human survival mentality. It is full of sound and fury, but it signifies nothing. I do not want to be betrayed by the religious opiate of my generation. That is, however, not what I am seeking to articulate. I have found in the quest for personhood an ability to embrace infinity, which leads me to the conclusion that I can and must share in that infinity. I am a person who can transcend time. I can study centuries long past and I can anticipate and even plan for a future that is not yet. Those are the things which lead me to the conclusion that I do, I can and I will escape the barriers of both time and space.

The discovery of the eternal is something that can be and is found as we go deeper and deeper into ourselves. Eternity is within us. That is what makes these conclusions intensely personal. That is what enables us to enter both a new meaning for personhood and a new understanding of what it means to be human. I turn once again to St. Francis of Assisi for the words found in a prayer attributed to him which captures this concept for me: "It is in giving that we receive, it is in loving that we are loved, it is in forgiving that we are forgiven and ultimately it is in dying that we live." When I am free to give my life to others, I will also be free to die without either fear or regret, for I will be in the possession of that which is eternal. Through that lens I now embrace the words attributed to Jesus by the Fourth Gospel alone. For then Jesus, the fully alive one, does become "the way, and the truth, and the life" (14:6), for it is the enhancement of the human that I see in him that becomes the only doorway into what "God" means.

Third and finally, the question people constantly ask about life after death is, Will I know my loved ones? I do not know how to answer that, for it assumes that there is a place where all the deceased are somehow physically gathered in recognizable forms and we begin the process of seeking out the ones for whom our hearts ache. I understand that yearning, but I am not drawn to such meaningless spatial images. What I can say to this yearning is that none of us becomes human in isolation. We are rather the creations of those who have loved us. That is how we have been introduced to life, to timelessness and to that which we mean by "God." In the process of having our own lives created by the love of others, we have become part of their lives and they have become a part of ours. We cannot separate ourselves from them, since the very being of all human life has been joined and intertwined. So if any of us is to share in that which we call the eternity of God, these lives that are so deeply a part of who we are must also share in that eternity with us. I cannot say more. I feel no need to say more. That is quite enough for me. I prepare for death by living. My commitment, which I see as the heart and meaning of worship, is to live as completely as I can and to drink in the sweetness which that particular day has to offer. While I am alive I will plumb life's depths, scale life's heights, and share my life and my love with those who are fellow pilgrims with me in my time and space. When I die I will rest my case in the "being" of which I am a part. That is where my faith has taken me. I can see more than I can say. I can experience more than I can describe. That is as far as words can carry me. I step beyond words at this point into the wonder of a wordless reality.

I have been engaged in the process of living for a long time. I have even enjoyed growing old and being old. I have enjoyed seeing grandchildren reaching maturity. I have enjoyed seeing young colleagues assume huge responsibilities. I am especially proud of the eight clergy who served with me in the Diocese of Newark who are now bishops of the Episcopal Church, and I am confident that eight is not their final number. One of these eight is now my own bishop, serving as my second successor in that office. I rejoice in his graceful and magnificent abilities.

I am glad I have experienced these "golden years." They have been the happiest and even the most creative and productive years of my entire life. I am still sorry my own father did not have the chance to know what I have known about the aging process. If the end of my life comes soon, I have no regrets. If I am able to live longer, I welcome it. I cannot imagine a life more blessed than mine, so even the chronic signs of age serve to remind me of how wonderful life is.

Finally, to state it as plainly as I know how to do, I believe deeply that this life that I love so passionately is not all there is. This life is not the end of life. I cannot articulate the content of this concept more than I have done, but I want my readers to know that my convictions, however poorly or weakly described herein, are real and they are convincing to me. The only way I know how to prepare for death is to live in such a way that I enable each day to participate in eternity. I enter the realm of eternity only by embracing the finite. I walk into life's meaning by being open to what lies ahead and beyond. I do believe that love is eternal and I am held in the bonds of love by my family, my friends and countless acquaintances. They are to me windows into eternal life. I embrace them and I embrace eternal life through them.

So I conclude with the question with which this book began. If someone were to pose to me the question that was posed by the mythical biblical character of Job so long ago— "If a man [or a woman] dies, will he [or she] live again?"—my answer would be yes, yes, yes!

That is as far as words can take me, but that is enough for me. So I end this book by calling you to live fully, to love wastefully, to be all that you can be and to dedicate yourselves to building a world in which everyone has a better opportunity to do the same. That to me is to be part of God and to do the work of God. That to me is to be a disciple of Jesus. Finally, that to me is the way to prepare for life after death. Shalom.

EPILOGUE

DEFINING THE CHOICE TO DIE

> *My life feels like it is concluding; this period has the feeling of a coda to it. I feel I've done what I needed to do. I look back without regrets, and I look forward without fear. I've never been more in the present.*
>
> **The Reverend Frank Forrester Church IV**[1]

There is one other aspect to death that confronts us in this contemporary world that, while not the theme or focus of this book, has become so widely and publicly debated and generally condemned by organized religion that I decided I must address it in an epilogue to this volume. It is found in the question: What choices are open to us morally, ethically and legally to bring our lives to an end by our own voluntary decision when circumstances make such a decision necessary and even desirable? That is an issue that our grandparents seldom had to confront.

I need to say first that I am passionate about life and about living. I view every moment of life as a privilege not to be missed, as an opportunity to be grasped. I am also comfortable with death and view it as a friend that must be creatively engaged. Having said that, however, I still recognize that one of humanity's most enduring characteristics is the tendency to run from, deny and ignore death, and even to pretend that death is not inevitable. People say such strange things as, "If I die, I want such and such to happen." Language is quite revealing. I wonder why they do not say, "*When* I die." Is there some question about whether it will happen?

The unwillingness to confront death is both conscious and unconscious. So is our expression of that unwillingness. With little conscious reflection, we spend much of life's energy building monuments that in some sense give us hints of immortality; at least we *hope* these monuments will extend our lives and survive us. Popular monuments include our reputations, our fame and our unique achievements. We never know what moment will lift us out of our anonymity. An obituary in the *New York Times* informed us recently of the death of the policeman who put the handcuffs on Lee Harvey Oswald. That was, as this article understood it, the defining moment of his life. It is interesting to note what fills up the fifteen-minutes-of-fame slot that supposedly each of us is granted. The popularity of photography is fed by the human sense that once we have been captured in a photograph, we have preserved our visage for all time, or at least from the ravages of age. Photography freezes time and makes it seem eternal. This meaning of photographs becomes quite apparent in times of disasters like fires and floods, when the possessions that people seek first to save are not those that might be the most valuable monetarily, but the photographs, their icons of immortality. If we achieve higher levels of affluence, we have our portrait painted, filling a hope that the portrait will endure for several generations, along with the interpretation of us through the eyes of the artist. In acts expressing the same hope for some semblance of eternity, we place our names on whatever we can—funds, libraries, memorial buildings, lecture series, foundations. All authors that I know have intimations of immortality when they dream of their books being read hundreds of years after their lives are over. Few of them will be, however. There is nothing quite so dead as a book on almost any subject about a decade after it has been published. Sometimes we strive for eternity by embracing causes that are larger than we are. By dedicating our energy to assuring the enduring influence of these causes, we have a sense that we have extended our lives beyond death, or at least the longevity of our values. Popular causes might include political parties, churches, universities, nations, parks and schools.

A surprisingly large number of people never quite get around to making out a will—another expression, typically unconscious, of an unwillingness to deal with their own mortality. Either they cannot face death or they like to pretend they can avoid it. In these and in so many other ways we seek to transcend or at least to mute the fact of death. This is a uniquely human trait and quite revealing of our human nature. Death casts a perpetual shadow over the life of self-conscious people.

In the animal world death is not anticipated nor does it normally come from natural causes since every living thing is in some other living thing's food chain. Death, therefore, typically comes prior to the winding down of that creature's biological clock, to meet the food needs of some other creature.

For the most part the same thing was also true in human life until relatively recently in our history. Throughout the sweep of time that human beings have been present on this planet earth, far more of us have died of various causes other than old age. We have been victims of violence, war, floods, accidents, starvation, disease, poison, infant, maternal and childhood mortality and that which we deemed natural enemies. Most of the things that killed us were interpreted by human beings as deserved or in some sense punitive, so that at least we believed we died for cause. I think that it was the largely premature aspect of human death that formed the pressure found in so many of humanity's religions, including Christianity, for death to be interpreted as an expression of divine disfavor brought about by our sins or as an enemy that should be resisted and, if possible, overcome. The biblical story of the Garden of Eden suggested that death was God's punishment meted out to Adam and Eve for eating the forbidden fruit. Eve made this clear when she told the serpent that God had said they would die if they ate or even touched the fruit (Gen. 3:3). Paul argues in I Corinthians (15:26) that death is "the last enemy" that must be defeated, and makes the claim that in Christ the victory over death has been accomplished. These are the things that made decisions about how to end our lives almost unthinkable to any of our ancestors.

In recent years, however, accelerating rapidly in the past century, the boundaries of death have been pushed back significantly. First, we subdued our environment and developed farming practices and food preservation techniques so successful that starvation began to recede as a possibility, at least in the developed parts of the world. The Irish potato famine could hardly blight a nation in the West today as it did Ireland in the nineteenth century. Second, we armed ourselves with weapons that have given us superiority over all of our natural enemies, rendering human life almost free from threat on the part of any non-human predators. Third, we expanded our medical knowledge, skill and technology, defeating disease after disease that once claimed us as its victims. Fourth, we learned how to chart the weather patterns, so that nature's more violent manifestations did not come upon us suddenly, which helped to maximize our ability to survive what we once called "an act of God."

The result of these, and many other factors that could be added to the list, was that human beings began to see new dimensions of life that had once been so rare. "Senior years," as we euphemistically called them, began to be viewed as another stage of life, like childhood or adolescence, that needed to be studied and understood and for which preparation was required. Senior citizens began to make their presence known politically through such organizations in America as the American Association of Retired People (AARP). More than anything else, however, the stretching out of the human life cycle forced us to begin to think about death in a way we had never done before. Death looks very different when it comes, not in the prime of life with swift suddenness, but at the end of life with slow decline. For the first time, then, we human beings had the opportunity to embrace the fact that we have some choices to make about when we die and how we die. This was a remarkably new phenomenon in human life and the necessity of dealing with this reality has become one of the unique responsibilities of our modern, or even postmodern, world. While there are many who are not eager to face these truths, a growing number of people are and that number is bound to increase. With that growth pressure will mount, as it is doing today, to allow individuals the right to make new decisions about death. It is simply another frontier that human beings will be called to cross.

With this new anticipation of a full life cycle, we are beginning to be aware of and to experience the transition moments that carry us quite naturally from maturity to death, just as we once studied the transitions from birth to maturity.

When is the peak of life, the moment in which we achieve our maximum potential? There is more than one criterion by which to measure. An athlete begins to decline in the late twenties or early thirties. Professional athletes still competing at age forty are so rare we can name them. I think, for example, of

Billie Jean King, George Foreman, Nolan Ryan, Brett Favre and George Blanda. Biologists tell us that males reach the height of their sexual prowess in their late teens and early twenties. The cycle seems slower and appears to last longer among females, who may reach their peak of sexual activity and pleasure in their late twenties or early thirties. We all know the meaning of the "dangerous forties" for men and the premenopausal fears for women. Both are death signs, the inescapable recognition of mortality, which drives us to seek reassurance with new sexual conquests or with plastic surgery.

Intellectually, the peak of life may well come much later. Most people now realize that university educations do not really educate; they only prepare students for the lifelong educational process. Undergraduate degrees serve primarily to make students aware of how much there is to know and how little of that knowledge they actually possess. The same is true even of graduate study. Graduate degrees, including PhDs, give one a familiarity only with one's field—its history, its parameters and its future. Knowledge is so vast that today we recognize that an expert has to be a specialist. The task of education is to carry us so deeply into the subject of our own field that we begin to see the whole of which our tiny insights are but a part. So the peak of one's intellectual life may well be much later in life's cycle.

No matter what criteria we use to determine our peaks, life always declines from these high points. The decline may be slow and smooth or it may be quick and abrupt, but it is inevitable. Physical strength can be maintained for years with proper diet and exercise, but its downward decline cannot be stopped. The same is true of one's intellectual strength. Neither the body nor the mind can do at seventy what it did at twenty or even at fifty. The process of accepting this reality is slow, but real. We stop cleaning our own gutters, shoveling our own walks and lifting our own suitcases. We give up late-night hours and long physical ordeals. We use golf carts instead of carrying our own clubs. We discover that there are some things that we can no longer eat without uncomfortable aftereffects. Antacids become a regular part of life. Sleep is no longer continuous. It becomes harder and harder to go through the night without relieving our less functional bladders of their excess. It takes more and more time to do what some women call "putting on my face." A look into the mirror, nonetheless, makes it obvious that this is a losing battle. Crow's-feet around our eyes, wrinkles in our faces and skin splotches called old-age spots all mark us as aging. Sometimes the varicose veins in our legs look like a secondary road map. The battles of our various bulges become first those that we cannot manage and then those that we cannot win. The mind follows a similar path. We begin to forget names and places when we tell stories. Our conversations are sometimes interrupted by blank spaces as we strive to recall. Some must struggle with early Alzheimer's. One person I knew waxed quite poetic when he informed his friends, "I am in the sunrise of my senility."

All of us develop physical symptoms that make hiding from the aging process impossible. I have now lived through two diagnoses that would have been considered fatal just one or two generations ago. On another occasion I developed a skin rash that itched terribly and would not go away. Finally, I went to the dermatologist, who biopsied the rash. When the pathology report came back my physician informed me that I had Grover's disease. "What is that?" I inquired. "Basically," she said, "it is a chronic, incurable, but manageable disease that tends to afflict elderly white men!" I accepted the fact that I now qualified for that disease. Other chronic diseases that can be managed but not cured take their toll and we adjust accordingly, but life still has great pleasure and we continue to live with as much gusto as we can muster.

Chronic diseases that can only be managed not cured, however, begin with the passing of time to be replaced with more serious diseases that are managed, not for containment, but only for delay. That is when the final horizons of our lives begin to come into our full view. That is also when the human capacity to make choices about life and death, about whether to accept or to forgo this treatment or that, whether to opt for quality of life or quantity of days, begins to come into play. By and large that is something with which earlier generations did not have to contend. Medical science and medical technology have given us choices that our grandparents did not have. I rejoice in this fact with enormous gratitude. I want to live each moment I am given to the fullest extent possible. I want to squeeze every ounce of joy I can out of every day. I want to live as long as life has meaning. I want to treasure this incredible gift of self-consciousness that I have been given. I want to transform its accidental nature into purposeful living. I want no one to think that I do not value as something of infinite worth the life that I live.

What happens, however, when medical science and technology cross the boundary that they now appear to be crossing? What happens when that wondrous ability to expand life to new limits begins to change into the process of simply postponing death? Expanding life and postponing death are not the same. Expanding life should always be celebrated. Postponing death should always be questioned. An unwillingness to postpone death beyond reasonable limits seems to me, therefore, to be a direct by-product of a commitment to the holiness of life.

What this means is that human beings have finally reached the point where we have a choice as to whether we will welcome and embrace death rather than postpone it. It becomes our choice to lay down the precious thing called life rather than to cling to it until it becomes a grotesque and pale replica of what it was intended to be. I believe, therefore, that I should have the personal and legal right to determine when I die and how I die. If I am fortunate enough to live long enough to face that decision, I want that decision to be viewed as a life decision, not a death decision; an ethical and moral decision, not an unethical and immoral decision; a decision to be celebrated and lauded, not one to be hidden, covered with shame and criticized. I want to cling to the possibility that the final decision I make in my life will be the decision to bring my life to an end, to lay it down with grace and beauty. I want a physician-assisted death end to my life to be my legal right and to be among the choices that I alone can make for myself.

I deliberately do not call this final act "suicide." "Suicide" in our society usually refers to a life-denying decision, while what I am discussing is anything but that. I believe it is a life-affirming decision. Suicide tends to be the conclusion to a life in which meaning and purpose have been lost to despair and meaninglessness. That is not what I am talking about. I think no one should give up on life when help is available that might still transform it, so I prefer other words, such as "choice in dying" or "compassion in dying."

Of course there are objections to a physician-assisted end of life, and these objections need to be listened to and understood. The louder voices raised in objection to choice in dying are normally religious voices. In some ways this seems strange because religious systems tend to claim that they have found the answer to death and the means of overcoming it. Once again that seems to reveal to me that religion is more about pretending to believe than about believing, more about erecting security systems than about seeking truth, more about developing a cultural mythology to manage the radical insecurity that life brings than about building convictions. The primary substance of their objection lies in the religious assertion that

human life is a gift of God and it is, therefore, not ours to ter-
minate. Only God should have the power to determine the
moment when death claims each of us, they assert.

Some years ago I became the first professional religious
person to be invited to address the national gathering of an organization known then as the Hemlock Society, named for the
hemlock that Socrates voluntarily drank to bring his life to a
close. In that address I attempted to speak to this religious concern that only God should have the power to end life. If only
God has the right to exercise life-and-death decisions, I argued,
why do so many religious people think they have the right to
end other people's God-given lives? History reveals that religious people have long claimed such a right for themselves. In
preparation for this address I searched through the scriptures
to see whether this claim is really biblical. I looked particularly
at those human behaviors for which the Bible, called "the Word
of God" by most of these critics, states that the death penalty is
appropriate. The list was both extensive and, by our standards
today, almost scandalously inappropriate. The Bible calls for the
execution of those of our offspring who are willfully disobedi-
ent and disrespectful of their parents (Deut. 21:18–21), those
who worship a false god (Deut. 13:6–11), those who commit
adultery (Lev. 20:10), gay and lesbian people (Lev. 20:13) and
anyone who has sex with his mother-in-law (Lev. 20:14), just
to name a few. It is quite clear from this litany of biblical narratives that, contrary to the way the Bible is generally quoted
in this debate, life-and-death decisions have never been left to
God alone. So this religious opposition to allowing one to make
one's own death decisions has got to rest on some other, unspoken (perhaps even unconscious) premise. This reveals yet one
more element of irrationality that needs to be sorted out in the
content of all religious systems. Religion is again revealed to
be a human creation designed to cover the threat of mortality,

which human beings are unable and/or unwilling to address. For people with deep religious ties to participate in a decision that their world has been organized emotionally to avoid thus becomes very difficult for most and impossible for many. That is not, for me, a determinative argument at all and I need to say so. I believe we can develop a different approach even for adherents of religion.

If we can grasp the vision of humanity to which I have pointed in this book, we will come inevitably to the realization that self-consciousness makes us aware that our seemingly individual and fragile lives are part of the very source of life that transcends all limits and shares in that which is eternal; then we ought to be able to move out of our survival-oriented mentality, which makes death our ultimate enemy. So when the time referred to in the ballad "September Song"[2] arrives and "the days dwindle down to a precious few," I can discover that I have the newly engaged responsibility of weighing quality against quantity. I can then let my days come to an end, voluntarily, appreciatively and purposefully. As I understand my Christian faith, that is a profoundly Christian decision that honors life; it does not diminish life.

To pose this issue in an existential way, let me offer an illustration. The deepest joy in my life is the deep connection I have with special people: my friends and loved ones, my children and grandchildren and, above all, the life-giving, life-sustaining and deeply meaningful relationship I have with my wife, Christine. Through those relationships I measure the meaning of life. To be specific, so long as I can see Christine smile and touch her hand, life has value and quality for me. If, however, I were to receive a diagnosis that was statistically fatal, in which medical experience suggested that time was limited and that the real medical issue was not healing, but the management of pain, then I would want the opportunity to review my choices and make a decision consistent with my values. If the drugs used to manage the pain would render me incapable of seeing Christine's smile or being aware of her presence, touching her face or experiencing her kiss, then I would not want to live any longer. While the presence or absence of the meaning in this primary relationship is the major issue for me, there are ancillary reasons that inform my decision. I want to preserve a memory among those who are my family and friends that resonates with who I am or who I was. I do not want my physical appearance or mental acuity to become so grotesque that my children and grandchildren do not want to look on my countenance or stare at my now dysfunctional body that once embraced them or through which my mind once was able to communicate. I do not want the uncontrollable functions of my body to render me burdensome to those I love the most. With medical care as expensive as it is under our particular system, I do not want the cost required to sustain those last few weeks or months of my life to cut into the financial security that my wife will need to live with the dignity that she has previously enjoyed. It is for these reasons primarily that I want the legal power and the moral authority to decide what is the loving and life-affirming thing for me to do. To live life in such a way as to actualize its deepest potential, one must take charge of this gift, claim it and hold it dear. Part of the way I do that is to have the freedom to lay it down, to place the well-being of those who have made my life worthwhile ahead of my basic survival needs. Human life, I believe, becomes whole and free when we transcend the drive to survive and discover that we can lay life down gracefully and give it away freely. Yes, I believe in and I support the idea that I must have the legal right to make choices appropriate to my circumstances at the end of my life. While I want that choice to be available to all those who are willing to accept that responsibility for themselves, I do not want it forced on anyone. Above all I want people to understand that my commitment to this choice is dictated not by a desire to die, but by my belief in life's holiness.

The other arguments mounted by fearful ones against this new and modern opportunity is some version of what is called the slippery-slope argument. This argument cannot see the ending of one's God-given life as an exercise of freedom; it sees only the potential for abuse. The slippery-slope argument suggests that once choice in matters of life and death becomes operative and legal, the value of life will be compromised and it will become easier and easier to do away with those who have become burdensome, expensive or just inconvenient. It always amuses me when this argument is advanced with "grave alarm" by specifically those with a religious agenda. When one looks at the history of religion and at the number of human beings who have been executed on religious grounds, killed in religious wars and persecuted for religious convictions, one wonders why suddenly believers are worrying about those whose commitment to life is so deep that they do not want to continue to live when life has become so compromised, both physically and mentally, as to be almost without meaning.

While I do not minimize the potential evil of which human beings are capable, I do not think this objection is worthy of much consideration. There is abuse already, on both sides of the issue. On the one hand there is a financial incentive for health care professionals and nursing homes to keep beds full and thus to keep people living. On the other hand I have known relatives who sought to rush the death process of one whose demise would result in increased riches for them. There are today some who work both sides of this street. I have known of unscrupulous nursing homes that drug the elderly to minimize the care required, thus hastening death as well as lowering the cost of the staff. I do not, however, think that we should refrain from making laws or changing mores because of potential abuse that might occur. We should rather seek to minimize the opportunity for abuse. It is, I believe, the attentiveness of loved ones, caregivers and pastors that provides the first line of defense against potential abuse.

The chief defense against the predatory exercise of life-ending decisions seems to me to be secured when the decision to end life is located in the person himself or herself. No one else should bear the ultimate emotional burden of that decision. If I have that privilege, I want to make this decision for myself. If I am no longer able to make the decision then I want the right to have my advanced directive honored so that I alone can delegate that decision to the one or ones I love the most. I trust my wife to make that decision for me at any time. We have shared life so deeply that we can surely share death and those stages toward the end of life as well. If she is too ill or is no longer living when that decision must be made, then I follow the law of primogeniture and vest that decision in my children, from the oldest to the youngest. I am confident that they will make it collegially. All of them are now fully mature and enormously competent. I trust them because I know them. To decide for someone else to end his or her life is a huge responsibility. I would prefer not to delegate so heavy a decision to my children, but I am confident that they will decide properly if the decision falls to them. Those people who have neither spouse nor child could designate their closest friend. If no one is available to fill that role for them, then I believe that the state and the medical profession have a responsibility to sustain that person as long as possible and in as much comfort as possible until the life processes themselves ring down the curtain. I do not believe that this intensely personal decision should ever be delegated to strangers, to doctors or to hospitals, because it is an act of love. If it is not an act of love then it violates the sacredness of life. Doctors, specifically, take vows to preserve life, so I do not believe they should be decision makers. I do believe, however, that all health care people, including doctors, ought to abide by and assist in facilitating the wishes of the patient. It is obvious that insurance companies and health insurance organizations that profit from death should be allowed no role, active or passive, in this end-of-life process.

Life is precious. I have loved my journey through it. I want the moment of my departure to be celebrated in a manner similar to the way the moment of my arrival was greeted, with joy and with great expectations. If in life we have touched the transcendent and the eternal, and have shared through self-consciousness in the life, love and being that flows through the universe, then I believe we can find the courage to lay this phase of that journey down when it is appropriate to do so and to enter what is to come. I would feel the same even if I were convinced that there was nothing more to come. I want the decision to end my life to be both my legal right and my ethical responsibility. I want to live well while I am living and to die well when I am dying, and both because I believe that life is holy.

John Shelby Spong

NOTES

Chapter 1: Setting the Stage—A Necessary Personal Word

1. From "Tracts," an unpublished poem written by Owen Dowling in September 2007 prior to his death in 2008. It is used by permission of Gloria Dowling, Owen's widow.

2. The reporter was Tim Russert of NBC.

3. Sally Quinn, a television personality (and wife of Ben Bradlee, the publisher of the *Washington Post* during the Watergate investigation), was the person on whom the controversy centered. Sally Quinn's religious background was shaped in interdenominational military chapels. Today she is known as a religious searcher with no known religious affiliation.

4. So stark was the ending of Mark, with no resurrection appearance stories, that several new endings for Mark were written. The Revised Standard and the New Revised Standard versions of the New Testament both attach two of these proposed endings, known as the "shorter ending" and the "longer ending," as footnotes. They are quite clear, however, that neither ending was part of the original corpus of Mark.

5. I refer especially to the tapes of lectures given at Oxford University in the United Kingdom by Daniel N. Robinson, published by the Teaching Company. The title of this course is "Consciousness and Its Implications." See bibliography for details.

6. Milton LeRoy, my other correspondent on death and dying, has had a rather remarkable revitalization. My wife and I drove to

his home in Bridgewater, Virginia, in November of 2007 to say good-bye to him. He did not believe that he would live until Thanksgiving Day. We talked deeply, as we always have, and that was when I invited him to chronicle his dying experience in regular letters to me. He made it, however, through Thanksgiving, Christmas, and Easter and into the summer of 2008 when we visited him again, this time with the first draft of this book. We discussed it in depth. On Christmas Eve of 2008 we visited him once more and he was as lively as I have seen him in years. So he does not qualify to be listed under the words "Rest in Peace." So to Milton I say, "Live with Confidence!"

Chapter 2: Life Is Accidental

1. Quoted from the *Book of Runes*, edited by Ralph Blum, page 44. See bibliography for details.

Chapter 3: All Life Is Deeply Linked

1. Taken from the online site www.quotationspage.com.
2. *New York Times*, October 16, 2008, page 29A. The author was John Wifford.
3. These words are part of a medieval Scottish prayer: "From ghoulies and ghosties and long leggedy beasties and things that go bump in the night, good Lord, deliver us."
4. *You Can't Go Home Again* by Thomas Wolfe. See bibliography for details.

Chapter 4: Dancing with Death: The Discovery of Mortality

1. From the Digha Nikaya ("Collection of Long Discourses"), page 16. Quoted from an unpublished paper written by one of my former students at Harvard, David Zuniga.
2. *The Episcopal Hymnal 1940*, number 87.

Chapter 5: The Lure of Religion

1. Taken from the online site www.quotationspage.com.
2. All Saints' Day is set on November 1. Halloween is thus All Hallows' Evening, the day before All Saints' Day. Normally, however, All Saints' Day tends to be observed in liturgical churches on the first Sunday of November.

Chapter 6: Life's Dominant Drive: Survival

1. Taken from the online site www.quotationspage.com.
2. Taken from Dr. Mardy's "Quotes of the Week," December 14–20, 2008. Found in *Escape from Freedom*. See bibliography for details.
3. *On the Origin of Species by Means of Natural Selection* by Charles R. Darwin. See bibliography for details.
4. *The Selfish Gene* by Richard Dawkins. See bibliography for details.
5. *The Book of Common Prayer 1928*. A phrase used in one of the occasional prayers.
6. This is part of Tillich's argument in the first section of his book *Systematic Theology*. That section is entitled "Being and God." See bibliography for details.

Chapter 7: Religion's Role in the Fear of Death

1. This quotation was taken from a birthday card, which attributed it, presumably accurately, to the great advisor to American presidents in the 1930s.
2. Izak Spangenberg is professor of Old Testament and Hebrew language and literature at the University of Pretoria, South Africa.
3. In the 1930s and 1940s Jack Benny was universally known as a popular comedian on radio. He played regularly on two themes: his age and his financial tightness.
4. *The Episcopal Hymnal 1940*, number 289.

5. I actually attended two more of these Lambeth Conferences, one in 1988 and one in 1998, and consequently went to high tea at Buckingham Palace with the queen on two other occasions. My wife Christine accompanied me to the last one. I can report that the menu at each was identical.

6. A familiar and often-quoted saying from Karl Marx, found originally in *Das Kapital*. See bibliography for details.

Chapter 8: The Faces of Religion

1. From *A History of God*, page 4. See bibliography for details.

2. I commend to my readers two of my books on this subject: *Rescuing the Bible from Fundamentalism* and *The Sins of Scripture*. Details on both are found in the bibliography.

3. Quoted from *The Episcopal Hymnal 1940*, number 519.

4. For those who would like to have a more substantive tour through the history of human religion I recommend the works of John Bowker, Karen Armstrong and Don Cupitt (especially *The Sea of Faith*), all of which are in the bibliography.

5. Chemosh was the God of the Moabites to whom reference is made in the Bible in Numbers 21:29 and in Jeremiah 48:7, 13 and 46. Baal was the God of the Canaanites referred to often in the Hebrew scriptures. Marduk was the God of the Babylonians.

6. I spelled out these vital transitions more fully in my book *Jesus for the Non-Religious*. See bibliography for details.

Chapter 9: The Tools of Religious Manipulation

1. From Augustine's work *Enchyridion*, pages 26 and 27. I have quoted it complete in its sexist language so that my readers might see the early Christian interpretations of human depravity, which underlie so much of the Christian theology of sin, sacrifice, blood and guilt that appears today to dominate religious systems, the nature of which I seek to expose for what it is in this

chapter. I do not believe that enhancing guilt will ever issue in
life here or transcendence beyond life.

2. This reference to Sigmund Freud and others that will be used
later are drawn primarily from three of his books: *The Future
of an Illusion, Moses and Monotheism* and *Totem and Taboo*. See
bibliography for details.

Chapter 10: Ridding Religion of Both Heaven and Hell

1. This was a conference of some fifteen hundred people from
across Australia and around the world that I was privileged
to keynote in 2007. The quoted speaker may have been either
Brandon Scott or Val Webb, both of whom made outstanding
contributions to this transformative conference.

2. Robert O. Kevin was my professor of Hebrew and the scriptures
of the Hebrew people. He was the one who first drew me into
looking at Jesus through Jewish eyes, an idea that has shaped my
approach to Christianity. Because he signed our papers with his
initials, ROK, our nickname for him was "The Rok of Ages."

3. I recall many conversations I have had with a close friend named
Ray McPhail, who lives in Highlands, North Carolina. Ray is a good
human being, gracious, generous and quite successful. He was raised,
however, in a debilitating southern religious tradition that burned so
deeply into his psyche the eternal flames of hell that he still reacts to
this threat in his maturity. His intellect is clear on this subject today,
but the emotional scar tissue will probably be there until the day he
dies. He illustrates for me how destructive the negative impact of this
kind of religion has been on many, many people.

Chapter 11: Putting Away Childish Things: The Death of Religion

1. Sarah Coakley, professor of systematic theology at Harvard Divinity School, referred to this quotation in a Chapel talk at Harvard University in 2000.

2. Gretta Vosper is the author of a book entitled *With or Without God*. This quotation comes from chapter 28, the first line. See bibliography for details.

3. These items are derived from a series of lectures entitled "Understanding the Universe" given by Professor Alex Filippenko on a Teaching Company DVD. See bibliography for details.

4. This was Michael Goulder's line in a book jointly written with John Hick entitled *Why Believe in God?* See bibliography for details.

5. *Time* magazine, the second week of July 1925.

6. This argument was developed by Professor Engel in a recorded public lecture that is available and is delightful. See bibliography for details.

7. It was after World War II in the middle of the twentieth century that state universities began to open their doors to women.

8. It was in 1920 that the Nineteenth Amendment to the Constitution of the United States granted the right to women to vote in national elections. Only one time did the vote of women actually determine the outcome of the election. That was in 1996, when President Bill Clinton defeated Senator Robert Dole.

9. The efforts to oppose *Roe v. Wade* are constant.

10. It was in 1976 that my church finally allowed women to be ordained. Some Protestant denominations reached that decision earlier. The Roman Catholic Church and the Eastern Orthodox Church do not yet recognize women as potential priests.

11. In Montgomery, Alabama, the chief justice of the Supreme Court, Roy Moore, refused to remove a three-ton statue of the Ten Commandments from his courtroom. He was removed as chief justice in November 2003.

12. This was one of the distinguishing marks of the reelection campaign of George W. Bush in 2004.

13. This is the title of Professor Cox's best-known book.

14. I think it is fair to say that Ogden nuances his argument more than the others, and Funk did not make an issue of it; but they are both in this camp nevertheless.

15. This phrase is borrowed with adaptations from Edna St. Vincent Millay's *Conversation at Midnight*. See bibliography for details.

Chapter 12: The Shift of the Religious Paradigm

1. This quotation was taken from page 76 of the *Book of Runes,* edited by Ralph Blum. See bibliography for details.
2. See bibliography for details.
3. See bibliography for details.
4. Michael Ramsey made these negative comments at the time of *Honest to God*'s publication. He later wrote, to his credit, that his treatment of John A. T. Robinson was one of the "two greatest failures" of his arch-episcopacy. "Better late than never," my mother always said.
5. See bibliography for details.

Chapter 13: Who Am I? What Is God?

1. *Hymns of Divine Love* 28, 114–115, 160–162. Quoted from *A History of God* by Karen Armstrong, page 224. See bibliography for details.
2. The professor's name is Alex Filippenko and he is both brilliant and clear, a rare combination in the field of education, but both traits are needed, if one wants to be an effective teacher. A good teacher must not only master the content of his or her field but be able to communicate that content to others. The course was taken on DVDs through the Teaching Company. See bibliography for details.
3. The title of this paper is "Cosmos to Consciousness: The Ascent of Humanity." The author is Daniel H. Gregory, M.D. To my knowledge this private paper is as yet unpublished.
4. Don Cupitt is a recently retired theologian at Emmanuel College of Cambridge University. He is still, however, a prolific writer. His 1984 book entitled *The Sea of Faith,* which grew out of a BBC television series, is the single most powerful statement that I have ever

read on the rise and fall of theistic religion. Cupitt today advocates, quite brilliantly, I might add, a point of view that he calls "non-realism." The debate between "realism" and "non-realism" turns on whether there is a reality to which our words point or whether our words are themselves the reality and human beings alone are the architects of all that they perceive. He and I presented the two sides of this debate in a meeting of the Jesus Seminar in New York City in the early years of the twenty-first century. Don's view on life after death is summed up in his own words: "That's all there is, folks." In the book to which I refer in this chapter, he proclaims that there is no God above the sky. I agree with this conclusion, but I do not think that our inability to locate God above the sky means that God is not real. Don Cupitt is a good friend for whose scholarship and ability I have enormous admiration. He has been formative in my own theological development and I treasure the time I spent working with him at Cambridge University. When we reach the core of what we each believe, however, we go in two different directions and I turn out to be, as he says, the "conservative clinging to the last vestiges of neo-Platonism"! Everything is truly relative, including theological nomenclature!

5. "Cosmos to Consciousness: The Ascent of Humanity"; see note 3.

6. *I and Thou* was the name of Buber's most famous book. See bibliography for details.

Chapter 14: The Approach of the Mystics

1. From an unpublished poem entitled "The Coming of Christ" by Maureen Ramsay Hughes of Fayetteville, Georgia. Used by permission.

2. The quotations from Meister Eckhart were all located on Web searches under "Meister Eckhart quotations." Tracking down quotations in their original source is quite difficult for this early-fourteenth-century mystic. If the words as quoted are not literally accurate, they are at least true to the remembered essence of Eckhart.

3. This phrase serves as the title of one of Tillich's most popular books. See bibliography for details.

4. The book of Zechariah is really two books divided by about a hundred years in time. Zechariah 1–8 should properly be referred to as I Zechariah, and Zechariah 9–14 should properly be referred to as II Zechariah. I have adopted that practice in this book.

5. *The End of Faith* by Sam Harris, page 204. See bibliography for details.

6. Quoted from *The Episcopal Hymnal 1940,* number 301. The words are by Walter Chalmers Smith, 1867.

Chapter 15: Resurrection: A Symbol and a Reality

1. This verse, the middle stanza of an unpublished poem entitled "Dreams of a Kingdom?" was written by David Stevenson, a member of a Methodist church near Loughborough in the English Midlands. He describes himself as one who writes "from an amateur perspective as a man in the pew." Used by permission.

2. Deepak Chopra's book *Life After Death* is in the bibliography.

3. I will inevitably treat the great events in our faith story only briefly in this section of the book. If my readers would like to look at these texts in more detail, for the birth narratives I refer you to my book *Born of a Woman,* for the details in the adult life of Jesus to my book *Rescuing the Bible from Fundamentalism,* and for the details about the cross and Easter stories to my book *Resurrection: Myth or Reality?* All are listed in the bibliography.

4. I attribute that phrase to Walter Wink, but whether I read it or heard him say it I do not know. I am confident, though, that I got it from him.

5. *Christpower* is a book of poems that I wrote with the assistance of Lucy Newton Boswell Negus, who shaped them into free verse. It has recently been republished by St. Johann Press in New Jersey. See bibliography for details.

6. From his book *The Art of Loving.* See bibliography for details.

7. The quotation from Eckhart is taken from Karen Armstrong's book *A History of God*, page 253, and was used by Don Cupitt as the title of one of his best books: *Taking Leave of God*. Both books are listed in the bibliography.

Chapter 16: Hiding—Thinking—Being

1. This quotation is from page 17 of Robinson's book *Honest to God*. See bibliography for details.
2. "The Secret Sits," from *The Collected Poems of Robert Frost*, page 214. See bibliography for details.
3. Her full name was Cynthia Shelmire Cook. When last I heard of her she lived in Florida. That was years ago. I have no idea whether she is still among the living. She might be quite surprised to know what a vital role she played in my growth and development.
4. Darwin was a great writer. His *On the Origin of Species by Means of Natural Selection* and *Notes from the Voyage of the Beagle* are in the bibliography.
5. Robert Fitzroy, the captain of the *Beagle*, wrote against Darwin's conclusions. See bibliography for details.
6. Heinz Pagels was a world-class physicist before his untimely death in a mountain climbing accident. My favorite of his books is *The Cosmic Code*. See bibliography for details.
7. Paul Davies has become a friend over the years. I rejoiced when he was given the Templeton Prize. His books, including *God and the New Physics* and *The Mind of God*, are listed in the bibliography.
8. Isaac Newton's masterpiece, *The Principia*, is listed in the bibliography.
9. Albert Einstein's book on the general theory of relativity is listed in the bibliography.
10. Stephen Hawking's book *A Brief History of Time* is in the bibliography. It is one of the most difficult books I have ever read.
11. I investigated this area primarily by taking courses from the Teaching Company that featured Robert Greenberg of the San

Francisco Conservatory. Professor Greenberg, a native of New Jersey, may be the best lecturer I have ever encountered.

12. Alex Filippenko. See bibliography for details.

13. This was a 48-lecture DVD by William Kloss. See bibliography for details.

14. Francis Thompson's poem "The Hound of Heaven" can be found in a volume entitled *The Complete Poetical Works of Francis Thompson,* page 88. See bibliography for details.

15. This was the motto of the Virginia Theological Seminary in Alexandria, Virginia, and it became a mantra to my career.

16. The title of one of Paul Tillich's three most popular and nontechnical books was *The New Being.* See bibliography for details.

17. Richard Bach's book is entitled *Jonathan Livingston Seagull.* See bibliography for details.

18. Joel Osteen is the current popular preacher of success and plenty.

19. Paul Tillich's best-known theological work is probably his book *The Courage to Be.* See bibliography for details.

20. Edgar Bronfman's book *Hope, Not Fear: A Path to Jewish Renaissance* is listed in the bibliography.

Chapter 17: I Believe in Life Beyond Death

1. Quoted from page 254 of John Hick's book *The Fifth Dimension.* See bibliography for details.

Epilogue: Defining the Choice to Die

1. Forrest Church is the well-known and highly respected former senior minister at All Souls Unitarian-Universalist Church in New York City. These words are quoted from the *New York Times* on page B4, September 29, 2008, in a story about his impending death.

2. The music for "September Song" was composed by Kurt Weill and the lyrics were written by Maxwell Anderson. It was first introduced in the 1938 Broadway musical *Knickerbocker Holiday.*

BIBLIOGRAPHY

Albright, Madeleine, with Bill Woodward. *The Mighty and the Almighty: Reflections on America, God, and World Affairs.* New York: HarperCollins, 2006.

Altizer, Thomas J. J. *The Gospel of Christian Atheism.* Philadelphia: Westminster Press, 1966.

———. *The New Gospel of Christian Atheism.* Aurora, Colorado: Davis Group, 2002.

Aquinas, Thomas. *Summa Theologica.* Vol. 55. New York: and London: Blackfriars and McGraw Hill, 1963.

Ardagh, Arjuna. *The Translucent Revolution.* Novato, California: New World Library, 2005.

Arendt, Hannah. *The Human Condition.* Garden City, New York: Doubleday/Anchor Books, 1959.

Armstrong, Karen. *The Great Transformation: The Beginning of Our Religious Traditions.* New York: Albert Knopf, 2006.

———. *A History of God.* New York: Ballantine Books, 1993.

Bach, Richard. *Jonathan Livingston Seagull.* New York: Scribner, 1972.

Bacik, James J. *Apologetics and the Eclipse of Mystery: Mystagogy According to Karl Rahner.* Notre Dame, Indiana: University of Notre Dame Press, 1980.

Blum, Ralph, ed. *The Book of Runes*. New York: St. Martin's Press, 1984.

Bonhoeffer, Dietrich. *Letters and Papers from Prison*. Edited by Eberhard Bethge. Translated by Reginald Fuller. New York: Macmillan, 1952.

Bowker, John. *God: A Brief History; The Human Search for Eternal Truth*. London: DK Publishing, 2002.

———, ed. *The Cambridge History of Religion*. Cambridge: Cambridge University Press, 2002.

Bowman, George W. *Dying, Grieving, Faith and Family: A Pastoral Care Approach*. New York: Haworth Pastoral Press, 1998.

Bronfman, Edgar M., with Beth Zasloff. *Hope, Not Fear: A Path to Jewish Renaissance*. New York: St. Martin's Press, 2009.

Brown, Raymond. *The Gospel According to John*. Vols. 1 and 2. Garden City, New York: Doubleday, 1966–1970.

Buber, Martin. *I and Thou*. Translated by Walter Kaufman. New York: Scribner, 1970.

Bultmann, Rudolf Karl. *The History of the Synoptic Tradition*. Translated by John Marsh. Oxford: Basil Blackwell, 1963.

Calvin, John. *The Institutes*. Library of Christian Classics. Edited by John J. McNeill. Translated by Ford Lewis Battles. 2 vols. Philadelphia: Westminster Press, 1975.

Cerminara, Gina. *Many Mansions: The Edger Cayce Story on Reincarnation*. New York: New American Library, 1999.

Chopra, Deepak. *Jesus: A Story of Enlightenment*. San Francisco: HarperOne, 2008.

———. *Life After Death*. New York: Random House, 2006.

Clark, Neville. *Interpreting the Resurrection*. Philadelphia: Westminster Press, 1967.

Cox, Harvey. *The Secular City*. New York: Macmillan, 1965.

Cullman, Oscar. *Christ and Time*. Translated by Floyd Filson. Philadelphia: Westminster Press, 1964.

Cupitt, Don. *Above Us Only Sky.* Santa Rosa, California: Polebridge Press, 2008.

———. *The Great Questions of Life.* Santa Rosa, California: Polebridge Press, 2005.

———. *The Sea of Faith.* London: BBC Publishing, 1984.

———. *Taking Leave of God.* London: SCM Press, 1980.

Darwin, Charles R. *The Journal of the Beagle.* Edited by Paul H. Barrett and R. B. Freeman. London: William Pickering Press, 1986.

———. *On the Origin of Species by Means of Natural Selection.* Philadelphia: University of Pennsylvania Press, 1959.

Davies, Paul. *God and the New Physics.* London: Dent, 1984; New York: Simon and Schuster, 1992.

———. *The Mind of God.* New York: Simon and Schuster, 1992.

Dawkins, Richard. *The God Delusion.* London: Bantam Press, 2006.

———. *The Selfish Gene.* New York: University Press, 1976.

Dodd, Charles H. *The Interpretation of the Fourth Gospel.* Cambridge: Cambridge University Press, 1968.

Dollar, Jim. *The Evolution of the Idea of God.* Greensboro, North Carolina: Outlands Press, 2006.

Einstein, Albert. *Relativity: The Special and the General Theory.* Translated by Robert W. Lawson. London: Methuen, 1920.

Elias, Norbert. *The Loneliness of Dying.* Translated by Edmond Jephcott. Oxford: Blackwell, 1985.

Engel, Elliot. *Queen Victoria and the Victorian Novel.* Taped lecture. Cary, North Carolina: Authors Ink, 2002.

Epperly, Bruce G., and Lewis D. Solomon. *Finding Angels in Boulders: An Interfaith Discussion on Dying and Death.* St. Louis, Missouri: Chalice Press, 2004.

Erikson, Erik H. *Identity and the Life Cycle.* New York: Norton, 1980.

Farrer, Austin. *Saving Belief: A Discussion of Essentials*. London: Hodder and Stoughton, 1964.

Filippenko, Alex. *Understanding the Universe: An Introduction to Astronomy*. Lectures recorded on DVDs from the University of California in Berkeley. Chantilly, Virginia: Teaching Company, 1998.

Finn, Charles C. *Embraced It Will Serve You: Encounters with Death*. Bloomington, Indiana: Milton Keynes; UK: Author House, 2006.

——. *For the Mystically Inclined*. Privately published, 2002.

Fitzroy, Robert. *An Essay by the Captain of the Beagle*. Recorded in a taped reading of the *Voyage of the Beagle*. Tantor Unabridged Classics. Phoenix Recordings, 2006.

Frankel, Victor. *Man's Search for Meaning*. Boston: Beacon Press, 1959.

Freud, Sigmund. *The Future of an Illusion*. Translated by James Strackey. New York: Norton, 1975.

——. *Moses and Monotheism*. Translated by Katherine Jones. New York: Vantage Books, 1967.

——. *Totem and Taboo*. New York: Norton, 1956.

Friedman, Edwin H. *From Generation to Generation*. New York: Guildford Press, 1985.

Fromm, Erich. *The Art of Loving*. New York: Harper and Row, 1956.

——. *Escape from Freedom*. New York: Avon Books, 1941.

——. *The Heart of Man: Its Genius for Good and Evil*. New York: Harper and Row, 1964.

Frost, Robert. *The Collected Poems of Robert Frost*. New York: Holt McDougal, 2002.

Funk, Robert, and Roy Hoover. *The Five Gospels: The Search for the Authentic Words of Jesus*. New York: Macmillan Press, 1992.

Goulder, Michael Donald, and John Hick. *Why Believe in God?* London: SCM Press, 1983.

Grof, Stanislav. *Beyond the Brain: Birth, Death and Transcendence in Psychotherapy.* New York: State University of New York Press, 1984.

Groopman, Jerome, M.D. *The Anatomy of Hope: How People Prevail in the Face of Illness.* New York: Random House, 2004.

Guilding, Aileen. *The Fourth Gospel and Jewish Worship.* Oxford: Clarendon Press, 1960.

Hamilton, William. *Radical Theology and the Death of God.* Indianapolis, Indiana: Bobbs-Merrill Press, 1966.

Harpur, Tom. *Life After Death.* Toronto: McClelland & Stewart, 1992.

Harris, Sam. *The End of Faith: Religion, Terror and the Future of Reason.* New York: Norton, 2004.

Hawking, Stephen. *A Brief History of Time: From the Big Bang to Black Holes.* Introduction by Carl Sagan. New York: Bantam Books, 1988.

Hedrick, Charles W., ed. *When Faith Meets Reason: Religious Scholars Reflect on Their Spiritual Journeys.* Santa Rosa, California: Polebridge Press, 2007.

Hegel, G. W. Friedrich. *Early Theological Writings.* Translated by T. M. Knox. Chicago: University of Chicago Press, 1948.

———. *The Phenomenology of Spirit.* Translated by J. B. Baillie. New York: Macmillan, 1949.

Heidegger, Martin. *Being and Time: A Reading for Readers.* Translated by E. F. Kaelin. Tallahassee: Florida State University Press, 1987.

Hick, John. *Death and Eternal Life.* San Francisco: Harper and Row, 1976.

———. *The Fifth Dimension: An Exploration of the Spiritual Realm.* Oxford: One World Press, 1999.

———, with Michael Goulder. *Why Believe in God?* London: SCM Press, 1983.

Horgan, John. *The Undiscovered Mind: How the Brain Defies Replication, Medication and Explanation.* New York: Simon and Schuster, 1999.

Hoskyns, Sir Edwyn. *The Fourth Gospel.* London: Faber and Faber, 1947.

Ireton, Sean. *An Ontological Study of Death: From Hegel to Heidegger.* Pittsburgh: Duquesne University Press, 2007.

James, William. *Pragmatism: A New Way for Some Old Ways of Thinking.* London: Longman's Green, 1949.

Jaspers, Karl. *Nietzsche: An Introduction to the Understanding of His Philosophical Activity.* Translated by Charles F. Wallraff and Frederick J. Schultz. Tucson: University of Arizona Press, 1965.

Johnson, Steven. *Mind Wide Open: Your Brain and the Neuro-Science of Everyday Life.* New York: Scribner, 2004.

Jonas, Hans. *The Gnostic Religion: A Message of the Alien God and the Beginnings of Christianity.* Boston: Beacon Press, 1958.

Kloss, William. *A History of European Art.* Lectures recorded on DVDs. Chantilly, Virginia: Teaching Company, 2001.

Kohn, Rachel. *Curious Obsessions in the History of Science and Spirituality.* Sydney: ABC Publishers, 2001.

Kung, Hans. *Eternal Life: Life After Death as a Medical, Philosophical and Theological Problem.* Translated by Edward Quinn. Garden City, New York: Doubleday, 1964.

Lake, Kirsopp. *The Historical Evidence for the Resurrection of Jesus Christ.* New York and London: G. P. Putnam Sons, 1907.

Leadbeater, C. W. *The Life After Death.* Madras, India: Theosophical Publishing House, 1912.

Lewis, C. S. *A Grief Observed.* New York: Phoenix Press, 1961.

Lewis, H. D. *The Elusive Mind*. London: George Allen and Unwin, 1965–1968 (The Gifford Lectures).

Luther, Martin. *Luther's Works*. Vol. 28. Edited by Hilton C. Oswald. St. Louis: Concordia Press, 1923.

Madigan, Kevin J., and Jon D. Levenson. *Resurrection: The Power of God for Christians and Jews*. New Haven: Yale University Press, 2008.

Marx, Karl. *Das Kapital*. Edited by Frederick Engels. Translated by Ernest Untermann. Vols. 1–111. Chicago: Charles Kerr, 1906–1910.

Meredith, Lawrence. *Life Before Death: A Spiritual Journey of Mind and Body*. Atlanta, Georgia: Humanics Publishing Group, 2000.

Meyers, Robin R. *Saving Jesus from the Church*. San Francisco: HarperOne, 2009.

Millay, Edna St. Vincent. *Conversation at Midnight*. New York: Harper and Brothers, 1937.

Miller, J. Kenneth. *The Secret Life of the Soul*. Nashville, Tennessee: Broadman and Hardan, 1997.

Mitford, Jessica. *The American Way of Death*. New York: Simon and Schuster, 1963.

Moltman, Jurgen. *The Crucified God*. London: SCM Press, 1974.

Moody, Raymond A., Jr. *Life After Life*. New York: Bantam Books, 1976.

Moule, Charles, ed. *The Significance of the Resurrection of Jesus for Faith in Jesus Christ*. London: SCM Press, 1968.

Neuhauser, Robert G. *The Cosmic Deity: Where Scientists and Theologians Fear to Tread*. Lancaster, Pennsylvania: Mill Creek Publishers, 2005.

Newton, Isaac. *The Principia*. Edited by Alexander Kayre and I. Bernard Cohen. Cambridge, Massachusetts: Harvard University Press, 1972.

Newton, Michael. *Journey of Souls: Case Studies of Life Between Lives.* Woodbury, Minnesota: Llewellyn Publications, 1994.

Nietzsche, Friedrich. *Thus Spake Zarathustra.* Translated by Walter Kaufman. Princeton, New Jersey: Princeton University Press, 1974.

Nineham, D. E. *St. Mark.* London: Penguin Books, 1963.

Novak, David. *The Soul's Refinement.* Chicago: Non Fir Press, 1996.

Nuland, Sherwin B. *How We Die: Reflections on Life's Final Chapter.* New York: Alfred Knopf, 1994.

Ogden, Schubert. *The Reality of God and Other Essays.* San Francisco: Harper and Row, 1963.

Ogletree, Thomas W. *The Death of God Controversy.* Nashville, Tennessee: Abingdon Press, 1966.

Pagels, Elaine. *Beyond Belief.* New York: Random House, 2004.

Pagels, Heinz R. *The Cosmic Code: Quantum Physics as the Language of Nature.* New York: Simon and Schuster, 1982.

Pannenburg, Wolfhart. *Jesus, God and Man.* Translated by Lewis Wilkins and Duane Priebe. London: SCM Press, 1968.

Pike, James A. *If This Be Heresy.* New York: Harper and Row, 1967.

———. *A Time for Christian Candor.* New York: Harper and Row, 1964.

Pittenger, Norman. *God in Process.* London: SCM Press, 1967.

Robinson, Daniel N. *Consciousness and Its Implications.* Twelve lectures delivered at Oxford University. Chantilly, Virginia: Teaching Company, 2003.

Robinson, John Arthur Thomas. *Honest to God.* London: SCM Press, 1963.

———. *The Human Face of God.* Philadelphia: Fortress Press, 1974.

———. *In the End: God.* London: Collins, 1968.

Ruth, John L. *Forgiveness: A Legacy of the West Nickel Mines Amish School*. Scottsdale, Pennsylvania: Herald Press, 2007.

Sartre, Jean Paul. *Being and Nothingness: An Essay on Philosophical Ontology*. Translated by Hazel E. Barnes. New York: Philosophical Library, 1956.

Schleiermacher, Friedrich. *The Christian Faith*. London: T. & T. Clark, 1908.

———. *The Experience of Jesus as Lord*. New York: Seabury Press, 1980.

Schulenberg, Michael. *Getting to the Promised Land Without Spending Forty Years in a Wilderness*. Pittsburgh: Dorrance, 2005.

Segal, Alan F. *Life After Death*. New York: Doubleday, 2004.

Smart, Ninian. *Philosophy and Religious Truth*. New York: MacMillan, 1964.

Smith-Tilly, Kelly. *At Life's End: A Portrait in Living and Dying; The Story of Dr. Maynard Adams*. Privately published. Raleigh, North Carolina: North Carolina State University, 2003.

Smoley, Richard. *Conscious Love: Insights from Mystical Christianity*. San Francisco: Jossey-Bass, 2008.

Spong, John Shelby. *Born of a Woman*. San Francisco: HarperSanFrancisco, 1992.

———. *Christpower*. Arranged by Lucy Newton Boswell Negus. Richmond: Thomas Hale, 1975. Republished Haworth, New Jersey: St. Johann Press, 2007.

———. *Here I Stand: My Struggle for a Christianity of Integrity, Love and Equality*. San Francisco: HarperSanFrancisco, 2000.

———. *Jesus for the Non-Religious*. San Francisco: HarperSanFrancisco, 2007.

———. *Rescuing the Bible from Fundamentalism*. San Francisco: HarperSanFrancisco, 1991.

———. *A New Christianity for a New World*. San Francisco: HarperSanFrancisco, 2002.

———. *Resurrection: Myth or Reality?* San Francisco: HarperSanFrancisco, 2005.

———. *The Sins of Scripture*. San Francisco: HarperSanFrancisco, 2005.

———. *Why Christianity Must Change or Die*. San Francisco: HarperSanFrancisco, 1998.

Strauss, David Friedrich. *Leben Jesu, or The Life of Jesus Critically Examined*. 1834 reprint. London: SCM Press, 1973.

Streeter, B. H. *Immortality: An Essay in Discovery*. New York: Macmillan, 1922.

Tattersall, Ian. *Becoming Human: Evolution and Human Uniqueness*. New York: Harcourt Brace, 1998.

Taylor, Charles. *Hegel*. Cambridge: Cambridge University Press, 1975.

Temple, William. *Readings in St. John*. New York: Macmillan, 1945.

Thielicke, Helmut. *Death and Life*. Translated by Edward Schroeder. Philadelphia: Fortress Press, 1970.

Thompson, Francis. *The Complete Poetical Works of Francis Thompson*. New York: Modern Library, 1913.

Tillich, Paul. *The Courage to Be*. New Haven: Yale University Press, 1952.

———. *The Eternal Now*. New York: Scribner, 1963.

———. *The New Being*. New York: Scribner, 1953.

———. *The Shaking of the Foundations*. New York: Scribner, 1948.

———. *Systematic Theology*. Vols. 1–3. Chicago: University of Chicago Press, 1951–1963.

Tippler, Frank J. *The Physics of Immortality*. Garden City, New York: Doubleday, 1994.

Tolle, Eckhart. *A New Earth: Awakening to Your Life's Purpose*. New York: A Plume Book, Penguin Press, 2005.

Tournier, Paul. *The Seasons of Life*. Translated by John S. Gilmore. Richmond, Virginia: John Knox Press, 1961.

Vahanian, Gabriel. *The Death of God: The Culture of Our Post-Christian Era*. New York: George Braziller, 1964.

Van Buren, Paul. *The Secular Meaning of the Gospel*. New York: Macmillan, 1963.

Von Hügel, Baron Friedrich. *Eternal Life: A Study of Its Implications and Application*. Edinburgh: T. T. Clark, 1912.

Vosper, Gretta. *With or Without God: Why the Way We Live Is More Important Than the Way We Believe*. Toronto: HarperCollins, 2008.

Wilber, Ken. *A Brief History of Everything*. Boston: Shambhala Press, 1996.

Wolfe, Thomas. *You Can't Go Home Again*. New York: Harper and Row, 1934.

INDEX